AVON
LOCAL HISTORY
HANDBOOK

AVON
LOCAL HISTORY
HANDBOOK

Edited by
J. S. MOORE

B.A.(Lond.), F.R.Hist.S.
(Lecturer in Economic History, University of Bristol,
and President of Avon Local History Association)

Published for
Avon Local History Association by

PHILLIMORE

1979

Published by
PHILLIMORE & CO. LTD.
Shopwyke Hall, Chichester, Sussex

© Avon Local History Association
and the contributors, 1979

ISBN 0 85033 318 0

Printed and bound in Great Britain by
UNWIN BROTHERS LIMITED
At The Gresham Press, Old Woking, Surrey

Contents

Acknowledgements

It is my pleasant task as editor to thank the many people involved in the production of this *Handbook*. The Avon Local History Association, which is sponsoring its publication, owes much to the original encouragement given by Major Richard Hungerford, formerly Regional Officer of the N.C.S.S., and the continued interest of Mr. Kenneth Nealon and Major Ian Wethey, respectively Chairman and Director of the Avon Community Council. Our particular thanks are due to Mr. John Arbuthnot, Principal Assistant of A.C.C., for his hard work as Hon. Secretary of A.L.H.A.

The successful production of the *Handbook* owes much also to the services of Mr. Graham Dear as Hon. Treasurer and especially to the energetic work of Mr. Fred Rapsey as Public Relations Officer of A.L.H.A. and *de facto* advertising manager for the *Handbook*. I am grateful to all my fellow-contributors for their hard work and patience with my editorial demands, and to Mrs. Leila Evans (Department of Economic and Social History, University of Bristol), Mrs. Lucy Hamid and Miss Caroline Bayford (A.C.C.) and Mrs. Rita Crowe (Frampton Cotterell and District Local History Society), for coping with the typing of the *Handbook* and the correspondence involved. Messrs. J. H. Bettey, Tom Crowe and Fred Rapsey acted as a final editorial committee and greatly assisted me, whilst two friends and colleagues at Wills Hall, Messrs. Sean Gill and Chris Harries, by casting fresh eyes over the text, eliminated errors both factual and stylistic. In particular I owe much to Mrs. Ruth Miles who, quite apart from all her other virtues, took on at very short notice the tiresome task of proof-reading and correction. The encouraging interest of all these people, and of my colleagues on the Executive Committee of A.L.H.A. and the representatives of local constituent societies of A.L.H.A., sustained me when it seemed unlikely that the *Handbook* would ever be published.

The grant of £200 towards the cost of publication by the Development Commission is acknowledged with gratitude, as is the support of our local advertisers. Without this financial assistance the *Handbook* either would not have been produced at all or, if produced, would have cost considerably more. Finally, nothing could have been achieved without the interest, friendship and co-operation of Mr. Noel Osborne, Editorial Director of Phillimore and Co. Ltd., whose continued services to the cause of local history are again demonstrated.

Bristol, Avon
February 1978   JOHN S. MOORE

Notes on Contributors

John S. Moore, B.A.(Lond.), F.R.Hist.S. Awarded the Alexander Prize of the Royal Historical Society and the John Nichols Local History Prize of the University of Leicester. Lecturer in Economic History, University of Bristol, Chairman of the Avon Local History Association, 1974-78, and President from 1978. Author of *Laughton, a study in the evolution of the Wealden landscape* (1965) and editor of *The Goods and Chattels of Our Forefathers* (1976). Now editing the Gloucestershire volume of Domesday Book for Phillimore's *History from the Sources* series. Continuing work on the economic and social history of South Gloucestershire since Roman times.

J. H. Bettey, M.A.(Birm.), Ph.D.(Bristol). Senior Lecturer in Adult Education and Staff Tutor in Local History, Department of Extra-Mural Studies, University of Bristol. Member of the Executive Committee of the Avon Local History Association. Author of *English Historical Documents* (1967), *The Island and Royal Manor of Portland* (1970), *History of Dorset* (1974), and *Rural Life in Wessex* (1977).

R. A. Buchanan, M.A., Ph.D.(Cantab.). Senior Lecturer in History, Head of the Humanities Group in the School of Humanities and Social Sciences, and Director of the Centre for the Study of the History of Technology at the University of Bath. Founding member and first President of the Bristol Industrial Archaeological Society. President of the Association for Industrial Archaeology, 1975-77. Author of *Industrial Archaeology in Britain* (1972) and other works in this field.

Graham P. Davis, B.A., M.Sc. Lecturer in History at Bath College of Higher Education since 1968. Member of the Executive Committee of the Avon Local History Association. Author of *The Langtons at Newton Park* (1976). Currently engaged in research for a Ph.D. at Bath University on a slum district of Victorian Bath.

Robert W. Dunning, B.A., Ph.D.(Bristol), F.S.A., F.R.Hist.S. Editor of *Victoria County History of Somerset* since 1967. Hon. Editor of Somerset Record Society since 1969. Author of *Local Sources for the Young Historian* (1973) and *Christianity in Somerset* (1976); joint author of *Victorian and Edwardian Somerset* (1977); editor of *The Hylle Cartulary* (1968); joint editor of *Bridgwater Borough Archives, 1468-85* (1971); editor of and contributor to *Victoria County History* *of Somerset,* vol. 3 (1974); contributed new introduction to Hale's *Precedents and Proceedings in Criminal Causes, 1475-1640* (1973).

John Haddon, B.A.(Bristol). Principal Lecturer in Geography, Bath College of Higher Education. Author of *Local Geography in Rural Areas* (1964), *Discovering Towns* (1970), *Bath* (1973), *Fieldwork in Geography* (1974) and *Local Geography in Towns* (2nd ed. 1975).

Royden B. Hope, M.A., M.Ed.(Manchester), Ph.D.(Bristol), A.R.Hist.S. Head of Education and Social Sciences, Bath College of Higher Education. Part-time tutor for the Open University. Recognized teacher of Bristol University. Local history work has included research studies concerning educational developments in Manchester and Bath.

Geoffrey Langley, B.A.(Lond.), F.L.A. Reference Librarian, Bristol Public Libraries, 1961-74. County Reference Librarian, Avon County Library, since 1974. Member of the Executive Committee of the Avon Local History Association. Author of professional papers in Library journals and anthologies. At present working on a handlist of maps of Bristol.

Walter E. Minchinton, B.Sc.(Econ.)(Lond.), F.R.Hist.S. Awarded Alexander Prize of the Royal Historical Society. Professor and Head of the Department of Economic History, University of Exeter, since 1964. Chairman, Standing Conference for Devon History since its foundation. Chairman, Exeter Industrial Archaeology Group. Author of *The British tinplate industry, a history* (1957); *The port of Bristol in the 18th century* (1962); *Industrial Archaeology in Devon*(1968); 'Patterns and structure of demand' in *Fontana Economic History of Europe,* vols. 2 and 3 (1973-4), and *Devon at Work* (1974). Editor of *The trade of Bristol in the 18th century* (1957); *Politics and the port of Bristol in the 18th century* (1961); *Essays in agrarian history,* 2 vols. (1968); *Mercantilism, system or expediency* (1969); *The growth of English overseas trade in the 17th and 18th centuries* (1969); *Industrial South Wales* (1969), and *Wage Regulation in Pre-Industrial England* (1972). Continuing work on 18th-century commercial and maritime history, including the Atlantic slave trade, privateering and the port of Bristol, industrial archaeology, particularly the history of tidemills in Europe and America, and the history of the cider industry in Europe.

Derek M. M. Shorrocks, M.A.(Cantab.), Diploma in Archive Administration, Liverpool University. Deputy County Archivist of Somerset 1957-77, now County Archivist. Somerset Editor, *Somerset and Dorset Notes and Queries.*

Brian S. Smith, M.A., F.S.A. County Archivist of Gloucestershire since 1968. Author of *History of Malvern* (1964); *Gloucestershire Local History Handbook* (1968, 2nd ed. 1975) and, with Miss E. Ralph of *History of Bristol and Gloucestershire* (1972). Editor of *Transactions of Bristol & Gloucestershire Archaeological Society* since 1971. Part-time lecturer in local history for University of Bristol since 1962.

C. J. Spittal, A.L.A. Librarian-in-charge, Queen's Building Library, University of Bristol. Member of the Executive Committee of the Avon Local History Association. Compiler of glossary in *The Goods and Chattels of Our Forefathers* (1976).

Mary E. Williams, B.A. (Wales), Diploma in Archive Administration, Liverpool University. City Archivist of Bristol since 1971. Vice-Chairman of Avon Local History Association, 1974–78. Joint editor, with Miss E. Ralph, of *The Inhabitants of Bristol in 1696* (1968).

Turn over a few pages of Bristol's history

Here are four books published by Bristol & West as part of the conservation effort.

They've been well received, and we hope to publish more in the coming years.

The prices quoted include post and packing.

Send cheques or postal orders for the books you would like to:

Press and Information Services, Bristol & West Building Society, Broad Quay, Bristol 1.

Bristol & West
BUILDING SOCIETY
A MEMBER OF THE BUILDING SOCIETIES ASSOCIATION

Trends in housing and conservation. 1978 issue **35p**

Tomorrow's history today. A selection of some of Bristol's best modern buildings **35p**

A comprehensive survey, well illustrated, of a period only now receiving the critical attention it deserves **£1.20**

A collection of work by Bristol artists, from the collection of the City Art Gallery **80p**

Why Charles Good rode the Bristol Bridge tram in 1886.

The Company was already 104 years old when Mr. Good was the local secretary of the Phoenix Fire Office in the High Street.

Our sign there was quite a landmark for a lot of Bristolians on the Bristol Bridge route.

Today, the trams are gone from Bristol. But not the Phoenix.

You'll find us high on Redcliff Hill, at the new Phoenix House, national centre for many of the Phoenix's control operations.

Though we've changed our address, we still give the same expert service to you or your business as we did when Mr. Good rode the Bristol Bridge tram.

PHOENIX ASSURANCE

Phoenix House, Redcliff Hill, Bristol BS1 6SQ.
Tel: Bristol 294941.

One plant that's always flourished at Avonmouth.

It started to grow in the area as long ago as 1743 when Europe's first large zinc plant was established at Bristol.

We continued the tradition over sixty years ago when the National Smelting Company acquired land for zinc smelting at Avonmouth.

And steadily Avonmouth became the centre of the zinc industry.

Since then we've grown and grown, with the expanding uses of zinc.

For diecasting, galvanizing, alloys, chemicals and components.

The Avonmouth plant is the only primary zinc smelter in Britain and we've spent millions helping it to flourish.

A fine port, motorways and other amenities have been good for our growing plant. We like to think that in terms of employment and industrial growth, backed by care for the environment, it's been good for Avonmouth too.

1

Local History: Ends and Means

J.H. BETTEY and J.S. MOORE

What is local history and why should we bother about it? In one sense of the word, history is the total human past, but this is not very helpful as a definition since 90% or more of our actions go unrecorded and at best can only be inferred. It would be a very obsessive and meticulous diarist who noted his total activities day-by-day, and it is doubtful if he would have time for anything else besides keeping his diary. A more useful definition of history would be the total recorded human past, but even this represents an impossible ideal in practice: some actions, some thoughts, some people are more important than others, and all historians have therefore to be selective in their use of available facts. They must strive to answer what seem to them to be the most significant questions about the society they are studying. It is for this reason that this *Handbook* is organized in chapters covering the major topics that together constitute the life of local societies in the past, because these are the matters that most concerned past inhabitants in every locality: how to earn their living, how to feed, clothe and house themselves and their families; and how to organize themselves or be organized for various communal and individual purposes, both material and spiritual. This is not to say that all local historians will find all these questions of equal importance, or even equally answerable for their own localities, nor to suggest that all local historians ought to write their histories according to the same model. But these are the sort of questions they ought to consider and try to answer, otherwise they will become mere antiquarians hoarding facts as squirrels hoard nuts, but without the squirrels' eminently practical purpose: at the end they will only be able to say, like the Welsh chronicler Nennius, 'I have made a heap of all I have found'. And even the heap will be useless to more acute users if the sources of the information are not precisely recorded in footnotes so that others can check where they got their information—this is why amateur local historians should be scrupulous in recording their sources. As W.G. Hoskins has said, amateurs need not be amateurish.

So much for the questions: what about the area of study? Local history has been classically defined as the origin, rise and development of the local community, and by convention and customary usage the local community is generally equated with the parish or town where the local historian lives. There is much to be said for this definition: where one lives does have a special significance for the individual. Hoskins aptly quotes Horace: 'it is that place that has a special smile for me', and whether one was born there or has chosen to live there is immaterial: often, indeed, it is the newcomers, anxious to put down roots, who are more concerned with the history of their adopted locality than the old-established inhabitants who take it for granted out of long familiarity. Again, precisely because of local loyalties, local history organizations flourish most easily if based on the village or town: the region or county (old or new) does not attract anything like the same degree of attachment. Nevertheless, because of the process of historical evolution, today's social unit may well not be meaningful in the past, and *vice versa.* To take one particular case to illustrate the general point: Frampton Cotterell parish in Northavon nowadays consists, in the main, of a built-up residential area including the whole of Coalpit Heath, though technically half of Coalpit Heath is in Westerleigh parish to the east. Historically this link goes back no further than the development of the coalpits of Coalpit Heath in the 17th century. Before then, Westerleigh had little connection with Frampton Cotterell, and much more with its mother parish of Pucklechurch; equally Frampton seems originally, from a study of interlocking parish boundaries, to have included Stoke Gifford and Winterbourne to the south in Saxon times, probably dependent on the great royal manor of Bitton, also the centre of its hundred and deanery, as Winterbourne still remained down to the mid-12th century. Yet in the Roman period, to judge from the location of suspected Roman sites in relation to later parish boundaries, Frampton seems to have been linked not with Stoke Gifford and Winterbourne but with Iron Acton to the north in an estate centred near Cogmill, which, significantly, was the one part of Frampton which down to the 17th century was included not in one of the two manors of Frampton, but in Iron Acton manor. Here, then, the modern area of Frampton Cotterell parish has in the last 2000 years been successively part of equally valid local communities but with very different boundaries in different periods, and this example could be endlessly multiplied throughout the area of Avon. And Avon itself, though often denounced as an artificial creation of 1973, could also perfectly well be portrayed as a belated administrative recognition of a long-standing economic and social reality, the Bristol region, cutting across 'old' county boundaries which, no doubt, 10th century patriots of Mercia and Wessex vigorously denounced as 'artificial' innovations.

There are two further, practical reasons why local historians, even though legitimately concerned in the main with their parish or town, should not be too parochial. As one of us has frequently remarked, 'after all, one parish pump is very like another': the parish or town did not exist in splendid isolation. It was always linked to its neighbours by bonds of common interest (trade and security, to name just two) and superior allegiances (to county, diocese, kingdom for example): it shared the common physical characteristics of its geographical region. Unless the local historian is aware of the larger world, and of its constant reinterpretation by regional and national historians, he is likely to attach undue importance to the commonplace that to him is apparently exceptional, or to assume that interesting or unusual practices of his own locality were in fact universal. This is why the bibliographies in this *Handbook* include general works as well as works relating specifically to Avon: so that local historians can become aware of the general historical background to their area's development. The second reason is based on a problem faced by most local historians, the uneven survival of historical evidence. Supposing the historian of a given area wishes to produce a rounded account of the major features in its history, he will frequently be confronted with insufficient facts or no facts at all. Put most starkly, how often does the parish historian have at his disposal equally good manorial and estate records on the one hand, and good parish records (apart from registers) on the other? Is he to say, in the absence of the former, 'I cannot deal with the agricultural history of my area, even though I know that for centuries farming was the principal occupation of its people' or, in the absence of the latter, 'I shall entirely ignore local government and the relief of the poor, despite the known fact that one-third of the local population at some time in their lives were in receipt of parish relief'? In either case the result would be a sadly unbalanced and unsatisfactory compilation: the remedy surely is to look for the nearest comparable evidence, very probably abundant in the next parish. The local historian must therefore beware of adopting too narrow an approach to his subject, and must always be interested in the adjacent parishes, the whole locality, whether region or county, as well as the history of his own chosen parish. There is much to be said for studying a block of two or three parishes together or choosing some other unit such as a river valley rather than sticking too rigidly to the history of one narrowly defined area.

We conclude, therefore, that local history is about local people, though the boundaries of the locality have probably altered more than once in the past; it is about the major concerns that affected that local population in the past, even though the evidence may exist only for a nearby area in some cases. Above all, we would emphasize, it is about people, though thankfully local historians are less likely to need reminding of this than other historians. Industrial archaeology, for example, has sometimes been dubbed 'the new antiquarianism' because too frequently it has concentrated on things rather than the people who made, used or worked in them. Much economic and social history written by professionals also often loses sight of the people who made that history.

Given the interest, what do we do about it? Where do we start? The first step is to acquaint oneself with the necessary background knowledge, which is quite within every intelligent person's capability. One should read some of the standard guides, starting probably with those of Hoskins or Celoria, progressing via Rogers to the detailed heights of Stephens. Do not be put off by footnotes (see above) or bibliographies (they are there to help you). Do not assume that without a knowledge of Latin or Old French or Anglo-Saxon you are totally damned: you are in fact in the company of 99% of your amateur colleagues and at least 50% of professional historians. Above all, do not be frightened by old handwriting, much of which is more readable than that of most modern doctors! Again, there are good guides (e.g. Grieve and Emmison), and with practice, commonsense comparison with known words, and increasing familiarity with the purpose and content of various documents, success will come. One of us remembers being told by his postgraduate supervisor that learning to read old handwriting was precisely like learning to ride a bicycle—one falls off time and time again, picks up self, bike and bruises, and climbs on repeatedly, until, without realizing exactly how, one is riding and wondering only why one did not do it before. This advice is wise, encouraging and true!

Furthermore, unless special circumstances or living in a tiny community prevent it, do not work alone: find like-minded enthusiasts and work with them. Contact first the Avon Local History Association to see if a local history group already exists in your area; if not, either apply for individual Associate Membership of the A.L.H.A., or try to set up your own local group (again, the A.L.H.A. will gladly help and advise) by means of personal contact, local notice-boards or correspondence columns in the local press. Seek professional help from the University of Bristol's Department of Extra-Mural Studies, from local Record Offices, Museums and Libraries, and consult existing societies who will also be only too pleased to help.

Above all, define your objectives, whether as an individual or as a group. Not all group members for a variety of reasons can devote the same amount of time with the same degree of enthusiasm to local historical research and writing, but many who cannot will nevertheless attend lectures, join in on social events, help with fund-raising activities, and generally assist the good cause. Even if your own interests are centred on research, the other activities are necessary if societies are to flourish, not least by recruiting new members.

Whether as individual or as society member, the first stage in research is to discover what is already known and in print by consulting the standard bibliographies and the indexes to the main county historical periodicals. The second is to find out what manuscript materials exist, recognizing that 100% coverage even of what still exists today is never likely to be achieved—because of staff shortages, the constantly growing collections of the Public Record Office in London will never be fully indexed, and all that can reasonably be hoped for is that the major series likely to be of use will have been examined. For a variety of reasons, local records may have migrated far outside Avon—Bristol MSS. exist in the Scottish Record Office in Edinburgh, Bitton documents in the Lincolnshire Record Office, Frampton Cotterell records in Stockport Public Library: whether or not such 'strays' will be located elsewhere is largely a matter of luck coupled with persistence and a growing awareness of local historical developments leading one to a suspicion of possible locations to be checked by enquiry. Since the search for source materials will never be concluded, once the obvious places have been checked (the local record offices, the local library, the parish church, the local estate office if one exists), the next step is to consider what use is to be made of them.

Unless your group is large (say, over two dozen working members) and contains at least one expert (e.g. a history master) or is serviced by an extra-mural tutor, it is probably unwise immediately to think in terms of publishing a full-scale history, for two good reasons. The first is the time involved (at least 5–10 years for part-time work) before the end product emerges, with consequent disillusion, loss of interest and declining membership in the interim. The second is the difficulty in present economic circumstances of getting a full-scale history published. A much more practical scheme, bearing in mind the interests of group members and the known availability of records for the area, is to start simultaneously on several projects of limited scope, of which one or two should be designed to be finished quickly, within at the outside a year or so. This will encourage members to take on and persevere with longer projects, and can also be used as a recruiting stand: visual impact should be emphasized, e.g. a series of coloured historical maps based on estate, Tithe or Ordnance Survey maps (see chapters 2 and 4), a family reconstruction exercise on a well-known local family or a study of the parish from the 1841 or 1851 census enumerators' books (see chapter 3), photographs and plans of local houses and other buildings (see chapters 2 and 7). An exhibition is by far the best immediate aim for a new local history society; it publicises the work of the society; it introduces people who have local records, memories, etc.; it swells the society funds, and, above all, it provides the society with an immediately successful start. For already existing societies, an exhibition which concentrates on a particular aspect of the former life of the community—farming, industry, recreations, etc.,—is a particularly useful and worthwhile group project. The group organizer in arranging longer projects has to tread a delicate line between not boring his members with such projects that may take years to complete, especially if these involve working in record offices for a large number of visits of limited duration, and not deluding his members into thinking that certain essential jobs such as full studies of parish registers or series of wills and probate inventories (see chapters 3 and 7) can be skimped or ignored. That there is such a line is certain: finding it and keeping to it is a matter of luck and experience. Finally, there is no need to assume that full chronological coverage is either feasible or necessarily desirable: lack of evidence may make this near impossible, as may lack of aptitude. Especially in the early days of a new group, there is much to be said for tracing the history of a local community backwards, beginning with the relatively familiar and copious material relating to the recent past, and gradually working back to the more difficult periods. Above all, local historians should avoid beginning by trying to understand the difficult technical language of an Anglo-Saxon charter, Domesday Book, or a medieval court-roll. Such material is much better approached after the later history of the community has been investigated.

This suggestion receives added weight from publishing economics (see above). Wherever possible, local history groups should aim to publish their work, both for their own satisfaction and for the use of other interested persons outside their area. Commercial publishers, generally speaking, will not consider publication of local history works, without a subsidy or at least a guaranteed number of orders, and in any case professional advice should always be sought before entering into a contract or paying over any money as a subsidy. Some form of serial publication is therefore the answer, either in a county historical series (though their editors rightly insist on very high standards and may have a backlog of articles awaiting publication) or as a privately produced effort for mainly local distribution (though copies should be sent to the county record offices and libraries). The problems here are vetting the proposed production (A.L.H.A. will help with this), costing it efficiently in the light of realistic expectations of sales, effective reproduction (love and cherish secretarial members, girl friends, wives and daughters, especially those with access to electric typewriters which produce much clearer stencils than ordinary machines) and vigorous selling and promotion.

Despite the problems we have outlined above, we do not believe that their solution is impossible if goodwill, enthusiasm and reasonable efficiency exist. There is increasing interest in local history at all levels of society, and with the aid of the professionals (academic historians, archivists, librarians and museum-curators) the amateurs can be enabled to pursue their interests in local history effectively and pleasurably. In pursuance of these beliefs the A.L.H.A. was founded to bring together all those (whether amateur or professional) interested in local history in Avon: whether it succeeds largely depends on the support given by its constituent societies and their members. We hope that all who are seriously interested in Avon local history will find this *Handbook* useful to them in their future work and will in return, by promoting the work of the A.L.H.A., help us to help you still more.

One final point remains to be emphasized, namely that of chronological coverage. We have deliberately omitted treatment of the prehistoric and Roman periods, not because these periods are unimportant but because the evidence for them is almost completely derived from archaeology. We have tried to produce a *Handbook* for local historians in which the usefulness of archaeological evidence is stressed where it is appropriate for later periods. But the techniques for discovering and interpreting such evidence in the earlier periods require very different skills from those of the historian, and perhaps in the future our sister body, the Avon Archaeological Council, may produce its own guide to the rich local archaeological resources.

2
The Rural and Urban Landscape

J. HADDON

Landscape patterns

Within the quite wide limits set by the physical nature of the land, landscapes are the product of human decision-making and are therefore indicators of a complex inter-related system of economic, technological, social, and political forces, whose analysis is made the more difficult by the irrationality of some human action. As these forces change during time it follows that landscape has a proper place in historical study. The contrast, for example, in the lowland levels between the irregular fields of the medieval piecemeal drainage and the rectangular pattern of the 19th century enclosures reflects a change not only in technology but in farming methods, social structures, and legal processes. Similarly, the Georgian squares and crescents of Bath are the product of a society very different from that which built the neo-Gothic and 'Jacobethan' villas of Clevedon and Weston-super-Mare. The remains of moated farmsteads, isolated churches, green roads, old railway lines, and abandoned collieries are among the relics of past landscapes which serve as clues to history. This 'history on the ground', so skilfully analysed by such writers as Hoskins, Beresford, and Finberg, is vanishing at a great rate and there is an urgent need to record it fully and accurately. Similarly, the present rate of change is such that there is a pressing need to record eye-witness accounts and to gather together copies of materials still in private possession.

In studying landscapes, past or present, we are describing and analysing patterns composed of areas of differing textures and colours separated by boundaries of different natures and developed on varying slopes. These include, particularly in townscapes, the nature of vertical surfaces as determined by building materials and architectural style. Much of this can be expressed in the form of maps, but these need to be augmented by photographs, drawings, and verbal descriptions. There is as yet no generally agreed notation for recording townscape, and this is something which might well be pioneered in Avon. In the countryside, texture and colour are largely provided by vegetation, with a basic division between grass, cereals, roots, or any other crop where the plants are of some size, and trees. These patches are lined and their shapes determined by walls, hedges, fences or ditches, and may be separated by roads. Thus a land-use map is a good guide to appearance and a comparison between the maps of the first (pre-war) and second (post-war) *Land Utilisation Surveys* showing, for example, increasing acreages of grass, decrease of orchards, and amalgamation of fields would form a good basis for description of change in the landscape the reasons for which the historian must seek. The same approach can be taken further back in time with a study of tithe maps and, where applicable, enclosure and drainage awards. Useful, but less comprehensive cover comes from estate management maps.

The coarser web of road, canal and rail can also be pieced together from map evidence back to at least the beginning of the 19th century, using Ordnance Survey maps and deposited plans (usually held in County Record Offices) of canal, turnpike, and railway undertakings and the empowering Acts of Parliament. Local details may be found in enclosure awards, and in the records of the parish Waywardens, Highway Boards, County and Town Councils and Improvement Commissioners. Mapping of main roads first appeared with the Elizabethan cartographer, John Norden, and this continued in Speed's *Theatre of the Empire of Great Britain,* published in 1611 and containing useful town plans. In 1675 came Ogilby's 'strip' road maps which were incorporated in 1695 in Morden's maps for Camden's *Britannia* and in Bowen's *Ogilby Improved* (1720) and *The Large English Atlas* (1750–2). Transport is dealt with in detail in Chapter 5, and Agriculture in Chapter 4, and the local historian concerned with landscape will need to be familiar with these so that he may call on workers in those fields for material which he can co-ordinate for landscape study.

Similarly, Industry (Chapter 6) produced remarkable changes in landscape patterns, whether it was extractive (mines, claypits and quarries), manufacturing (e.g. brass-working, shipbuilding, paper-making, industrial Severnside), or distributive (warehousing), and often gathered around it housing and services (for example at Filton). With the growing interest in Industrial Archaeology an increasing amount of information is being collected which is being co-ordinated by Dr. R.A. Buchanan at Bath University. Other information may refer to specific activities, such as Mrs. Joan Day's book on brassworks in the lower Avon area, Down and Warrington on the Somerset coalfield, or histories of firms such as Wills. What the landscape historian has to do is to gather together and augment this information in terms of regional complexes which include not only industry but the matrix of geology, topography, farming, communications, and settlement in which it stands, or stood.

Local and Regional Studies

In regional differentiation a basic problem is that of scale. The tendency is for local historians to work on a very large scale of map for a very small area of land, such as a parish, and this leads to an uneven coverage of information for a county and the loss of the broad picture of distribution which would result from working on a smaller scale, although it is a useful corrective to the work of national historians whose accounts may give a completely false impression of what was actually happening in one small part of the nation. Even at regional level the scale may be too small to reveal important sub-regional differences, as for example, in Darby's otherwise excellent *Domesday Geographies* of Midland and South West England or reports such as 'Severnside'. Indeed the latter example highlights one of the fundamental problems of obtaining agreement between planners and people; the former work on large area, small scale objective maps while the latter live, as it were, on large scale, small area, mental maps and the two groups therefore see planning problems in quite different contexts.

The question of scale also applies to the visual impact of landscape. Thus a view of the lowland levels from the Cotswold edge is very different from a view of the same area taken from within it when the observer can often see no further than the nearest hedge, and the visual impression of the hill-and-valley country between Bath and Radstock from the main road, which tends to keep to the higher ground, contrasts with the impression from minor roads which wind along the valleys. Bristol from a distance appears as a uniform mass of buildings with parts differentiated only by height of land or of individual structures; inside the city the view may be restricted to a single street.

Rural Landscapes

The great merit of the local historian is that he or she works on a scale which enables him or her to become an expert, indeed the expert, on the history of a small area of country or town, someone to whom the maps and documents and other sources have a living reality because they are illuminated by a detailed knowledge of the land to which they relate. The recording of the local area is the primary and invaluable function of the local historian, but an added contribution to historical understanding could be made by the collation of individual studies into a study of change over a wider area.

In planning such a research programme for Avon the right scale must be determined for two types of work, the immediately local and the county, and a mechanism designed by which information is transferred from one to the other, involving a decision on how much detail may suitably be lost. In doing this, consideration must be taken of the scale on which maps are to be drawn for record; and distinction must be made between the scale of 'spot-light' studies which illustrate in detail the past landscapes of a small area and of 'floodlight' studies which bring out the general characteristic of a larger one—thus, a detailed study of Marshfield might be included with a general study of the visual characteristics of the Avon villages of Cotswold (Southwold), or an in-depth study of the Royal Crescent presented in conjunction with a general survey of the basic characteristics of the Georgian urban scene in Bath.

Whatever scale is chosen, a uniform method of representation of landscape features must be adopted, and this could be the responsibility of a co-ordinating committee.

Basically, the study of a specific period in history would require:

1. An introductory account of geology and physical features.

2. A map showing a pattern of fields, boundaries, buildings, land use.

3. A set of illustrations of appearance of buildings, etc., including old photographs for the more recent periods and landscape sketches for the older ones. There are many excellent sets of topographical drawings, engravings, and paintings from the 18th and 19th centuries.

4. Copies of any written descriptions from the period. Here private letters, diaries, reports, and topographical guide books are useful. For example, works of Daniel Defoe, Celia Fiennes, Arthur Young, William Marshall and John Billingsley (on agriculture).

5. A written analysis of the historical forces which created the landscape under study. This would include a study of the aesthetic principles which were in fashion at the time, relating mainly to architecture.

The amount of material available before the 19th century is quite limited and there is a good deal to be said for concentrating studies initially on the later period. Tithe maps and awards, together with estate or enclosure maps and awards, glebe terriers, auctioneers' sale particulars, road and other plans deposited with the County Record Offices, and other sources detailed in Chapter 4, provide basic information for reconstructing past landscape patterns which should be related to detailed study on the ground. This may well provide clues to the explanation of obscure documentary references and may correct erroneous conclusions reached from documentary study—the patterns laid down by the Enclosure Commissioners, for example, were often different from those which actually developed.

Detailed study of the shapes of fields in earlier maps and in early editions of 6 and 25 inch Ordnance Survey maps may enable the local historian to identify fossilised common field strips, later piecemeal enclosure of irregular fields, and more rectangular enclosure made still later by Act of Parliament. It is this kind of local detail which underlies, for example, Finberg's *Gloucestershire: the history of a landscape.*

Another source of information comes from the names of fields, lanes, villages, hamlets, farms, etc. but this needs to be treated with care, as names have often changed their form and interpretation calls for specialised knowledge—and the experts do not always agree. Local historians should not guess at the original meaning of names, but should collect the earliest known forms for interpretation in the light of A.H. Smith, *The Place-Names of Gloucestershire*, especially volumes 3–4 (English Place-Names Society, 1963–4). Volumes for Somerset have not yet been published, though preliminary work is in progress.

Though the period before 1086 is basically the province of the archaeologist, local historians should be aware that many parish and field boundaries are now thought to be older than used to be assumed and may date back to Roman or pre-Roman times (see the works of D. Bonney and P. Fowler in the bibliography). They should look for field-names such as Blacklands, Chestles, Oldfield, and Oldland which may well indicate Roman or earlier sites still recognisable in the Anglo-Saxon period, and should consider the location of Roman or prehistoric sites in relation to later parish and manorial boundaries.

Buildings are considered in the Townscape section and in Chapter 7, but it is worth noting that rural buildings, which may include industrial establishments such as mills, often have indications of change—blocked-in windows and doors, for example, old lintels, changes in floor and roof level, and changes in pattern of stone-work—which help to reconstruct their history. Other clues to be looked for are old foundations (sometimes indicated by crop-marks and aerial photographs, or revealed at low light), the presence of garden flowers, pattern of bumps and hollows in fields, which may indicate the sites of long-lost buildings. A useful book here is M.W. Beresford, *The Lost Villages of England*.

The ancient past has great appeal, but it is worth noting that some of the greatest changes in the rural landscape have taken place in the last 30 years with a revolution in farming methods, a decline in demand for farm labour, and the development of villages as commuter settlements. There is hardly a village in Avon without its addition, sometimes considerable, of post-war housing and re-furbishing of old properties; and detailed study of change in the post-war period would be of interest and value, particularly in its examination of the processes by which such change has been wrought, which can be studied in particular in relation to planning processes. So rapid is the rate of change that yesterday is history.

Townscapes

Reconstruction of past townscapes involves a study of ground plans, both of street patterns and of plot boundaries, for which a useful start has been made in the recent publication of *Small Medieval Towns in Avon*, though this must be used with caution. Some of this can be done from present map and field evidence, some from old maps and writings—for example, William of Worcester's meticulous study of Bristol in 1480 and Joseph Gilmore's map of Bath in 1694 with its border of drawings of contemporary buildings. We then need to know how the spaces, including those left open, were used. Here, until the advent of photography, we have to rely on written descriptions, topographical drawings and whatever buildings still remain, a source made scanty in Bath by the almost complete 18th century reconstruction, and in Bristol both by reconstruction and by wartime bombing. As a great deal of property in both cities was owned by their Corporations important information is available in the local archives, but for private land we must turn to other sources. In Bristol, for example, important developments, particularly in Clifton, were carried out by the Merchant Venturers, and in Bath an area was developed by the Bathwick Estate. Much research is needed into the activities of private builders and developers, an area of study where records tend to be very scanty, and, where discovered, need to be preserved. There are a number of printed sources for individual buildings, including Ison's work on Georgian architecture in Bath and Bristol, and Clare Crick's excellent *Victorian Buildings in Bristol*, for which we need a Bath counterpart, and various architectural studies of Bath, including Peter and Ruth Coard's *Vanishing Bath*. There is not a great deal on townscape as a whole, although there are useful studies in Bryan Little's books on Bath and Bristol, Tudor Edward's *Bristol*, the perambulations in Pevsner's *Buildings of England* and the interesting studies which are being made by the History and Conservation Group at Weston-super-Mare.

Although it is to be hoped that architects will concern themselves with the analysis of buildings and their history there is no reason why amateurs should be put off by a feeling of inadequacy. Initially, all that is required is a real interest in townscape, a clear eye for detail, and a basic architectural vocabulary which will be rapidly enlarged as the study progresses. A background knowledge of the main historical styles is useful both in description and in dating, but dating should not rely on style alone. Ability to use a tape measure, take a photograph, and make a sketch is obviously a help. Basically a building consists of a roof and walls with holes in them. What distinguishes one type from another are the materials of which the elements are constructed, the proportions of the elements, their shape, and their decorative treatment. From the point of view of townscape we are only interested in the interior if in some way it affects the exterior visible form, although if we are studying the history of an individual building most of the clues will come from interior variations such as changing floor levels, wall thicknesses, disposition of hearths and staircases, and roof construction—for this see the Fieldwork: Buildings chapter in Hoskins' *Local History in England*, and Iredale's little book *This Old House*. For a general study of townscape see Ewart John's *British Townscapes*; Cullen's *Townscape* is more concerned with the aesthetics of townscape design.

Much of the work will be concerned with 'ordinary' or vernacular buildings from the few surviving medieval cottages to the multitude of modern housing estates. A pioneer study was *Monmouthshire Houses* by Sir Cyril Fox and Lord Raglan, National Museum of Wales, 1951-4, and some other work has been published (see lists by the Vernacular Architecture group) but a great deal remains to be done and there is hardly anything on the inter- and post-war housing which has transformed much of our scenery. Useful books are *The Pattern of English Building* by Alec Clifton-Taylor, and *An Illustrated Handbook to Vernacular Architecture* by Dr. Ronald Brunskill. The two authors have also collaborated to provide a very useful book on English brickwork.

As in the rural scene there is a great deal to be studied in recent development, from the major transformation of Victorian times to the post-war flood of suburban building and inner city redevelopment. Detailed studies of small areas and of the engulfed villages such as Fishponds and Kingswood in Bristol or Weston and Twerton at Bath would be most valuable in identifying the forces of change, the instruments with which they have worked, and the townscapes which they have produced.

The study could be along the following lines:

1. Select an area of consistent townscape. This may be uniform (as in much byelaw 19th century or post-war estate building), or it may be a mixture of styles which constitutes an area distinctively different from adjacent ones.
2. Find out when, why, by whom, and for whom it was built.
3. Record its characteristics. Individual buildings may be selected for detailed study.
4. Record evidence of change and analyse reasons for change.

Alternatively:

1. Select a year.
2. Reconstruct the townscape of the area for that year, following the sequence outlined above.

Regional patterns

Once again it is a question of spotlight and flood light, the collation of detailed work done by individuals or groups for small, manageable areas, and the transference, with important decisions to be made on what detail is to be lost, from large-scale to small-scale; the small-scale in the urban case being larger than in the rural where the detail is less closely packed. A similar landscape may extend over several miles whereas townscape may change markedly within a few hundred yards. In deciding on a pattern of regionalisation of townscape within a city useful guidelines are already in existence in planning maps and reports. Some suggested regions are as follows:

Landscape regions

The basic regions, which can be sub-divided, are:

Coastal lowlands

Coastal uplands

Northern triangle, hill and valley (including Frome valley system)

Cotswold (or Southwold) (scarp foot, scarp, top)

Avon valley

Southern hill and vale (eastern and western parts differ—sub-divisions include Wrington Vale and the valleys of Cam, Wellow and Chew)

Mendip fringe

Winscombe Vale

Carboniferous limestone plateaux (Lulsgate, Failand, Kingsweston, Durdham Downs)

Townscape regions

Central core (includes the Central Business District)
Georgian extension
Regency/Victorian suburbia (villa land, terrace land)
Inter-war suburbs and infill (Council and private)
Post-war suburbia (Council and private)
Urban villages (e.g. Kingswood)
Industrial (heavy, light)

3

Population and the Structure of Local Society

J.S. MOORE

The size and composition of the population of the local community are two of the most important topics confronting the local historian; they are also topics in which recent advances in demographic methods have shown that progress at a national level is largely dependent on previous work at regional or local level, so much so that at the present time our knowledge is largely based either on Laslett's hundred local samples or on Wrigley's study of Colyton parish in Devon. Here, therefore, is an area in which the local historian has a very real contribution to make; not only locally, but also in building up a more soundly based revision at national levels. Again, however, the local historian must not be too parochial, since no parish was a totally isolated unit: as we shall see, members of its population moved across its boundaries either temporarily or permanently, so that here, as with other topics, a more suitable unit of study is the group of two or three adjacent parishes.

The level of population

The first question that the local historian needs to answer is, quite simply, how many people were there in his area at different times in the past. Several records enable estimates to be produced at intervals, starting in 1086. Domesday Book will provide, on a manorial basis, figures of villagers (*villani*), cottagers (*bordarii* or *cotarii*), freemen (*liberi homines, radknechti* etc.) and slaves (*servi*). We may assume that all these figures except the slaves, and priests if these occur, refer to heads of households, and to obtain total population figures these must be multiplied by a factor of four-and-a-half to five. In some parishes, certain population groups will not be enumerated in *DB*, in particular the inmates of castles and monasteries, and allowance must be made for these omissions (see Knowles for monastic population). Similar estimates can be made later in the medieval period from the total number of tenants recorded in manorial 'extents', rentals and surveys, but in all these instances two problems must be borne in mind: first, the relationship between manor and parish has to be established; second, the total number of tenants is not necessarily the total number of heads of households, either because there are independent freeholders in the parish or because there may be subtenants of the manorial tenants not recorded in manorial surveys, though court rolls or other records may reveal their existence (see chapter 4). Other sources for medieval estimates are subsidy rolls (up to 1327) and the poll-tax returns of 1377 to 1381, but in these cases inaccuracy is likely to arise either because part of the population were too poor to be taxed for subsidy purposes or because of tax-evasion. More reliable estimates can be calculated from the subsidy rolls of Henry VIII (1524–46) and the 'military survey' of 1522 where this survives: later subsidy rolls can be disregarded since the poor were deliberately excluded from assessment after 1546. Tudor and early Stuart muster rolls (notably for Gloucestershire John Smyth's *Men and Armour*) may be useful provided that it can be demonstrated that all adult males were included. In estimating total population from subsidy and muster rolls, allowance must be made for exclusions: women (probably 50% of the total population), children (probably 30% to 40% of total population), and in muster rolls men over 60 (about 5% of total population). From the mid-16th century, more abundant sources become available: the 'chantry certificates' of 1547–8 provide estimates for many parishes of 'houseling people', i.e. men and women over 16: these must be adjusted as above to include children; returns were made to the Privy Council of families in 1563 and of communicants (over 16) in 1603; a further return of families was made in 1650, whilst in 1676 the 'Compton census' gives figures of people over 16 divided between Anglicans, Catholics and Protestant Dissenters. (For Gloucester diocese the figures exist on a parochial basis: for Bath and Wells and Bristol dioceses, only the diocesan totals survive.) These can be compared with the total number of householders given in the 'Hearth Tax' returns of 1662–74, provided that the returns include both taxable and exempt householders. Certainly for Bristol and Gloucester dioceses, similar population estimates may be found in unprinted diocesan surveys in the 18th century, though a comparison may show that some figures were copied from earlier versions without revision; county histories and other printed works are a further source of figures to be explored. An example of how early modern population figures have been derived for part of south Gloucestershire is given in J.S. Moore, *The Goods and Chattels of Our Forefathers*, pp. 10–11. From 1801 onwards, total population figures can easily be extracted from the decennial censuses: for the 19th century these are conveniently tabulated in the second volumes of the *Victoria County History* of Gloucestershire and Somerset. Given a reasonable degree of record survival and of persistence by the local historian, a number of population estimates for each parish should be possible at intervals between 1086 and 1971.

Unless hundred account rolls are available giving figures of 'hundred penny' payments from each male over 12 in the area (see Titow), it is doubtful whether medieval estimates can be linked together to produce a continuous population curve; and certainly, then or later, straight line interpolation on graphs should be avoided: at national level, however, a continuous medieval series is available for comparison (appendix in Hollingsworth). From the 16th century onwards, however, more continuous figures can hopefully be produced by a graphical presentation of annual baptisms and burials ('aggregative analysis') derived from the Anglican parish registers, though such figures cannot hope to be equally reliable everywhere. Much depends on the unknown degree of conscientiousness of incumbents and parish clerks in compiling the registers: trends in baptisms and burials are not the same as trends in births and deaths, though they are unlikely to be radically divergent in most parishes. Some specific factors may nevertheless cause problems: burials of people from some chapelries may by custom take place in the mother church, and other local difficulties may lead to anomalous situations. In Stoke Gifford, for example, a small churchyard was frequently completely full, and burials had to take place in Almondsbury, Filton or Winterbourne, thus artificially inflating the burial figures for these parishes. But the major difficulty in using Anglican registers, particularly after 1660 and even more so after 1688, is the existence of Protestant Dissenters both 'old' (Baptists, Presbyterians and Quakers) and 'new' (Methodists etc). Unless the Dissenters' registers are also available, this difficulty cannot completely be overcome, but it may be doubted in most cases whether either the number of Dissenters was so large that population trends were likely to be seriously affected, or the population trends of the Dissenting population were likely to be radically different from those of the Anglicans. In any case, the local historian, from his study of the ecclesiastical sources (see chapter 9), is the person best qualified to assess the local importance of Dissent, which in terms of numbers has almost certainly been grossly overstressed and overall rarely exceeded 10% of the local population. But for all the above reasons the annual totals of baptisms and burials from the Anglican registers should not be taken as absolutely reliable guides, only as relatively good indicators of the general population trend: if the resulting long-run series seriously diverge from the trends indicated by the individual estimates, both trends and estimates must be reconsidered to determine which is more likely to be in error and why. At best, given now uncheckable errors in the original records and inevitably imprecise multipliers for family size and age composition in the local population, we cannot hope to produce more than a good approximation to the actual demographic situation before 1801. Again, a comparison of the series from similar adjacent parishes may reveal that, on occasion or consistently, one series is exceptional and anomalous, either because the development of this parish was genuinely different or because its recording was eccentric. The difference between 'open' and 'closed' parishes (see chapter 4) or between mainly agricultural and mainly industrial parishes may be a relevant factor: equally, the interaction between individual incumbents and their populations may cause exceptional problems: during part of the 18th century, for as yet unknown reasons, many Mangotsfield baptisms and burials were being recorded at Almondsbury and Winterbourne; on the other hand, very conscientious parsons, as at Westerleigh, might record baptisms and burials of their parishioners occurring in neighbouring parishes.

Causes of population change

Having done our best to trace the evolution of local population over time, we must now try to explain the changes observed: in the main, this is only possible after the Anglican parish registers start in 1538. The annual (and in large parishes quarterly or even monthly) tabulation of baptisms and burials is the first step: local historians should remember that down to 1752 (apart from a few years between 1653 and 1660) the church of England used the 'Old Style' calendar, in which the New Year began on Lady Day (25 March). To obviate difficulties in comparing developments before and after 1752, events before 1752 should be redated so that each year begins on 1 January. Also, baptisms of older children or adults whose ages are given should be moved from the year of baptism to the presumed year of birth: at times, religious enthusiasm created by a new incumbent resulted in sudden upsurges of baptisms of such children and adults, whilst some poorer (or less pious) families developed the practice of baptising all surviving children when the last infant was baptised. Such removals should always be noted in the tabulation (e.g. '1754: 40 baptisms (including 5 children aged 4 baptised in 1758)'); the reason for the whole operation is to reveal the trend in births, not the trend in religious enthusiasm, important though the latter is in its own right. It is generally assumed that all other baptisms are of infants under about a month old: but any evidence in registers of birth-dates alongside dates of baptisms should be noted. It will also be found in the course of family reconstruction that some children are buried whose baptisms are not recorded: if these baptisms cannot be traced in a neighbouring parish, these children probably died before being baptised, and their births should be added to the number of baptisms in the year of their burial. The tabulation and graphical presentation of baptisms and burials will immediately reveal abnormalities to be investigated. In the case of baptisms, it may well be that some months are especially well represented, and this may result not from any seasonal distribution of births but from local customs which restricted baptisms to certain months in the year. In the case of burials, 'bad years', in which the number of burials was more than one-and-a-half to two times the average number of burials in the five years before and after those years, represent exceptional mortality which can often be attributed to known causes, such as plague, influenza or bad harvests. If the cause is not known either from local mentions or national works, the monthly pattern should be investigated, since many diseases (e.g. plague) have a marked seasonal pattern of occurrence. Even in normal years, a sharp concentration of deaths in one or two months almost certainly indicates an infectious or contagious disease at work, and the local historian should also investigate whether the deaths are confined to a few families either living close to each other, or to the poorest classes, those most liable to deficiency diseases. Birth and death rates should not be calculated from the annual tabulations, since in most cases before 1801 there are not enough population figures to provide a firm basis for such calculations; to calculate such rates, and to delve further into the causes of population change, the more refined method of 'family reconstitution' should be used.

This involves reconstructing each family, generation by generation, on a series of index cards (at least 8″ × 6″) in which the baptism and burial of each member of the family is noted: this enables the age at marriage and death of each member to be calculated (which are not normally given in the registers until after 1837 and 1813 respectively), and it also gets round the problem of a fixed population basis for calculating birth and death rates, since in any one year that basis will be the total number of people alive in all the reconstructed families. In constructing this index, allowance has to be made for alternative forms of christian names (e.g. Ann/Hannah; Fanny/Frances), variant spellings of surnames (these should be cross-referenced to the preferred form), and some degree of mistakes, especially in easily confused wives' names (e.g. Mary/Martha). An example of a family reconstruction card worked out by the Almondsbury Local History Group is given below: an index of such cards also forms a very useful basis for the addition of other information from wills, marriage licences, probate inventories and administration bonds, poor-law records, gravestones and monumental inscriptions (M.I.'s).

Front of Card:

SMITH, BENJAMIN Baptised at Almondsbury 3-3-1776, son of BENJAMIN and BETTY SMITH. Buried at Almondsbury, aged 66, 29-11-1841. (M.I.: died 22-11-1841; 1841 Census: aged 65)

MANNING, SARAH Buried at Almondsbury, aged 73, 14-4-1851 (M.I.: died 7-4-1851, aged 72; 1841 census: aged 63; 1851 Census: aged 73, widow, annuit- ant, born Kenn Court, Somerset)

Married at Almondsbury 6-1-1801 (∴ Wife 4 months pregnant) (Age at marriage: H:24¾; W: *ca*.23)
Carpenter and builder (Alm.C.Reg., 1813, 1816), 'the builder engaged about the church when it was renovated' (Alm.B.Reg., 1841); (M.I.: Yeoman)
Husband: Signs. Wife: Signs. (Alm.M.Reg., 1801)

Back of Card: (All baptisms and burials at Almondsbury).

ELIZABETH Baptised 2-6-1801
Buried, aged 47, 7-4-1849 (M.I.: died 31-3-1849, aged 48)

WILLIAM Baptised 28-8-1803 (1841 Census: carpenter, aged 35; 1851 Census: carpenter, aged 47)
Married CHARLOTTE [   ]

JULIA Baptised 6-1-1805
Buried, aged 45, 13-5-1850 (1841 Census: aged 30)

JANE Baptised, 3 years, 11 months old, 26-8-1810
Buried, aged 18, 24-10-1824 (∴ born September 1806)

HESTER   Baptised 26-8-1810 (1841 Census: aged 25)
MARGARET   Baptised 28-3-1813
                      Buried, aged 8, 23-10-1821
BENJAMIN   Baptised 8-12-1816
                      Buried, aged 4 months, 3 weeks, 4-5-1817

If the occupational or social status of the husband is also entered on the card (see below), it will be possible to investigate how far certain trends were confined to certain groups of the local population.

The use of this method enables much more precise calculations to be performed which may reveal factors of considerable local importance, particularly whether or not more children were being born; if they were, whether this was because couples were marrying younger or were moving in from outside; whether those dying were mainly older people (the normal modern experience) or mainly children under 1 year old (the norm before the 19th century). Because of its prevalence, migration should always be investigated: if young couples were moving into a parish, birth rates would be abnormally high and death rates (apart from infant mortality) artificially low, whilst if such couples were moving out, the opposite would be true. Where available, poor-law settlement records (see chapter 8) will indicate the major directions of migration; the prevalence of migration will also be revealed in family reconstitution cards lacking the burials of children (who have presumably emigrated) or the baptisms of parents (who had presumably moved in). Again, if a group of parishes is chosen as the unit of study, some of the data missing from one set of parish registers may well be recovered from neighbouring sets: unless lines of communication (see chapter 5) or economic opportunities elsewhere (see chapter 6) are especially good in a particular direction, most families before 1900 did not usually move more than about 10–20 miles from their place of birth, but the first independent check on this will be obtained from the analysis of birth-places in the census enumerators' books from 1851 onwards. Another very valuable source of information on migration is contained in ecclesiastical deposition books, which survive in bulk for Bath and Wells and Gloucester dioceses, or in loose depositions in the diocesan courts: witnesses ('deponents') are usually identified not only by present but also by past occupation and residence. It is impossible in this short chapter to indicate all the possible methods and lines of research in local demography: readers should refer to the books and articles listed in the Bibliography for further guidance.

Household and family

It is rarely possible before the census enumerators' books in the P.R.O. become available after 1841 to investigate the size and structure of the family and household. Yet this subject is of great importance, not only for population history (as we have seen, a family or household 'multiplier' is essential for obtaining many population estimates before

1801, and an age-composition 'multiplier' for others), but also for social history, the quality of life and the upbringing of children. Generally, it has been suggested that for England the normal family was on average a unit of about four-and-a-half to five people, usually headed by a married couple or a widowed survivor, rarely containing more than two generations and almost never more than one married couple: outsiders, if any, usually comprised only a few servants, apprentices and occasionally lodgers. Local historians should investigate the census enumerators' books for their parishes (most are now available on microfilm in the Avon Central Library), possibly adopting the following form of tabulation for each family: H, W, xC, yO (H = Husband, W = Wife, xC = no. of children, yO = no. of outsiders); family-size will be the total H + W + C, household size size the total H + W + C + O. Age composition can also be studied from the original census records after 1851; in 1841, however, the ages of people over 15 was usually only given to the lowest term of five years, e.g. a 23 year old would be entered as 20. Another source of information on this subject is, of course, the family reconstitution cards where the families have been completely reconstructed. Any great divergence from the normal family size and age composition should be investigated, as it may reveal special local circumstances of significance for the historical community. Any detailed 'listings' of local families before 1841 (e.g. the Olveston parish census of 1742) should be analysed and if possible printed: these records are both rare and valuable for the insights they give into the early modern family. Finally, although the 'extended' or multi-generation family was rare or non-existent in England, kinship and propinquity were important links between family and community. The former can be documented from marriage links given in parish registers, whilst linking together the information on occupiers from Tithe Maps and Awards and the heads of households in the near-contemporary 1841 Census will reveal to what extent parents, married children and in-laws lived near each other, and also how far certain occupational groups tended to cluster in specific parts of the local area: some useful insights here can come from modern investigations of working-class families, e.g. in Bethnal Green.

Occupational and Social Structure

Important though this subject is throughout local history, it can rarely be investigated in detail before the early modern period. Some light can be thrown on the medieval community by a tabulation of the size of holdings in manorial surveys (see chapter 4), though what allowance should be made for the incidence of personal freedom and free tenure before, say, 1400 is singularly unclear. The subsidy rolls before 1327 and the Poll Tax returns of 1377–81 will also reveal some degree of stratification, though the lowest social groups in the former records are likely to be understated or omitted altogether; some Poll Tax returns also give valuable information on later medieval occupational distribution. The tax assessments in the subsidy rolls of 1524–46 again reveal the total social structure of their time, as do those in the poll tax returns of 1666–94, where these exist, and in the Hearth Tax returns of 1662–74; the later subsidy rolls from 1548 to 1663, whilst excluding the lower social groups and becoming increasingly unrealistic as a guide to absolute wealth, nevertheless enable us to identify the richer groups in local history vis-à-vis each other. In the 18th century the returns to the assessed taxes on horses, windows, servants and hair-powder, where they survive, fulfil the same role.

The local historian is much less well provided with sources that instantly reveal the occupational structure between the 16th and the 18th centuries, unless the rare returns to the 1522 'Military Survey' exist including occupations or this information is incorporated in the 1524–5 Subsidy Rolls, which is also rare; the most likely sources are the poll books for Bath and Bristol between 1711 and 1870, and any returns made under the Militia Acts from 1754 onwards, though the latter are also rare. Otherwise, before 1841, apart from the unique version of the 1608 Gloucestershire muster roll annotated by John Smyth and printed as *Men and Armour for Gloucestershire*, the local historian must reconstruct the occupational structure of his community at intervals for himself by taking a full list of males (e.g. the 1524–46 Subsidy Rolls or the Elizabethan and early Stuart muster rolls) or of heads of households (e.g. the 1662–74 Hearth Tax returns and parish rate-books), any 'Easter Books' (lists of communicants) or parish 'listings', and annotating these himself, following in the steps of John Smyth. In default of any such lists, particularly in the 18th and early 19th centuries, the local historian must first compile his own, for example by extracting from parish registers the names of all fathers of children baptised over a 30 year period. Occasionally, he will find that the registers are sufficiently consistently annotated with occupations for this task to be accomplished quite speedily (e.g. J.S. Moore, *The Goods and Chattels of Our Forefathers*, Tables 5–7); otherwise the parish registers are only one of the many classes of record which must be combed for the required information. The reason why many classes of record have to be examined is that no one class will cover the whole local population: some, such as wills and marriage licences, relate mainly to the upper groups of local society.

The single most valuable class is that of probate records, since at least in theory all dead adult males and independent widows and spinsters should either have left a will or had an administration bond made after their death: both wills and bonds should include the occupation of the deceased, and the bonds in addition nearly always give the occupations of the two administrators. From about the mid-16th to the mid-18th centuries, again in theory, the moveable estates of all dead adults should be listed in probate inventories, the headings of which normally mention the occupation of the deceased. For Bristol and Gloucester dioceses these records are in the B.R.O. and G.R.O. respectively, but nearly all the Bath and Wells probate records were destroyed in Exeter in 1942: the S.R.O., however, has a card-index to surviving copies of probate records.

Records relating to the settlement of the poor are the best supplementary source of data on the lowest social groups, whilst marriage licences and bonds provide additional information for the upper social groups: down to 1822, the marriage bonds, like the administration bonds, give the occupations of the bondsmen as well as the prospective grooms. Especially for towns, apprentice registers of indentures and the records of the many urban courts reveal valuable additional occupations, but even urban apprentice registers can be useful for rural historians, since certainly in the 16th and 17th centuries many country children were apprenticed to urban masters; from 1711 onwards all apprenticeships, rural and urban, were also recorded for tax purposes in registers now in the P.R.O. Apprentice registers of whatever kind are especially valuable for occupational history because in addition to giving the trade of the master and apprentice they also give the occupation and parish of the apprentice's father. Even in the countryside, court records are valuable, especially when the main registers or rolls are supplemented by indictments and depositions, since these also, whether in secular or ecclesiastical courts, virtually always include the occupation of the accused or witness. Finally, despite their voluminous nature, estate records should not be overlooked: deeds and leases generally give the occupation or status of buyers, sellers and tenants, and detailed surveys, particularly in the 18th century, may do so as well.

In the last century and a half, the sources for occupational history become much fuller: after 1813, the occupations of all fathers are recorded in the Anglican baptismal registers, and for 1841, 1851, 1861 and 1871 the census enumerators' books provide complete coverage: similar books will be made available in the P.R.O. 100 years after their compilation. For the modern period, town and country directories will give the callings of all local residents who are self-employed or professional people, and nonconformist registers and membership lists may also yield occupational information. On a regional basis, the occupational distribution is analysed in the printed *Census Reports* since 1841.

Wearisome though the collection of all this information is, it is undoubtedly vital to local history, since its analysis will determine the direction of later, more extensive research on the economic development of the area by pointing to the major sources of employment to be investigated. Also, whilst the collection of the basic information will be confined to the more mobile members of local history groups able to consult the necessary record evidence, the indexing and analysis of this information can usefully be farmed out to those group members whose circumstances do not allow them to work much or at all outside their own homes: this is also true regarding the analysis of most of the information collected on local population trends.

A final, significant, indicator of social structure can be obtained from an analysis of personal wealth, though no records cover both land ('real property') and other property.('moveables'). The 13th–14th and earlier 16th century subsidy rolls are useful here, as are the Poll Taxes, both those of the 14th and the 17th centuries; the Hearth Taxes are less valuable because of the wide range of houses with only one hearth. The

NAME: MALE/FEMALE   STATUS/OCCUPATION:
PARISH: PLACE OF RESIDENCE:
DATE OF INVENTORY: DATE PROVED: REF:
APPRAISORS:

I PERSONAL ESTATE

WEARING APPAREL:
MONEY IN PURSE:

HOUSEHOLD	NUMBER	£. s. d.
Beds and appurtenances:		
Tables, chairs, benches, etc.:		
Cupboards, Chests:		
Cutlery/Crockery:		
Kitchen implements:		
Luxury Goods (carpets, silver, paintings, books, etc):		

Total Household:

NUMBER OF HEARTHS: NUMBER OF ROOMS:
NAMES OF ROOMS:
OTHER PROPERTY—HOUSE/SHOP:

TOTAL PERSONAL ESTATE:

II CAPITAL ESTATE (INCOME PRODUCING)

LIVESTOCK	NUMBER	£. s. d.	COMMENTS
Oxen:			
Heifers:			
Cows:			
Bulls:			
Sheep:			
Horses:			
Pigs:			
Poultry:			
Others:			

Total:

CROPS	ACRES	£. s. d.	IN STORE	QUANTITY	£. s. d.
Wheat on Ground:			Wheat:		
Rye on Ground:			Rye:		
Barley on Ground:			Barley:		
Peas/Beans on Ground:			Peas/Beans:		
Others on Ground:			Hay:		
Orchard/Fruit:			Others:		
Common rights/herbage:					

Total: Total:

MISCELLANEOUS	TOOLS
Timber/Wood:	Agricultural:
Dung in yard: ·	Craftsmen:
Buttery:	Craft Materials:
Brew House/Malt House/Other:	Other:
Stored Food and Liquor:	
Other:	

LABOUR/SERVANTS: INVESTMENTS:
                                   TOTAL CAPITAL ESTATE:

DEBTS:
SUM DEBTS OWED TO TESTATOR: SUM TOTAL OF GOODS:
SUM DEBTS OWED BY TESTATOR: PERSONAL AND CAPITAL
(See overleaf for details)   (PLUS OR MINUS DEBTS):

most worthwhile source is again the probate inventories (though these exclude freehold and copyhold land), and a suggested form for summary analysis, originated by Mr. James Horn of the University of Sussex in the course of work on the Vale region of Gloucestershire, is shown opposite. A study of the composition of wealth in different social groups within the local population will throw much light on the accumulation of capital and the standard of living in Avon in the past.

4

Agriculture

G. DAVIS and J.S. MOORE

Of all the economic aspects of local history, agriculture is undoubtedly the most important: excluding Bath and Bristol, every parish in Avon depended on agriculture to provide food and employment for the bulk of its population until well into the 19th century, except where rural industrialization had started earlier (see chapters 3 and 6). The evolution of local agriculture was therefore basic to the economic history of the region and must be considered by all local historians; even if the evidence is defective in a particular parish, agriculture had a marked regional character, the result partly of the natural environment (see chapter 2), partly of the development of a regional market (see chapter 5), so that considering the evidence from neighbouring parishes is both desirable and necessary. What then are the questions the local historian should be asking? First, he needs to consider the agrarian structure, to find out who at different periods owned and farmed the land, the conditions of tenure, the size of estates and farms. Second, he ought to study the broad agricultural background, changes in predominant land use and the ways in which the major elements of agricultural land (arable, pasture, meadow, orchard, woodland) were integrated over time. Third, he should study how farms operated within this background, discovering the main crops, livestock and techniques in use in each major period. Fourth, he should strive to explain why changes in all these aspects occurred, bearing in mind major factors such as trends in population and occupational structure (see chapter 3) and the availability of alternative sources of both supply and demand (see chapter 5), but also remembering that very specific local factors may produce exceptions to general practice, whilst throughout agrarian history the role of the large estate may mean that major administrative decisions have been made outside the region entirely. As a further result, agricultural records more than most may be preserved outside the county, in the Public Record Office and in non-local record offices (e.g. the large collection of Thornbury archives in the Staffordshire Record Office).

Agriculture before 1750

The structure of landholding both before and after the Norman Conquest is revealed in Domesday Book, though even in translation this source is not easy to use. The large estates of 1086 are easily revealed by the layout of *DB* itself, but indexing the 1066 landholders reveals many large estates already in existence. The best indicators of the size of individual manors are the values, the ploughlands (in Somerset) and the ploughs (in Gloucestershire): in both counties, the ploughs are divided between demesnes and tenants, and these figures give the best available idea of the average size of both demesnes and tenants' holdings, assuming that one plough (team) usually implied one field-hide (the *DB* hides are fiscal units and should be ignored for agrarian purposes). Later in the medieval period the number and size of demesnes are revealed for secular estates in the 'extents' often attached to inquisitions post mortem, and for ecclesiastical estates in the *Taxatio. . . Papae Nicholai IV* of 1291; more detailed surveys may exist for all estates either in the P.R.O. (especially for ecclesiastical estates) or in the archives of their present or later owners. These more detailed surveys, and sometimes also the extents, are also the main sources of information on the size of peasant holdings, and are often termed 'custumals' because of their detailed description of the rents and customs (labour-services, etc.) by which the peasants held their lands. Inspection of printed examples such as the *Red Book of Worcester*, the rentals and custumals of Glastonbury Abbey estates, or the extents in *Gloucestershire Inquisitions Post Mortem*, vols. 4–6, will show the sort of data contained in them. In the absence of such documents, the services and rents can be discovered from the court-rolls and account-rolls if these exist; however, it should not be taken for granted that the tenant named in surveys or court-rolls is necessarily the actual farmer of the holding in question, as sometimes he will have sublet to one or more undertenants. Calculating the size of both demesnes and peasant holdings also presents difficulties: the 'acre' in medieval records is more often than not a customary measure, not a statute acre, and customary units such as the hide or virgate (¼ hide) vary in area according to local soil conditions; only the carucate is likely to approximate closely to 120 acres. Nevertheless, the local historian should not shirk attempting to arrive at some rough and ready conclusions, since the size of holdings is a major factor determining the economic and social position of individual peasants in local society. After the early 14th century, demesnes were increasingly let to tenants rather than being operated by bailiffs on behalf of manorial lords, a change traceable from account-rolls: local historians must try to find out when and how this change occurred (were demesnes let *en bloc* or piecemeal?) and to whom demesnes were leased or 'farmed', to local men or outsiders. Because of the size of most demesnes, these changes may have a great effect on agrarian and agricultural development locally. Where the evidence survives (court-rolls, account-rolls and comparable surveys), an attempt should also be made to discover how and when the structure of land-holding is changing over time: are small farmers maintaining their position, or are they being superseded by a smaller number of large farmers, with the smallholders being downgraded to labourers? Are these or similar changes, e.g. from copyhold to leasehold, being encouraged by landlords able to charge higher rents from more efficient large farmers? It should be remembered, however, that the very existence of records may indicate atypicality, and it is suspected that 'open villages' or 'freemen's villages' may have very different histories from 'closed villages' dominated by one or two large landlords: unfortunately the latter are likely to be far better documented than the former.

The principal questions to be answered about the regional background are the existence of a 'common' or 'open-field' system during the period; the existence concurrently of compact farms alongside that system; the extent to which, by purchase or exchange, the first system was evolving into the second; and whether or not local agriculture was mainly arable-based, mainly pastoral, or mixed farming. *DB* and the extents show that meadow and woodland normally accounted for only a small proportion of the total cultivated area, but the failure of *DB* to mention either should not be taken as conclusive proof that none existed in 1086. If either a two- or three-field system existed (which can be discovered from the details of demesne crops sown in the account-rolls, from detailed descriptions of peasant holdings in court-rolls or deeds, from extents mentioning half or one-third of the demesne as lying fallow or *in warectam*, and from later evidence such as maps or enclosure awards) the land-use of the demesne is likely to be similar to that of the peasants' holdings, unless other records make it clear that the demesne has been consolidated within a ring fence outside the open-fields. Otherwise, it is fairly safe to assume that the balance between arable (normally simply termed 'land', *terra*, in medieval records), meadow (*pratum*) and pasture (*pastura*) revealed in demesne extents and account-rolls applied throughout the local open fields, though *pastura* does not include commons and wastes unless it is explicitly termed *communis*. Particularly after demesnes have been leased out in the later Middle Ages, manorial surveys may give a total conspectus of land use holding by holding, and such records should be fully analysed: generally speaking, if arable constitutes 75% or more of the cultivated area, open fields still exist; if less than 50%, probably enclosure is under way (see *The Goods and Chattels of Our Forefathers,* Table 10). Glebe-terriers, describing the composition of the glebe-lands attached to local parsonages, are another source which indicate the existence of common fields or enclosed farms: these exist from the 1570s to the 19th century and are now in the diocesan archives.

It is rarely possible to discover much about peasant agriculture, unless a long series of court-rolls exist, in which details of cases of theft or trespass brought up in manorial courts may throw some light on this dark subject. From about the mid-16th to the mid-18th century, however, an incomparable source is available in the probate inventories. These are lists of a dead person's goods made by friends or neighbours which include crops sown or in store, livestock, farm tools and equipment, and farm produce awaiting sale (especially cheese, bacon and cider). Unfortunately, the destruction during World War II of the Exeter Probate Registry (to which most Somerset probate records were transferred in 1858) has meant that only a few inventories survive for

Somerset in Taunton, but several thousands survive at Bristol and Gloucester for south Gloucestershire. These need to be fully analysed both on a parochial and a regional basis (see chapter 2), and on an economic basis: husbandmen and craftsmen will probably be farming mainly for subsistence purposes, whilst the larger yeomen will probably be producing for market consumption. The type of farming by each group may therefore differ considerably, as will the apparent results from inventories taken at different times of the year, but the underlying basic character of local agriculture will be revealed by a total review of all the available inventories. Conclusions cannot safely be drawn from individual inventories: Joan Thirsk has made much of two Winterbourne inventories in the first half of the 17th century mentioning turnips, but these inventories relate to a clearly exceptional father and son, and turnips are not commonly found in south Gloucestershire until after 1750. Nevertheless, inventories are by far the best guide to early modern farming practice, as opposed to the precepts of reformers only slowly adopted in the countryside. Farm accounts both before and after 1750 are rare, and should always be studied in detail by local historians, though they may possibly represent exceptional rather than normal practice and should always be interpreted in the light of the local inventories. Some guidance on the use of probate inventories is given in the introduction to *The Goods and Chattels of Our Forefathers.*

The explanation of observable changes in local agriculture may not be completely possible until research on other aspects of the local economy and society is nearing completion, since agriculture did not operate in a vacuum. It is only possible here to point to some of the factors which elsewhere have been found significant. The major determinant of and constraint on agricultural change is undoubtedly geographical: the physical and chemical quality of local soils, relief and drainage, the existence of water supplies and transport facilities, simply because these are factors least likely to be technically or economically capable of alteration. Of historical factors, population change is probably the most important: increasing population pressure is likely to lead to smaller holdings and increasing burdens on their holders (higher rents and services), whilst concomitant price rises, by widening profit margins, will encourage larger farmers to produce for market consumption; falling population will have the opposite effect. The structure of the local economy is also significant: the development of rural industry and of urban markets will stimulate local agriculture to produce more both absolutely (to feed a growing non-agricultural population) and relatively (since surplus population will be siphoned off to supply the labour requirements of rural and urban industry). Finally, the development of transport facilities (see chapter 5) will affect local agriculture for good or ill depending on its efficiency: it may open up larger markets outside the region, it may enable more efficient regional specialization, it may also provide alternative sources of employment for the local population which may either weaken local agriculture or force it to be more efficient with higher levels of productivity, and it may expose local agriculture to the unwelcome blast of competition from other areas able to supply produce more cheaply, because their labour costs (in the absence of alternative sources of employment) are lower.

Finally, the evidence of field archaeology and maps should be integrated with the documentary evidence: relict-features such as ridge and furrow or other indications of former field systems; common meadows (often recorded on Tithe Maps even after enclosure), as at Keynsham. Long narrow fields possibly indicate fossilized strips of common field arable, as in the north-west of Frampton Cotterell, often of a 'reversed-S' pattern, whilst fields of irregular shape may suggest early enclosure. The counting of hedge-species may help to date hedges and therefore enclosure (see Hooper), and local historians should test and amend Hooper's hypothesis by applying it to local hedges which can be independently dated from documents. Above all, the physical evidence of farms and farm-buildings is important for many developments in local agriculture throughout Avon, but especially in the south where inventories are sparse.

Agriculture since 1750

In the period after 1750, some new sources become available to the local historian, who must recognise the background of continuous change that characterises modern agriculture. Three topics will serve as examples of how a range of sources might be used to increase our understanding of agricultural development in the region. In each case some of the appropriate sources will be suggested, and although some overlap is inevitable, it is a reminder that the same sources can be used for different purposes. The three topics are enclosures, farming practice, and the condition of the farm labourer.

Enclosure, where it took place, either by private treaty or by means of Parliamentary legislation, often brought profound changes in the pattern of landholding, but could also mark a turning point in the life of a rural community. It used to be held that enclosures in the period 1760 to 1850, although necessary to implement changes in agriculture sufficient to feed an increasing population, destroyed peasant agriculture and produced widespread misery among the newly created mass of landless labourers. Many were consequently driven from the villages of their birth to seek employment in the industrial cities. This view has been challenged in recent years. It appears that, in some cases at least, enclosure generated more employment, and evidence on the number of smallholdings seems to suggest that enclosure may only have continued existing trends. Certainly, the average size of holdings remained small, even after the impact of enclosures.

The counties of Somerset and Gloucestershire were affected by early enclosure in the late medieval and early modern period, but from the late 18th century onwards a new round of enclosures of commons and wastes took place. To find out if a particular village was affected, the lists of Parliamentary Enclosure awards should be consulted. These record the parish and the date of enclosure. The details of a particular enclosure will be given in the enclosure award. These may be supplemented by surveys, commissioners' minutes, and field books to provide a fuller background to the event of enclosure. In the absence of enclosure awards, estate and tithe maps contain useful evidence of newly enclosed common land or the disappearance of the strip system, in field names, and changes in their size and shape. However, to obtain a proper perspective of the effect of enclosure in one parish or a group of parishes, a reasonable length of time has to be studied. An attempt might be made to plot the pace and extent of changes that occurred in the size of agricultural holdings for a generation before and after the date of enclosure.

To this end, a number of sources can be used to complement each other—land-tax assessments, poor-rate books, and the tithe schedule, in close association with the available maps. Land-tax assessments are full of pitfalls. Where valuations for individual holdings remained constant for many years, an increase in the size of the holding was concealed by deliberate under-assessment. The returns could be misleading on the extent of smallholdings because they included such properties as inns, smithies, or even gentry houses with their pleasure gardens. In an individual parish, a closer check can be made on the number of smallholdings by a familiarity with the names of the inhabitants. This can be achieved through extensive use of the parish registers and the enumerators' census schedules between 1841 and 1871.

The information on occupations will be the most valuable in the 1841 census schedules. Farmers were normally styled as such, but many craftsmen and tradesmen, such as millers, publicans, carpenters and blacksmiths, occupied smallholdings, which they farmed as a sideline. Until the early 20th century the village parson was most likely to have been supported by a smallholding, the glebe land. The share of the total farm acreage in a village occupied by tenant farmers, by tradesmen and craftsmen, and by members of the professional classes such as clergymen or solicitors, would indicate how far agriculture had developed from the mixed pre-enclosure pattern to the 19th century domination by tenant farmers. Bound up with this trend, the size of holdings, as farming commentators believed, was a guide to how far progressive methods were being adopted.

From 1851 on, in addition to the information on occupations, census enumerators often included details of farm acreage, and the number of men, women, and boys employed by the farmer. This may not always coincide with the size of individual farms within a single parish, as land in an adjoining parish could be included in the farmer's total acreage. Here, a reference to the Poor Rate books of adjoining parishes would help to disentangle the occupation of individual parcels of land. The fullest single view of ownership and occupation is found in the tithe schedule and the tithe map. The schedule lists owners and occupiers separately, records the extent of acreage and describes the land usage, including that of buildings. Each parcel of land is numbered on the tithe map.

If a study of the above sources indicates clear changes in the number and size of agricultural holdings within a parish in the period affected by enclosure, an attempt might be made to estimate levels of migration in and out of the village. This is a daunting task, but one that is central to the question of the impact of enclosures. It ranges beyond the parish boundary in that demand for labour in the nearby towns prompted migration as much as poverty in the countryside. A first step towards estimating migration levels would be to record the population size of the parish and adjoining parishes, from the printed census returns beginning in 1801 and taken subsequently every ten years. A significant change in the rate of population increase, or decrease, would suggest that migration was, at least in part, responsible. The growth of population in most agricultural villages in south Gloucestershire and north Somerset between 1801 and 1841 was probably below the rate of growth of the towns in the area. After 1841, many villages experienced an absolute decline in population size. How far were enclosures and changes in farming responsible for this transfer of population away from the countryside (see chapter 3)?

A check on the frequency of surnames in the parish registers at regular intervals can provide a rough indication of any marked turnover in population. Marriage registers reveal the extent of contact between different parishes, urban as well as rural. The birthplaces of members of families recorded in the census schedules from 1851, and an analysis of the age and occupational structure of the village population between census dates will indicate the trend of past movements. The relative absence of young people in the age group 15–30, is a strong indication of migration out of a village. If agriculture is the main employer, changes in its organisation and practice may go a long way to explain migration to the towns.

The subject of farming practice is closely allied to that of enclosures, but is not to be confined to a generation or two. Changes in farming methods have continued to play a vital role in determining not only the appearance of the countryside, but also the size of rural communities. It has far ranging implications. It takes into consideration such developments as the application of science in superseding traditional customs, and improvements in transport which at once opened up more distant markets and undermined the self-sufficiency of village communities. In 1800, most villages grew their own wheat, irrespective of the quality of the local soil. By the mid-century, it was no longer necessary to feed a village population from produce predominantly grown in the village. Increasing mechanisation, and a move to less labour intensive farming, for instance a reduction in arable farming, may be connected with the renewed drift from the land after 1870 in Somerset and Gloucestershire. These 19th century trends have continued into the 20th century, farm workers making way for the tractor and the combine harvester.

Changes in a particular rural community should be measured against the general regional pattern. The farming returns, recorded for most parishes during the Napoleonic Wars, provide a basis for later comparison in the acreage devoted to livestock, cereals and winter feed crops. A generation later, the tithe schedule will give fuller information from which to calculate the proportion of arable, pasture, meadow and woodland. The associated tithe file in the P.R.O. may provide additional information on the variety of soil in the parish, on particular problems, such as drainage or flooding in winter. It will also have livestock figures and these may be usefully compared with the annual returns for crops and livestock which begin in 1866. A fuller picture of the region's agricultural structure can be obtained in the 1874 *Return of Owners of Land* in each County, and in Bateman's survey of landed estates, which went through several editions in the 1870s and 1880s.

For the regional background, there are the county surveys. For Somerset, there is Billingsley, written in 1795, and Acland and Sturge, written in 1861; for Gloucestershire, there is Turner, written in 1794, Rudge, written in 1807, and the county is featured in Sir James Caird's *Survey of English Agriculture* in 1851. Both counties are covered by Marshall's *Rural Economies c* 1790 and his county reports to the Board of Agriculture in 1818. In addition, Cobbett's *Rural Rides* and Rider Haggard's *Rural England* contain colourful descriptions that may prove useful, as may other travellers' narratives. Lastly, the chapters on Agriculture and on Social and Economic History in the respective *Victoria County Histories* are still worth consulting. For examples of new developments in farming practice in the region, the *Journal* of the Bath and West of England Society, and the *Annals of Agriculture* should be examined. These may involve much labour for little reward. This could equally be said of *Parliamentary Papers*, which demand a careful selection. A useful list of these can be consulted in W.R. Powell's *Local History from Blue Books* (1962).

One of the questions that remains to be fully explored in a local context is how long it took for new ideas in agriculture to become accepted farming practice. There is some evidence in the first half of the 19th century that agricultural reformers, particularly with their emphasis on corn crops, found little enthusiasm among the despised cowkeepers of Somerset. Yet, by the mid-century, dairy and fatstock farmers, who formed the majority in North Somerset and South Gloucestershire, were reaping the benefits of market prices in their favour, as corn crops became relatively less profitable.

Some indications of the relative prosperity of different types of farming would be found in the county surveys, but for an individual parish one has to look again at a number of sources in combination. Rent levels of individual farms and changes in acreage can be traced from a run of Poor Law rate books, if they survive. Where the evidence is scanty, the tithe schedule and Poor Law Valuation Lists will provide the same information. Increases in rent and acreage, sustained over a generation or two, through good and bad times, would indicate increased profitability. In the mid-19th century, the farm rent was, as a general rule, reckoned to equal half the tenant's gross income, so that his profit, labour-costs, taxes and other expenses had to come out of the other half of his income. On a dairy farm, he might expect an income of £4 to £5 an acre, while his rent would range between 40 and 50s (£2 to £2.50) an acre. A holding of 100 acres might produce a 15% return on capital employed at £4 an acre, or as much as 30% on a farm of several hundred acres. With dairy and fatstock farming becoming more profitable than arable farming, this was reflected in the level of farm rents. This is the background to the substantial decline in acreage devoted to cereals in the last quarter of the century.

If there are records relating to a particular farm, perhaps where a family has occupied the land for many generations, it may be possible to reconstruct the business operations of the farm, at least for a limited period. Further information may be obtained from local newspapers, where the level of local market prices, the condition of the harvest, the introduction of farm machinery and, of course, the sale of farms, were all reported. Sale advertisements contain valuable information about buildings, stock and machinery that can all be related to the size of the holding. These might be supported with the records of auctioneers and estate agents that handled agricultural properties. Even surviving farm buildings can provide clues to the dating of new developments in local agriculture—new farmhouses and barns at a time of enclosure, and new cowsheds and stockyards marking the change to a pattern of mixed farming.

By the Edwardian period, the persistence of depression in agriculture brought an increase in the number of farms for sale. Reduced rents meant that the large landed estates often found it necessary to begin the process of selling off outlying farm properties. The extent of that process would be a fascinating study in itself. It also serves to remind us that the records and family papers relating to a particular estate can provide very detailed information on rent levels, the size of holdings, the system of tenure, and farming methods, possibly over a long period. Estate maps, rent rolls, cash books, letter books, stock books, and records of sales could be employed in extracting detail on the prevailing farming practice in the area covered by the estate. The management or mismanagement of the estate, possibly linked with the fortunes of the estate family, might itself make an absorbing piece of historical research.

In the late 1930s, a comprehensive national survey of agriculture in each county was undertaken. The details are contained in the reports of the Land Utilisation Survey of Britain, 1937–1940. Some valuable historical background is provided on the farming practice in the region, with land utilisation maps for Gloucestershire and Somerset. A similar survey was carried out in the 1960s, which records the result of changes in the countryside since World War II. Existing occupiers of farms may well go back several generations, but even within one generation, since 1945, agricultural practice has become increasingly dependent on scientific advice and improved machinery. Indeed, within living memory, there has been an agrarian revolution quite the equal of its more widely recognised counterpart in the 18th century. Particular examples of local evidence on this rapid change may be uncovered in the form of farm account books, farming implements, and old photographs.

Changes in farming practice clearly influenced the lot of the agricultural labourer. Public concern increased from the time of the 'Swing' riots in 1830, just at the time when conditions began to improve. Real wages rose slowly, but in the middle decades of the century the labourer was to gain from improved cottage accommodation and the provision of field gardens or allotments, particularly on landed estates. The drift from the land that accelerated after 1870 was not confined to men. Employment of women and children in agriculture diminished under the increased pressures of domesticity and educational provision.

The most detailed contemporary sources for investigating the life and labour of farm workers and their families are found among the Parliamentary Papers. Some of the most valuable are the reports of committees on agricultural distress in the 1830s, 1880s and 1890s, the reports of the Select Committees on Agricultural Customs for the 1840s and 1860s, and the reports on the employment of women and children in agriculture in 1843 and 1867–70. Information on agricultural wages can be found in various reports. Apart from the reports of the Commissioners themselves, they contain the recorded testimony of numerous witnesses, including farm labourers and their wives. These may refer to the locality of interest, but are more likely to describe the general condition of the region. Similarly, the county surveys, already mentioned, contain general detail on wage levels, cottage rents, and the custom of payments in kind.

For an individual parish, the level of cottage rents can be found in the Poor Rate Books. It may also be possible to link these up with the accommodation provided by cottages, comparing those that can be dated from the 19th century with those of earlier origin. Some cottages might be dated by written sources and maps where available, or their dates could be determined from external evidence by reference to works on vernacular architecture (see chapter 7).

The condition of agricultural labourers as a group might be studied within a single parish, or throughout the region. The printed census returns provide aggregate totals of occupations by county. For the parish, the census schedules contain the raw data for an analysis of the size and composition of the agricultural labour force. For this purpose, the number of shepherds, cowmen, blacksmiths, wheelwrights, etc., would be included with farmers and agricultural labourers. Agricultural labourers commonly had large families. The size and structure of labourers' households, the numbers of children, dependents and lodgers, would provide a measure of overcrowding and insights into living conditions. It may be possible to construct case studies of individual families from the parish registers, census schedules, and poor law records.

In the 20th century, much information might be obtained from the collective folk memory of retired farm hands. The nature of the work, the hours worked, the levels of wages, the numbers of hands employed, relations between the farmer and his men, and individual perspectives on the inevitable drift from the land might all be profitably explored. It should be acknowledged that some information gained in this way is only vaguely or mistakenly recalled, but every man remembers the size of his first wage packet, the hours he worked, and the conditions he endured. Indeed much that is remembered in this way never will be written down unless it is recorded from the memory of a contemporary witness. Where oral evidence can be checked against written sources, this should be included as an essential part of oral history. The pioneering work of George Ewart Evans and, more recently, that of Ronald Blythe and Raphael Samuel, will provide inspiration and example for those equipped with much time and patience, and a good tape recorder (see chapter 12).

Collective folk memory, besides recalling individual past experiences, may help to reconstruct the life of the old village community, one that was based on the common dependence on agriculture. In many villages, it was disappearing by the outbreak of the Great War; in others, in remote areas, it lingered until the Second World War. Gradually, changes in farming methods and the growth of private transport have brought a new social composition to many villages. Commuters have replaced farm hands as villages have become dormitories for nearby towns.

Reconstructing the agricultural past need not be merely an exercise in recording crops, rents, and the size of the labour-force: it can also be rediscovering how for centuries mainly self-sufficient communities survived and flourished. This is our common past. It may, given some of the problems of our modern industrial society, be a guide to our common future.

5

Trade, Transport and Communications

W.E. MINCHINTON

How did goods, people—and news—move in and out and within what is now the county of Avon? A major influence, whose importance has altered with developments in the means of transport available, has been the topography of the county. With the Severn forming its western boundary and the Avon almost bisecting it as it runs WNW through Bath and Bristol to the Severn, in the period before the railway and the internal combustion engine, water transport was of prime importance to the county. Within the county, movement by road was not facilitated by the undulating nature of the ground, with the Mendips forming the southern boundary and the Cotswolds the eastern. And the marshy coastlands south of Clevedon and north of Avonmouth were particularly difficult to cross in winter.

Because the source material is different, the subject matter of this chapter will be considered under three main headings: foreign trade and transport; inland trade and transport; and the movement of goods and persons within towns. A final section will deal with some of the residual matters. Source material and secondary accounts will be mentioned on the way but suggestions for further reading will be found in the Bibliography.

First, the foreign trade and transport of the region. This was confined to Bristol, which occupied a defensible position eight miles from the mouth of the Avon. So far the earliest indication that a trading centre had grown up on the peninsula between the Avon and the Frome, trading particularly with the southern and eastern coasts of Ireland, is provided by two silver pennies minted at Bristol in the reign of Ethelred II (979–1016). Further evidence of Bristol's trade before the Conquest will not be easy to find. About 1145 Bristol is already described in the 'Gesta Stephani Regis Anglorum' as a city nearly the richest of all the cities of the country, receiving merchandise by sailing ships from the neighbouring counties and from foreign countries. Evidence for Bristol's trade in the 12th and 13th centuries with Ireland and in wine and woad with France can be found in the charters and inquisitions *ad quod damnum*, while the growth of trade in woollen cloth in the 14th and 15th centuries can be traced in the Staple Court Books (see *B.R.S*, vol. 5, edited by E.E. Rich), the Constables' Accounts (*B.R.S*, forthcoming vol,

ed. Margaret Sharp) and in the customs records, some of which have
been published by Professor Carus Wilson (*B.R.S*, vol. 7, and, with Olive
Coleman, *England's Export Trade, 1275–1547*). In the 15th century
Bristol traded with Iceland (see Carus Wilson, 'Overseas trade of Bristol
in the 15th century', in Power & Postan) but whether Bristol ships
pressed on to discover the new world in 1480–1 (see Quinn) is still a
matter of debate. Certain it is that when Cabot sailed from Bristol in 1497
he relied on the skill and knowledge of local seamen. The outline has
been set out most recently by J.W. Sherborne, *The port of Bristol in the
middle ages*, but there is still scope for detailed work on particular
branches of trade and commodities.

The enrolled customs accounts for the 16th century support Roger
Barlow's comment in 1540 that Bristol was a noble town of great trade
and many ships, though, as Jean Vanes shows in *The port of Bristol in the
sixteenth century*, the trade proved less buoyant in the later 16th century
and particularly in the 1560s than it had been in the earlier part of the
century. The cloth trade particularly suffered from the effect of war and
from competition from other areas, so that by 1600 Bristol could no
longer claim to be a major cloth exporter. In using the customs records of
this—and other periods—account needs to be taken of smuggling.
Broadly speaking the generalisation can be hazarded that the higher the
duties the more was the incentive to smuggle. Trade recovered with the
peace with Spain in 1604 but until the mid-17th century Bristol
merchants kept largely to their traditional markets in Spain and
Portugal, France and Ireland. Cloth was the most important export while
a variety of other goods, as the Port Books (PRO E 190) reveal, was
imported and exported. Already foreshadowed by mid-century, a
radical shift in Bristol's foreign trade occurred after the Restoration.
While the old trades expanded, Bristol was one of the western ports
which rose as her trade with West Africa, the West Indies and the
American mainland colonies grew. While a variety of largely
manufactured goods and foodstuffs were exported, imports were
dominated by the new colonial products, tobacco, sugar, rice, indigo and
dyewoods. Bristol merchants also took part in more roundabout trades
like the Newfoundland fish trade with the Mediterranean and the
Atlantic slave trade. To the greater wealth of records available, the *B.R.S.*
volumes edited by McGrath and Minchinton provide excellent guides.
But while the outline picture of Bristol's trade until 1800 as set out in
Walter Minchinton, *The port of Bristol in the 18th century*, is reasonably
clear, the detailed chronology and trade in particular commodities and
in particular directions requires further study.

While maintaining its volume of trade, Bristol lost ground to other
ports in the early 19th century due in the main to two factors, the absence
of industrialisation in Bristol's hinterland and the decline of trade with
the West Indies. Then in the second half of the 19th century, Bristol's
trade began to expand, with tobacco and grain prominent amongst
imports. A satisfactory study of Bristol's trade in the 19th century,
together with more detailed discussions of trade in particular
commodities and with particular countries, is much needed. Material is

available in the Bristol Presentments (ACL), from 1830 in the Board of Trade published returns and from 1855 in the monthly and annual statistics issued by the Customs and Excise. The traditional view that Bristol had a reasonable economic performance in the 19th century has recently been challenged by Dr Alford who believes all the evidence shows that it was generally mediocre (*BGAS*, 1976), a viewpoint which deserves further scrutiny. Nor should students spurn the 20th century. For a study of the changing volume, direction and commodity composition of Bristol's trade since 1900 there is abundant material in official sources and in newspapers.

The movement of persons is a different question. Over Bristol's long history not many people appear to have entered the county by sea for permanent residence. But Bristol was reputedly an exporting centre for slaves in Saxon times. In the 17th and 18th centuries people emigrated, freely, as indentured servants, or as convicts, on which some information is available. But no connected account of emigration or passenger traffic in the 19th and 20th centuries has been written.

Besides its commerce, other aspects of Bristol as a port deserve investigation. A variety of vessels, many of which were built in Bristol, used the port. From the 1760s their history has been examined by Grahame Farr (*B.R.S.*, vol. 15), but information is available in official records, in *Lloyd's Lists* and from the mid-18th century in the newspapers, which will enable a fuller account of shipping using the port to be produced. Then, some attention has been paid to the pilots, based on Pill, who enabled vessels to navigate the treacherous waters of the Avon, Severn and Bristol Channel, but no full account drawing on the records of the city and the Society of Merchant Venturers has so far been produced. The port facilities themselves underwent improvement. As early as 1240 a radical decision was made to create a new channel for the Frome in order to provide better quays. When the new course of the Frome was completed in 1247 it made Broad Quay the main anchorage for ocean-going ships while the quays along the Avon were used for coasters. When these works were completed, Bristol Bridge was rebuilt and the old port above the bridge ceased to operate. As trade expanded and ships grew in size there was pressure on the port facilities for extension of the quays, for the provision of cranes and the construction of warehouses. Early in the 18th century a dock was built at Sea Mills and then in 1767 William Champion, who had earlier built a dock later known as Merchants' Dock, put forward a plan for a floating harbour and a dam near the present entrance. Though it was recognised by 1791 that the harbour was by nature inferior to that of many other ports, the construction of the floating harbour did not occur until 1804–9. After this, as a result of the heavy expenditure, the Dock Company tried to recoup its outlay by charging high port dues. The resultant protests led eventually to the docks, which had been improved by Brunel in the 1840s, being taken over by the Corporation in 1848. Further improvements of the channel took place and, with the recognition that the Avon was a difficult river to navigate, new docks were constructed at Avonmouth in 1877 and Portishead in 1879 which came under municipal control in 1884. Further construction took place in the 1920s and 1930s and in the 1970s, which have led to the closure of the city docks and the concentration of trade at Avonmouth and Portbury. Material in the Bristol Record Office, especially the papers of the Port of Bristol Authority, and the Society of Merchant Venturers' records should enable this history to be told in more detail.

Because it was free of national customs and records of local tolls are scarce, less is known about water-borne trade in the middle ages, though it is clear that Bristol was the focal point of the trade of a wide area including the Midlands within reach of the Severn and its tributaries, South Wales and the neighbouring counties of Somerset, Devon and Cornwall. Diligent research could no doubt reveal more of the story. Information is easier to obtain from the 16th century, for there are coastal port books which record the movement of commodities, and once newspapers and directories become available in the 18th century the documentation thickens. In 1788 it was estimated that 'upon the coasting trade from the various ports of England, Scotland and Wales, exclusive of the navigation of the Severn, about 1,300 vessels of various burthen arrived annually in the port of Bristol'. At this time the directories provide a timetable of the sailings of these vessels—the Severn trows for Bewdley or Worcester, the market boats for Caerleon, Newport or Chepstow and the constant traders for ports as far distant as London or Glasgow. Each trade had its special part of the quay, of which Welsh Back is the most vivid reminder. This traffic, which helped to make Bristol in the 18th century the metropolis of the West, continued into the 19th century, to be sharply reduced with the coming of the railway. Both its heyday and decline deserve to be chronicled.

Apart from Bristol and its outports of Portishead and Avonmouth, there were no ports of significance in Avon though Uphill was once a creek within the customs port of Bristol. But the development of pleasure shipping led to the construction of piers at Clevedon (now sadly damaged and disused) and at Weston-super-Mare. Upriver from Avonmouth there were no ports on the Severn within Avon, but until the construction of the Severn Bridge there was a ferry crossing from Aust to Beachley (see Jordan). The ferries across the Axe at Uphill and across the Avon at Shirehampton, Rownham and Hanham still await study.

The only river which provided inland communication within the county was the Avon upstream of Bristol. This underwent improvement in the course of the 18th century, when the weirs were by-passed by locks which enabled barges to journey between Bristol and Bath. In the canal mania of the early 1790s there were a series of projects which would have made Bristol the centre of a canal network linking the city with Gloucester, London, Newbury, Southampton, Poole and Taunton; but of these only the most ambitious, the proposal to link the Kennet and the Avon and so provide an inland waterway between London and Bristol, came to fruition. Completed in 1810, it was taken over by the GWR in 1852 and traffic virtually ceased on the canal by 1890. Longer-lived was the Somerset Coal Canal, built in 1800, which ran from Paulton (with a short-lived branch to Radstock) to link up with the Kennet & Avon Canal near the Dundas Viaduct over the Avon, which remained in use until 1902. To the history of the Avon navigation, the Kennet & Avon and the Somerset Coal Canal, Charles Hadfield provides an introduction, while Kenneth Clew has recently written a history of the Somersetshire Coal Canal. Both provide a guide to sources for further study.

As a pendant to the maritime history of the county, the story of the fisheries deserve attention. The Greenland and South Sea fisheries in which Bristol merchants engaged in the 18th century were the most speculative but, like the river and inshore fisheries of the county, they deserve a historian.

In studies of the Bristol region, attention has tended to be concentrated on sea and river transport, but land communication was also important for the carriage of persons and goods. Most of the traffic was within the present county of Avon or to the immediately neighbouring counties of Somerset, Dorset, Wiltshire, Gloucestershire, Oxfordshire and Devon. The collection of town-dues at the town gates (which elsewhere has provided invaluable information on the nature and extent of inland trade) was abandoned at Bristol in 1544, and no records of its collection survive. But the wide range of goods on which these dues had been levied by virtue of Bristol's medieval charters (see *B.R.S.* vols. 1 and 2) illustrates well the interdependence of town and country from early times. From the 16th to the 18th centuries the probate inventories of merchants, retailers, shopkeepers and craftsmen can reveal the variety of goods on sale in Bristol and the surrounding country towns and villages, as can farm and household accounts where these survive. Also by 1500 an extensive network of markets and fairs in the countryside provided the means for buying and selling basic commodities (see Finberg and Hulbert). Many of these institutions survived well into the 19th century and local historians ought to consider their decline, as well as the rise of new regional shopping centres in the 20th century (e.g. Yate) and the more recent hypermarkets on the edges of modern towns (e.g. Patchway). Up to the 20th century the operation of country carriers can be traced in the past through directories whilst, as Defoe reported early in the 18th century, Bristol traders maintained 'carriers, just as the London tradesmen do, to all the principal counties and towns from Southampton in the south even to the banks of the Trent in the north: and though they have no navigable river that way, yet they drive a very great trade through all those counties'. The low-lying ground along the Severn in the vale of Berkeley and in Somerset was difficult to cross in winter, and so carts and coaches tended to keep to the higher ground southwards across the Mendips to Shepton Mallet and northwards through Wotton-under-Edge and Dursley. Eastwards the three main routes lay through Chipping Sodbury to Cirencester, through Marshfield and Chippenham, the most important route which led to London, and south-east through Bath to Warminster, Salisbury and on to Southampton. From Bath, another nodal point of the road system, roads also ran to Radstock, to Stroud and to Chippenham. The upkeep of roads and footpaths and their changing pattern can be studied in the records of the highway authorities, the Quarter Sessions and in the deposited plans in record offices.

Early in the 18th century turnpike trusts were active in improving roads and by 1750 all the main routes from Bristol had been turnpiked. Further improvements came in the later 18th century, and by 1800 there were few places which were inaccessible to wagon traffic. By that date a regular network of passenger coaches (which also carried mail) had been established linking Bristol with the main towns of southern England. Each week 38 coaches left for London, 31 for Birmingham, and over 100 for Bath, while there were daily services to Exeter, Oxford, Gloucester and Wales. Eric Pawson, in *Transport and economy*, has provided an example of how 18th century records can be explored to show the relationship between the development of the local transport net and the growth of a local economy. In the 19th century the improvement of roads continued. The turnpike trusts were liquidated and, apart from a few isolated examples, road transport was relieved of tolls. Since 1960 the road situation has been transformed by the construction of the M4 and M5 motorways (with the M32 link into Bristol) which is likely to have a marked effect on the economy of Avon. With it has come an effective road link via the Severn Bridge—which is a toll bridge—with the Forest of Dean and South Wales.

The earliest railway in Avon was the tramway built in the 1730s by Ralph Allen to carry stone quarried on his Prior Park estate down to the Avon Valley, but it had no successors for almost a century. Then two horse tramways were built to carry coal from Coalpit Heath, one to St. Phillips, Bristol, the other, sponsored by the Kennet and Avon Canal Company, to the Avon near Bitton. Both were in operation by 1835. Although proposals were put forward earlier, the major railway proposal, the Great Western Railway to link London with Chippenham, Bath and Bristol, was not started until 1836. It was then extended as a broad gauge line to reach Exeter in 1842. The Bristol-Gloucester Railway was completed two years later in 1844, also using broad gauge track. Other towns in Avon were linked with the railway later. The arrival of the Midland Railway in Bristol in 1854 brought the standard gauge to the city. The battle of the gauges then ensued in Avon, until standard gauge finally won about 1875, though broad gauge traffic continued to operate through Bristol until 1892. A line was built from Frome to Radstock in 1854 and in 1857 a railway was opened from Trowbridge and Bradford-on-Avon to Bath. Clevedon was linked to the Bristol and Exeter line in 1847, the Bristol and North Somerset Railway was constructed to Pensford and Paulton and then on to Radstock in 1873 which was connected to Bath in the following year. Links with South Wales were built more slowly. In 1863 a line was built from Bristol to New Passage to connect with the Ferry to Portskewett, but the Severn tunnel, which was required to make an effective link between the two banks of the Severn, was not constructed until 1885. A year earlier the Weston-super-Mare loop had been completed, while a line was opened from Avonmouth to Pilning and the Severn tunnel in 1900. A light railway ran between Weston, Clevedon and Portishead which was connected to the Bristol and Exeter line by a railway constructed on the left bank of the Avon by the Portishead Pier and Railway Company. The direct London-South Wales line which runs through Avon from Chipping Sodbury to the Severn tunnel was built in the early years of this century. By 1845 main railway lines had joined all the larger towns in Avon and during the following five years the Somerset coalfield was reached. Since 1945 there have been three main developments. First, some branch lines—notably the Weston-Clevedon and Portishead light railway through the Gordano Valley—and stations—part of Temple Meads Station, Bristol, is now a car park—have been closed. Secondly, some stations have been modernized and new stations, notably Bristol Parkway, have been built. And finally, the improvement of track and signalling has enabled the British Rail high speed train to operate between London, Bath, Bristol and Cardiff.

Nor should the history of aviation in the county be neglected. The former Bristol airport at Whitchurch has disappeared and has been replaced by Lulsgate. Filton airport, the base of the Bristol Aeroplane Company, which saw the first flights of the ill-fated Brabazon and of the British Concorde, has probably a limited life. There is also a small airport at Weston-super-Mare.

Apart from Bristol and Bath, there was little need for urban transport before the 20th century, but within these two cities there were various facilities for the carriage of passengers and goods. In Bristol there were sleds as well as packhorses and wagons for goods, and hackney coaches for passengers; in Bath during the period of its vogue as a spa the sedan chair was a popular means of transport. In the later 19th century tramway systems were built in Bristol and Bath, the Bristol system being brought virtually to a halt during the second world war when buses took over the routes to add them to the existing network of urban services. Buses also linked the towns and villages within the county. Taxi services provided ancillary transport, and from the inter-war period motor charabancs enabled holiday-makers to enjoy day trips or longer holidays.

Not only was a means of transport necessary for the traveller, but he also needed accommodation and places of refreshment. Hotels, inns and boarding houses provided for different categories of traveller, for those on business and those on pleasure bent, for the wealthy and the poor, for the merchant, the retailer or the commercial traveller. And restaurants, cafes, public houses, tearooms and coffee houses provided in their different ways at different times of the day, food and drink for the traveller.

From the 16th century the merchants banded together (as described by McGrath and illustrated by the two *BRS* volumes edited by McGrath and Minchinton) in the Society of Merchant Venturers, as pressure group, lessees of the quays, supervisors of the pilots and as a social club. For business, merchants met in the Tolzey (which had its own court) and later in the Exchange. Much local trade was carried on in the various towns in the county in weekly markets. Seasonal business was carried on at the various fairs in the county, at Pensford, Keynsham, Chipping Sodbury, Marshfield, Wickwar, as well as in Bath and Bristol. Much business, which is only just beginning to be studied, was carried on in inns. The history of retailing is also a neglected subject to which the directories provide an entry. Here again recent developments, such as the replacement of the corner shop by the supermarket, as well as the more remote deserve their chronicler. The department store and the chain store also have their place in the story. In the whole range of business in trade, whether wholesale or retail, foreign or domestic, and in the various branches of transport, the history of the individual firm is worth studying. And while many records suggest that business was regular and orderly, law suits and the records of the bankruptcy courts are a reminder that the conduct of business could be both untidy and risky.

Information about markets, about cargoes, about prices, were spread by word of mouth in inn, coffee house or exchange. Then, with printing, broadsheets were posted, bills of entry were made available for subscribers and newspapers were published. The earliest Bristol newspaper dates from the first years of the 18th century, and local newspapers were established elsewhere in Avon before the end of the century. At first weekly, some of them became dailies in the course of the 19th century. For large towns like Bristol, the evening newspaper was of especial importance for local news. But there were also other agencies of communication. Out of the correspondence carried by the coaches came the general post, which provided both for the delivery of letters and the distribution of packets and parcels. Linked with the post office there developed the telegraph and the telephone with its business extension, the teleprinter. Radio has extended the range of facilities available and the development of local radio has given communities like Bristol a new voice.

The wheels of commerce were oiled by the means of payment. The way in which transactions were carried out and accounts settled before the 19th century has received scant attention, though the *Marchants Avizo*, a late 16th century handbook for merchants, contains advice on this subject. Periodically in the past there were times when coin in circulation was in short supply. One device developed to overcome this problem was the production of trade tokens. Examples survive for Avon, for both the 17th and the later 18th century. Currency was minted not only nationally but locally and there was a mint in Bristol. The need for better institutional arrangements led in the middle of the 18th century to the formation of banks. Bristol Old Bank, set up in 1750, was the first in the county and was followed by a number of others. Following the crisis of 1825, Bristol was one of the places where the Bank of England established a branch which still exists. At a different level, in the 19th century savings banks, building societies, burial clubs and sickness benefit societies were founded to mobilise savings for particular individual purposes. Such capital became available for investment both in trade and in industry. And since trade was risky, merchants tried to limit their risks first by sharing their investment with others and then by insurance. Marine insurance, a topic worth further scrutiny, was first effected on a personal basis and then insurance companies were formed for this purpose as they were for fire, life and other contingencies. The records of the Sun Insurance Company and other companies are in the Guildhall Library, London (see Cockerell and Green).

This chapter has only been able to indicate very briefly something of the range of topics which fall within a consideration of trade, transport and communications. While in a number of directions the general outline is known, in many cases the details deserve further investigation. Even so it ought to be said that the received interpretations should not be regarded as inviolate. With the growing range of material available about private business as well as official bodies, the number of topics capable of discussion has increased. And finally it ought to be said that with the fast pace of technological and physical change, the recent past merits the attention of the research worker as much as the more distant.

6

Industry

R.A. BUCHANAN

From the point of view of its industrial development, Avon County can realistically be regarded as the Greater Bristol Region, insofar as the industries of the region have always been very responsive to the economic opportunities created by the existence of the port of Bristol and the large urban market that grew around it. Two consequences stem from this Bristol-orientation of the regional industries: their longevity and their variety. Longevity is the result of the continuity of urban activity over a millenium, during which period Bristol has been an important town, stimulating industry and commerce. Few other towns in Britain possess such an unbroken tradition: most of the large medieval towns sank into comparative obscurity with the onset of rapid industrialization, while the great industrial towns of the Midlands and the North barely existed before the Industrial Revolution. Bristol, like London, is one of the handful of important cities which preserved its industrial base from the Middle Ages into recent centuries, and extended it to accommodate new industries and processes.

The other consequence of the Bristol focus of Avon industries is their variety. Unlike most of the great industrial cities of modern times, the prosperity of Bristol has never been identified with a single industry, but always with a multifarious collection of different industries. The contents of this collection have changed over the years, with some industries disappearing and others continuing to grow. Amongst the many 'lost' industries which once flourished in the city but exist no longer are soap-boiling, glass-making, pottery manufacture and the preparation of sugar. The latter was one of the lucrative plantation commodities which came in bulk to Bristol as a result of its notorious involvement in the Atlantic slave trade in the 18th century. Another such plantation product was tobacco, which remains as one of the major industries of the region. The disappearance of many older industries has been balanced by the development of new processes, especially in engineering, so that the region now possesses one of the largest complexes of aeronautical engineering in the country. Thus the variety of industries in the Bristol region has been continually restored and enriched, so that Avon County has fortunately never sustained the sort of crippling depression which has occurred elsewhere when a single staple industry has declined.

Both the longevity and the variety of industrial activity in the Bristol region have been related to the key function of Bristol as a port. Its strategic position at the lowest convenient bridge-site on the tidal Avon more than offset the disadvantage of its inland position, some eight miles from the deep water of the Severn estuary. For many centuries ships sought the shelter of its city-centre wharves, aided in their navigation of the tortuous River Avon by the tidal flow, the range of which is amongst the largest in the world. But the increase in the size of ships made this operation progressively more difficult, so that the city began the long process of dock improvement which led, first, to the construction of the 'Floating Harbour' in 1804–9, and then, from the 1870s, to the construction of deep-water dock facilities at the mouth of the River Avon, resulting in the development of the modern port of Avonmouth. The tardiness with which these improvements were undertaken reflected the complacency and conservatism of the dominant mercantile interests in Bristol during much of the 18th and 19th centuries, and caused Bristol to decline in importance relative to other ports such as Liverpool, Glasgow, and Hull which adopted more dynamic policies. But the innovations in the port of Bristol served nevertheless to keep the city in the premier league of British ports, and sustained thereby the rich variety of industries already noted.

Two categories of industries are directly related to the existence of a port, and both these have flourished in Bristol. In the first place are those industries and processes concerned with servicing the needs of the mercantile community, including ship building, ship repairing, and maintenance, and the provision of sailcloth, rope, pitch, and barrels. The 19th century revolutions in shipping, with steam power replacing sail and iron or steel construction replacing timber hulls, brought concomitant changes in these industries. Shipbuilding declined in Bristol, although it has only just expired completely, with the closure of Charles Hill's small ship yard in the Floating Harbour. Similarly, the manufacture of rope survived in the city until quite recently. But in general, these industries have diminished greatly in importance in the last hundred years.

The other type of port industries comprises those that derive from specific commodities imported. In this category, the wine trade has been one of the oldest and most resilient of Bristol industries, with the development of facilities for storing wine and of expertise in blending sherry and preparing other distinctive wines. Later, as we have noted, the growth of the Atlantic trade and the plantation economy of the New World brought abundant supplies of sugar and tobacco to the port of Bristol and stimulated important industries. Despite the success of Conrad Finzel's large enterprise on the Counterslip in the middle decades of the 19th century, the sugar refining industry in Bristol was an early victim of the forces of concentration and bulk-handling which caused its virtual extinction by the end of the century, although some more specialized aspects of sugar manufacture continued in business until quite recently. The tobacco industry, on the other hand, has grown from strength to strength, the latest expansion being the transfer of Imperial Tobacco from its traditional premises in Bedminster to a brand new factory at Hartcliffe. Tobacco was taken in the form of snuff in the early 19th century, and fragments of the snuff industry survive in mill sites on the Clifton Downs and in the Stapleton valley of the River Frome. Cocoa was another significant port industry in this category, although its raw material came from plantations in West Africa rather than America. Several important cocoa factories flourished in Bristol, the largest of which was that of J.S. Fry and Sons in the Pithay, which moved out to its present site at Somerdale near Keynsham between the wars. Other important port industries have been those providing for milling grain in bulk at Avonmouth, and for handling a wide variety of imported commodities.

Imports have for long figured more significantly than exports in the trade of the port of Bristol, and one reason for this has been the function of the port as the 'metropolis of the west', supplying a substantial urban market and rural hinterland with essential commodities. The food and drink industries have thus been prominent amongst the enterprises of the Bristol region, and remain so with important chocolate (Frys), jam (Robertsons), and brewing (Courages, until recently George's Brewery) industries. There is still some malting carried on in the region (Bath has a malting still in business at Lower Weston, but has lost its large Bairds maltings near Churchill Bridge, while the small Bairds malting on the Kennet & Avon Canal at Widcombe has been elegantly converted for residential use). On a lesser scale, but still interesting physical remains of a process which once figured prominently in the regional economy, were the dozens of small grain mills which flourished on the smaller rivers of Avon County, such as the Bristol Frome and the River Chew. These were comparatively easily converted to other uses (snuff mills, paper making, dyewood grinding) when stimulated to do so by market demands, and several of them changed their functions more than once.

Avon County has had a long association with the textile industries. The outstanding textile of the region has been wool, and all the processes of woollen cloth manufacture have been familiar here. The great medieval and early modern West of England broadcloth industry was centred not so much in Bristol as in Bradford, Trowbridge, and Bath, and also in Stroud and Dursley. To some extent this represented a definite move to escape from the restrictive influence of the Bristol guilds which had dominated the manufacture of woollen cloth in the region during the Middle Ages. But it also marked the introduction of a new water-powered technology to operations such as fulling the cloth to give the 'felted' quality typical of broadcloth, and the movement of the industry inland was thus encouraged by the search for reliable sources of water power. With the coming of large-scale mechanization and the factory system this dependence on ample water power reinforced the advantages of the inland parts of the region, while Bristol further declined as a centre of woollen cloth manufacture although it maintained strong mercantile links with the industry. In the 20th century, the industry has declined almost to vanishing point, unable to compete with larger-scale manufactures in a market which has become progressively more difficult as foreign producers have taken an increasing share of the available trade, and as other textiles have challenged the supremacy of wool. Only a single mill remains in business in Trowbridge, and none survive in Bradford or Bath. Clothing industries, such as the felt-hat factories at Frampton Cotterell and Winterbourne, have mostly disappeared. The most severe challenge to wool as an all-purpose textile material came from cotton. Early success in mechanizing processes for spinning and weaving this material led to it being adopted as the first great success of factory production methods in the Industrial Revolution. The Bristol region is not generally thought of as a centre for the cotton industry, and there are good reasons for this, as most of the available resources were devoted to the woollen cloth industry or elsewhere. But several small-scale attempts were made to introduce a cotton industry to the region, and in 1838 a large mill was built in Barton Hill on the best principles of fire-proof mill construction as devised in Derbyshire and Lancashire. This became the Great Western Cotton Factory which, despite financial and other difficulties, survived in business until after World War I. In some respects this may be considered as another port industry, depending upon an imported plantation crop from America, but as it proved more economical to bring the cotton overland from Liverpool to the Barton Hill factory rather than to ship it direct into Bristol, it cannot be claimed as an import of the port of Bristol.

One of the great assets of the Bristol region as an area of industrial enterprise was the existence, from the Middle Ages until the present century, of accessible supplies of coal. The use of coal spread slowly, as it was deemed suitable for most purposes only as a substitute for wood when this became scarce and expensive. But there seems little doubt that the Bristol region was one of the first places to experiment in the industrial applications of coal as a fuel, first in the business of soap boiling and then in brewing, glass making, pottery, and many other processes. The coal came at first from Kingswood, the area of heathland to the east of Bristol which had once been a Royal Forest. The coal measures outcropped here and were exploited by a host of small 'bell' pits. As the demand increased, the search for coal spread into adjoining districts, so that by the 19th century deep collieries were being worked over a broad area of what was then South Gloucestershire and North Somerset (now mostly included within Avon County). The exhaustion of easily available good quality coal, and the competition of supplies from South Wales and the Midlands, has caused the extinction of this industry in recent years: the last colliery closed at Kilmersdon/Writhlington, near Radstock, in 1975. But it deserves recognition as one of the vital sources of industrial enterprises in the Bristol region, and one which has left its mark in many ways on the character of Avon County.

Another important extractive industry of the region has been stone mining. Bath stone is a form of oolitic limestone which, if it is properly cut and worked, provides an excellent building material for ashlar masonry work (i.e. squared stone regularly jointed with only thin bands of mortar) and has been highly prized as such in London as well as in the South West. The stone was mined from the hills around Bristol and

Bath from the 18th century until the present day; one mine is still at work near Box. It was conveyed down to the valley-bottoms by tramways, of which Ralph Allen's ingenious line alongside his Prior Park mansion in the 1730s was the first. The stone lent itself superbly to the classical design adopted for Georgian Bath, and was also transported via the Kennet & Avon Canal to the London market, where it was used in several important buildings, including Buckingham Palace (but not the façade, which is in Portland stone). Pennant stone also was quarried in large quantities in the valleys around Bristol. This is a fine grained grey sandstone, widely used for facing buildings and for paving stones, but little if any is being currently quarried. Indeed, of all the extractive industries in Avon County, the only surviving enterprises are for roadstone, in the limestone quarries both north and south of Bristol; for celestine at Yate; and for fullers earth in shallow mines at Combe Hay, near Bath.

Metal working has given rise to important industries in Avon County since the earliest historical records. The Mendip plateau, on the southern edge of the region, was the home of a well organised lead extracting industry by Roman times, and some of the metal won at Charterhouse and elsewhere found its way into Bath where it provided a vital material for the elaborate plumbing of the baths there. More recently, lead working processes have survived in Bristol even though the Mendip sources of metal have been extinguished for many decades. The preparation of lead shot by pouring molten lead down a 'shot tower' was invented in Bristol, and continues today in a brand new shot tower on Cheese Lane, in a small factory where lead is also rolled into sheets and piping.

Another important Mendip metal was zinc, extracted from calamine ore which was mined in large quantities around Shipham on Mendip during the 18th century and supported the Bristol brass industry which flourished at that time. Brass is an alloy of copper and zinc which was produced as a metal suitable for table ware, wire, nails, and many other uses. The copper ore for the Bristol industry was imported from Cornwall and was smelted in the region, which accounts for the survival of many black blocks of copper-slag 'masonry' locally. Cast from the furnace waste, these blocks proved to be an extremely hard-wearing building material. The main sites of the Bristol brass industry were in the Avon valley between Baptist Mills, now in the City of Bristol, and Lower Weston in Bath, where the water power for the heavy brass-battery hammers was an important consideration. The last brass works closed at Keynsham in 1927, although small scale brass-working processes continued in the region thereafter, and together with other non-ferrous metals there has been a revival of large-scale manufacture recently with the development of a large zinc smelter at Avonmouth.

There is a long tradition of iron-working in the region. Iron was found in conjunction with the coal measures, particularly in the coalfield north of the Avon in Kingswood and around Iron Acton, Frampton Cotterell, and Pucklechurch. But the discovery of workable iron ores in the Ashton Gate area, south of the river, also led to a substantial iron-working industry. This has virtually disappeared from Avon County in the present century, although a number of small-scale foundries survive in the urban centres, and there are larger foundries associated with engineering factories such as Stothert & Pitt of Bath. The manufacture of high-quality steel does not appear ever to have taken root in the region, although there is some intriguing archaeological evidence that steel might have been made by Fussells at Mells, which is just outside Avon County in the south. Pin-making certainly flourished in the Kingswood area, surviving into the present century.

Engineering has had a natural affinity with the metal working industries, as it is concerned largely with converting metals into sophisticated hardware, such as railway locomotives and rolling stock, automobiles, aeroplanes, and ships. All these engineering processes and many others have flourished in the region in the last century. There were many traditional horse-carriage builders who moved easily into the business of manufacturing railway carriages, and others started up specifically to manufacture the new machines and their engines. The Bristol & Colonial Aeroplane Company, for instance, was established at Filton in 1910, and developed into the huge modern engineering complex of BAC and Rolls-Royce Engines. We have already noticed shipbuilding as a port industry, but when this industry was revolutionized by the conversion to steam ships with iron or steel hulls, some Bristol shipbuilders were ready to adapt to the new engineering requirements. The S.S. *Great Britain,* now restored to the dry dock made specially for her construction in the 1830s, survives as a splendid monument to Bristol shipbuilding. Amongst other prominent engineering industries of the region, Stothert & Pitt of Bath became world-famous as manufacturers of cranes and similar machinery in the 19th century.

The variety of industries in the Bristol region means that it is virtually impossible to contain them all within tidy categories such as 'textiles' or 'the metal industries'. We are obliged to allocate many to a broad category of 'miscellaneous' industries, although insofar as they have anything in common it is that they are concerned with some aspect or other of a chemical process. Soap-making, for instance, was an early Bristol industry, involving boiling a noxious brew of animal fat and potash. The need for a large quantity of cheap fuel led to early experiments with coal, the smoke from which intensified the problem of polluting the urban atmosphere. After several vicissitudes, the industry reached a peak of prosperity in the late 19th century, when the Christopher Thomas factory was built on Broad Plain to manufacture Puritan Soap. But like other Bristol industries (sugar refining has already been mentioned) this was a victim of concentration and rationalization in the present century, when Unilever first bought and then closed down the Bristol enterprise.

Glass-making probably began in Bristol in the 16th or 17th century, and by the late 18th century had become a large industry providing both high-quality 'Bristol blue' glassware and vast quantities of cheaper glass for windows and bottles. The typical glassworks of this period was the glass cone, of which a few fragments survive, especially that which has been built as a restaurant into the Dragonara Hotel next door to St. Mary Redcliffe church. In 1788 John Lucas moved his business out of Bristol to establish a prosperous glass industry at Nailsea, using the cheap coal mined locally. Again, however, the Bristol region lost out to the forces of centralization with the emergence of giant glassworks at St. Helens and elsewhere, and no glass is now made in the region.

Bristol was until quite recently the home of a flourishing pottery industry, but when Pountneys' Bristol Pottery moved to Cornwall in the 1960s, three centuries of an intimate relationship with the city came to an end. 'Bristol Delft', a distinctive white and coloured glaze on an earthenware body, was being produced at St. Anne's in Brislington in the middle of the 17th century. Many potteries flourished in Bristol in the 18th and 19th centuries, especially in the Redcliffe area. Most of their produce was domestic ware for a fairly local market, but it is worthy of note that the British manufacture of high quality porcelain was first established in Bristol in 1770, when Dr. Cookworthy, who discovered how to produce this beautiful ceramic, moved from Plymouth and entered into partnership with his fellow-Quaker, Richard Champion (the Champion family was also very active in the local brass industry). But the business was not a success, and the sale of the patent rights to a Staffordshire company in 1778 marked the extinction of another promising Bristol initiative. Cruder ceramic processes like the manufacture of bricks, tiles, and drain pipes survive in the region, although they have dwindled in importance. The production of clay tobacco pipes was for long an important industry in parts of central Bristol, the pipes being exported all over the world to survive as useful fragments helping modern archaeologists to date sites in the New World.

Paper-making, using rags to provide the basic cellulostic material, became widely spread in England following the introduction of the printing press in the 15th century. Wherever there was an urban market (and source of rags) and a clear stream (to provide the other raw material) it was possible to establish a paper manufactory, and dozens of them prospered around Avon County, especially to the south where the Mendip streams were particularly suitable. Some of them grew into quite substantial businesses and survive to the present: the Bathford Paper Mill east of Bath is a good example of a traditional paper mill, specializing in high quality 'Bible paper'. Others, like the St. Anne's Board Mill, specialize in the manufacture of cardboard, and the function of paper and board as packaging material in all aspects of modern retailing encouraged the development of one of the most successful specializations of modern Bristol, with firms like E.S. & A. Robinson (now part of the John Dickinson Group) and Mardons (now part of Imperial Tobacco) growing into very large concerns.

Amongst other processes which can be loosely classified as 'miscellaneous' or 'chemical-based' industries, Harbutts' plasticine is one of the more interesting. This firm, established at Bathampton, near Bath, in 1900, has continued to produce a single product ('plasticine' is a name for the wax-based malleable material) for a world market. There have also been more substantial chemical factories such as a polysulphate works at Keynsham, and the Albert Logwood Mill at the same place producing dye-stuffs from imported hardwoods, both of which have now closed down. A large chemical works was established in Crews Hole, where the River Avon emerges from a steeply sided valley at St. Anne's, which produced alkalis in the first half of the present century, but this has now disappeared like many of the other industries—lead works, copper smelting, brass works, coal mines—which once made this a flourishing industrial community at the east end of Bristol. Only Butler's tar distillery, itself an important chemical process, continues in large-scale business. The decay of these Crews Hole industries, however, has been offset by the development of large modern complexes on Severnside, north of Avonmouth, enjoying the advantages of a modern port and easy access to the motorway network. There are large oil storage and treatment facilities, with big I.C.I. and Gas Board installations making use of them.

With its urban 'core' running along the Avon from Avonmouth through Bristol and Keynsham to Bath, Avon County has long had need of those service industries which supply a modern urban community with vital resources such as water, gas, and electricity, and which undertake the removal of garbage and organic waste and provide other services such as municipal transport. These can only be mentioned briefly in this context, but insofar as they have become important industries in the region it would not be appropriate to ignore them. Water supply became a matter of urgent public concern in the middle of the 19th century, and the Bristol Waterworks Company was established in 1846 to supply good quality water to Bristol. It eventually came to possess several large reservoirs, pumping stations, and treatment plant, and similar although smaller-scale provision was made in Bath. Even earlier, from 1815, both Bristol and Bath had begun to acquire gas companies providing the innovation of gas street and domestic light. These companies became large enterprises, and several smaller companies operated in outlying communities such as Chew Magna. In time, amalgamation and nationalisation brought them together in a single enterprise, and the introduction of natural gas and North Sea Gas to replace coal gas has revolutionised the industry in the last decade, with the disappearance of the giant coke retorts and many other features of the traditional gasworks. Electricity generation began later, in the 1890s, when companies were formed in both Bristol and Bath. The forces of concentration have operated even more swiftly than elsewhere here. The introduction of the National Grid made the multiplicity of small generating stations unnecessary. The only coal-fired station now active in Avon County is at Portishead, although there are nuclear power stations at Oldbury-on-Severn (in Avon) and at Berkeley to the north.

A lot has been written about the industries of Avon County, and there is much primary material, both documentary and physical, still requiring attention. There is a great deal of interest in the Bristol Record Office although it is necessary to know what one is looking for because there is little attempt at an industrial classification of the material. The Sanigar

Up to 1850 no rationalyzed industries of sorts

Collection, for instance, contains some useful bundles on the Great Western Cotton Factory, and there is much to be gleaned from Port Books, Apprentice Books, Trade Directories, and so on. Similarly, both Somerset and Gloucestershire Record Offices contain industrial source material for those parts of Avon County which previously fell within their jurisdiction.

Several important collections of primary material remain in the hands of the firms and undertakings responsible for them. The records of the port of Bristol in the 19th century, particularly the fine run of Minute Books for the Bristol Docks Company from 1803 to 1848, and the PBA archives, as well as the records of the Bristol and Bath gas companies, have recently been deposited in Bristol Record Office. Many records have been destroyed, either by enemy action in World War II or as part of economy campaigns, so that the task of the historian in reconstructing the development of the enterprise is made very difficult. The important Bath engineering firm of Stothert & Pitt, for example, possesses virtually no records from the 19th century, and this case is by no means exceptional.

There are excellent local history sections in both Bristol and Bath Public Reference Libraries, but here again it is necessary to know what you are looking for to obtain full benefit from the collections, as much of the industrial material is fragmentary and widely scattered. General works such as Latimer's *Annals* provide a useful introduction, and incidentally give valuable clues to likely newspaper references. Buchanan and Cossons, in *Industrial Archaeology of the Bristol Region* (1969) defined their region in terms of Avon County several years before the administrative reorganisation, and provide short historical sketches of the main industries in addition to the more specifically industrial archaeological treatment.

On particular aspects of the industrial history, reference can be made to several important monographs published or in preparation (see Bibliography), but at this time the historical coverage of several important Bristol industries is either out-of-date or otherwise inadequate. In this category should be placed soap-making, the glass industry, the gasworks, water supply and most aspects of engineering. The port of Bristol is a prime subject for scholarly reappraisal, and most of the port industries are due for reassessment. Little analysis has been done on either the location or the organisation of local industry either in town or country, which is essential for the proper explanation of the industrial evolution of the region. Certainly, there is thus plenty of work to keep industrial historians busy in Avon County.

Editorial Note

In addition to the aspects of industrial history covered by Dr. Buchanan, the reasons for the location of particular industries in particular places also needs to be considered, and the history of labour-relations awaits detailed examination. As an example, the reasons for the rise of the felt-hatting industry in the Frampton Cotterell district of Northavon during the 17th century can be cited. This can be attributed to the occurrence in combination of a number of known factors: the decline of the South Gloucestershire woollen textile industry during the 16th century, already apparent to Leland *c* 1540, led to unemployment amongst skilled men and a declining demand for wool as the new superfine broadcloth industry was concentrated north of the Little Avon. Wool was therefore plentiful and cheap, and the many rabbit warrens, recorded in local field-names like 'coneygree', testify to the availability of rabbit fur, another essential raw material. Clean water in quantity was also required both for preliminary washing and for boiling the felt and steaming the 'forms' into shape on the blocks. Apart from the Frome and the Bristol Avon, none of the local streams could supply sufficient water, and the lower reaches of the Frome and the Avon were already polluted by sewage from Bath and Bristol and industrial waste from Bristol. Boiling and steaming also required plentiful fuel, and this again was readily available by the Restoration period in the adjacent area of the rapidly expanding North Bristol coalfield known as Coalpit Heath. Finally a combination of lack of clean water and the existence of guild restrictions led to the migration of the urban sector of the hatting industry, predominantly centred in Bristol in 1600, into the Frampton Cotterell area, where 90 per cent of the hatters were found by 1660. Shortly afterwards the opening up of the Canadian beaver resources made readily available the essential raw material for the production of high grade 'castor' hats, whilst Bristol's booming trade with the West Indian and American colonies after 1660 (see chapter 5) added export demand to home consumption in ensuring a steadily rising market for the products of the industry. A consideration of industrial needs on the one hand and the local resources available on the other thus satisfactorily explains the early industrialisation of the Frampton Cotterell area which has already been emphasised in the introduction to *The Goods and Chattels of Our Forefathers.*

The investigation of local labour history is another rewarding subject still awaiting students in Avon. The sources most likely to be useful are the 'Blue Books' in the 19th century, local newspapers, and, where they exist, records of local trade-union branches and party-political organisations. Oral memory should be valuable as the subject becomes increasingly important during the last 100 years with the growth of political democracy (see chapter 8). Certainly the area that produced Ernest Bevin and Ben Tillett should prove rewarding for local historians of labour.

7

Housing and the Standard of Living

J.S. MOORE

It has probably always been true to say that 'we spend a third of our lives in bed'; allowing for meals and the normal exclusion of work on Sundays, not far short of half the lives of most men in the past was spent in or around the family home which was normally a house, however humble. This, indeed, would be a minimum estimate: women would probably spend most of their lives in these surroundings, and so long as industry was organized on the 'domestic system', many men would have spent the bulk of their working lives in the home as well; for most children also, the home was the centre of their lives until they began work in their early teens. The house was therefore an extremely important element in everyone's past, just as the family was the basic social unit within historical communities: the history of housing is thus a major topic for the local historian. And the quality of life within the home would be affected more than anything else by the cost and standard of living, especially since most people in the past lived far closer to subsistence levels than they do now, yet very few local historians have even attempted to tackle these questions.

Housing

In considering past housing, the local historian must try to answer a range of questions, not all of which can equally satisfactorily be answered everywhere, and he must bear in mind, here as with other topics, that documents are not the sole source of information: the material remains must also be examined wherever they survive. In trying to answer the necessary questions, he must always remember the economic and social structure of his community: certainly by 1600 and later, the farmhouse will be very different from the labourer's cottage, and that in turn will be different from a craftsman's cottage which fulfilled the dual function of home and workplace. All these will be different in both scale and quality from the large homes, whether those of local squires or landed magnates, on which the attention of most architectural historians has been focussed: also, whilst medieval or early modern houses of that level may survive today, very few ordinary houses built before 1560 are likely to exist now. The history of the castles and larger houses has been deliberately omitted from this chapter precisely because plenty of information is available on them in works listed in the Bibliography. The size and layout of the house is the first important matter to be considered.

Most ordinary houses originated in the medieval hall-type house, in which virtually all family activities took place in the one main room: gradually, first cooking and then sleeping acquired their own specialized areas, defined initially by partitioning and lofting, later by permanent walls and upper floors. This original hall-type house and its gradual elaboration can be discerned in detailed estate surveys, for example that of Sturdon manor in 1573 (J.S. Moore, *The Goods and Chattels of Our Forefathers*, Appendix 1), whilst later surveys may reveal the increasing differentiation between farmhouses and cottages as a result of the 'great rebuilding of rural England' in the period 1560–1700, e.g. a survey of Almondsbury manor in 1767 (G.R.O. D.674a/E.40) details the size and construction of tenants' houses on the Chester-Master estate. But surveys giving such detail are rare even on well documented estates, and medieval housing below manor-house level is poorly documented unless the manorial lords by custom or necessity became involved in the repair or replacement of tenants' houses, for which court-rolls may yield some rare data. It should be remembered that 'the great rebuilding' also contained a revolutionary leap from the temporary peasant house lasting at most 2–3 generations to the much more permanent farmhouse and cottage often lasting for several centuries. Since manorial records have yielded such data in Worcestershire (R.K. Field) and Dorset (R. Machin), hopefully they will do so in the Avon area. Other possible sources in the P.R.O. are the series of 'extents for debts' (which exist for the period up to 1649) succeeded by 'extents of crown debtors' (1685–1842), and accompanied by extents of outlaws' and felons' goods from the 13th to the 18th centuries: these quite frequently include details of debtors' houses. Undoubtedly the major source of information on housing in the period 1550–1750 is the series of probate inventories (see chapter 3) in which, more often than not, the makers listed the dead person's possessions room by room. Not only are the number and names of the rooms discoverable from these inventories (and from similar secular documents such as bankruptcy examinations and schedules and insurance policies) but also, by close attention to the order of the rooms above and below stairs, the layout of the houses. An attempt has been made to analyse all the surviving inventories for part of Northavon (J.S. Moore, *The Goods and Chattels of Our Forefathers*, Table 12) and this preliminary analysis is now being extended to cover the whole of south Gloucestershire by Dr. Martin Baum of the Frampton Cotterell Local History Society. It should, however, be remembered that there was no compulsion on appraisers to list possessions room by room, and one should not in most cases conclude from the absence of room-headings in such inventories that one is dealing with a one-room hovel; also, headings can be silently omitted, when for example a chamber (bedroom) over a named downstairs room is mentioned but not the downstairs room itself. The inventories in addition list in greater or lesser detail the furniture, agricultural or industrial tools and equipment, and other possessions of the dead and thus enable some idea to be gained of the material environment of the local homes (see below). In the 19th and 20th centuries the chief documentary source of information is likely to be the sale particulars, and though these are more plentiful for manor-houses and farmhouses, when whole estates are being sold off, cottage properties are also included; particularly for urban houses, newspaper advertisements of property to let or for sale should also be considered. Insurance policies are another source of information, particularly for farmhouses, larger houses and inns: the location of registers of policies is given in Cockerell and Green. For one specific type of house, the parsonage (whether rectory or vicarage), glebe-terriers are a valuable source of information, together with the faculties authorizing alterations or rebuilding: both terriers and faculties are to be found among the records of the respective dioceses. These terriers and records such as surveys often enable an approximate idea of the physical size of houses to be gained by providing measurements in 'bays' or 'syldes' of building. The term 'bay', though derived from timber-framed building where it meant the area between two pairs of upright crucks, was later adapted to areas of brick or stone building where it seems to have become the area on one floor lit by one window-space in a long wall, but, especially with houses containing two or more bays, there could be more than one storey; the bay could be between 10 and 20 feet in length and breadth, perhaps most commonly about 16 feet square. Even when the details of housing in inventories and similar documents are missing or incomplete, wills can often be helpful, as in the case of Joseph Lewis of Iron Acton, whose will of 1728 dealt in detail with the division of his house and smallholding between his three sons Thomas, Joseph junior, and John. The will enables us to reconstruct the house fairly completely: Thomas was to get 'the little Tenement Containing one bay of Building lying southward with the little orchard therunto adjoining', whilst the younger Joseph was to receive 'the Middle Tenement Containing two bays of Building, Three Upper rooms and one over the Buttery with the Garden Ground there unto belonging and a little out house formerly the Stable and half the Little orchard', and John was allocated 'the little Tenement lying Northward Containing two bays of Building and one upper Room and half the Little orchard'. Here we have a fairly large house of five bays lying roughly north to south, with a separate outhouse near the middle; most if not all the house was of two-storey construction containing 11–12 rooms, whilst the mention of five bays of building suggests total dimensions of 60–90 feet by 12–18 feet. Documentary sources can thus facilitate a reconstruction of the size, construction and layout of much past housing, but examination of surviving buildings and the excavation, under proper supervision, of earlier housing sites is also necessary for a full analysis. Such archaeological techniques will tell us much about the use of local materials and building styles not recorded elsewhere: particularly if an older house is being demolished or radically rebuilt, it may be possible to examine it much more thoroughly than if it is still inhabited, and to reconstruct its development in detail.

The chronology and location of housing are questions primarily answerable by the archaeologist, architectural historian and the geographer, and field-work is again essential: the map, however large its scale, is not enough, since local patches of dry and firm subsoil, small springs and wells, may not be marked on the geological map; and locally important ridges, making all the difference between a damp, unhealthy house and a pleasantly dry home, may not be high enough to affect contour-lines on the Ordnance Survey maps. Likewise, only someone experienced in local vernacular architecture will be able to date the various stages of building from the styles employed, but this experience is largely acquired, not taught, by comparison of the styles of datable examples in each locality. In providing exact dates the historian is invaluable: datestones and stones with identifiable initials which can be dated will provide clues to either original building or major reconstructions in many cases; a series of deeds, leases or surveys may also provide if not precise dates at least a defined period within which the work took place, as may references to 'new' houses or rooms in wills and inventories. Finally, in answering why houses were built when and where they were, the whole history of the area is relevant: industrialization (see chapter 6) and consequent immigration (see chapter 3), enclosure of open-fields and changes in agriculture (see chapter 4), and the construction of canals and railways (see chapter 5) may provide relevant economic reasons, but the need to 'pack' local elections (see chapter 8) is also a possible motivation behind sudden upsurges in building, as is deliberate rebuilding in the 20th century to meet higher social norms or, given commuting, economic developments elsewhere in the region. On the negative side, the desire by landlords to retain the agricultural economy and deferential society of the old community may restrict or prevent new building, as at Stoke Gifford before the 20th century.

One last question about housing, and one nearly always neglected by most historians, is that of cost: who built houses for whom and for how much? In 'closed villages', or on leasehold sections of estates, the landlords, or in towns their nominated subcontractors, were the builders, whilst in 'open villages' or on freeholds and copyholds the individual owner would be responsible. The cost of new houses can usually only be recovered for 'closed villages', and then only if detailed estate accounts survive, but there is no reason to suppose that building costs would have radically differed in 'open villages' unless (which is possible) paternalistic landlords were building to higher standards than private individuals could afford. But inspection of surviving examples will usually show where this has occurred, for example, at Newton St. Loe, East Harptree or Clevedon (see Bettey). In the latter case, it may be possible to make some deductions from deeds where these are available, if an empty plot is sold for building, and the new house is sold shortly after building, but if the second sale is more than a decade later changing price levels may prevent any safe conclusions being drawn.

Even where all the above questions have been considered, much will still elude the historian: the quantitative aspects may be quite clear but not necessarily the qualitative. The differing size of the average family during various stages of its life-cycle will usually mean that houses may be too big for most families early and late in the family marriage, yet overcrowded in the period of childbearing (see chapter 3). Assessment of the quality of housing is also difficult when norms of adequacy have so radically increased in the last hundred years: however, we are unlikely to over-estimate the quality of most local housing if we remember that Winterbourne rectory, certainly in the top half-dozen houses in the village, was rebuilt in 1828–30 because, whenever it rained, the ground floor was several inches under water. Even without the evidence of successive Parliamentary enquiries in the 19th century into housing, we should have to conclude that the ordinary house of the past would by our standards be overcrowded part of the time, very often damp, poorly lit, badly ventilated and underheated in winter. The provision of heating is, indeed, one of the few qualitative aspects of housing which can be studied directly from inventories or in conjunction with the Hearth Tax returns of 1662–74 (fireplaces are rarely mentioned in inventories but their firedogs, andirons, etc., normally are): it will generally be found that the lower down the social scale a man was, the fewer his rooms had fireplaces (for this reason, the Hearth Tax returns on their own are not a safe guide to house sizes). But conclusions cannot safely be drawn from single cases or small groups of examples; yet again, the appropriate area of study is larger than the parish. What ought to be studied is the type: the Cotswold or Mendip farmhouse and cottage, the Vale or Avon Valley farmhouse and cottage, the Coalfield cottage, the urban house, workshop/cottage, and slum tenement.

The Standard of Living

The chief source of information on this topic is the probate inventories and similar documents already mentioned for the later medieval and early modern periods: by comparison the 19th and 20th centuries are poorly documented so far as direct information is concerned, though where probate records preserve total valuations of moveable property, some deductions could be drawn for the lower classes whose property will chiefly consist of furniture and domestic goods. Furniture is usually well covered by the inventories, though quantifiable comparison over time is difficult unless allowance can be made for changing general price levels in different periods. Clothing, however, is poorly documented even in the inventories, which normally summarize all clothing under some inclusive phrase such as 'the deceased's wearing apparell': whenever clothing is listed in detail the evidence must be studied closely, despite the danger of drawing conclusions from small samples. Unfortunately, there is little in print of value on this subject, since most 'histories of costume' refer solely to the colourful opulence of the upper classes, not to the drab and often threadbare clothes of the vast majority in the past. In general, however, most historians have approached the question of the standard of living indirectly, through the cost of living, to which we must now turn.

This question, moreover, is one that presents considerable problems to all historians, local or national, particularly those concerned mainly with the lower orders of society. What is required is a comparison over time between income and expenditure, but before very modern 'family expenditure' surveys this information is not available. As a result, historians have to compare the nearest possible substitutes, namely wage-rates in place of total earnings and cost of living indices in place of total expenditure. But wage-rates are only a completely satisfactory guide to earnings under full employment: otherwise allowance must be made for unemployment and for the length and number of working days per annum, on both of which data is defective. Earnings in bye-employments (the modern moonlighting or second job) and earnings by wives and children, all of which are known to be significant at various times in the past, are impossible to quantify. In the absence of family budgets, it is also impossible accurately to calculate the overall pattern of expenditure, though for most of the past food is known to have accounted for about three-quarters of most families' expenditure. If this assumption is generally true, nevertheless, indices of food prices in particular do give a reasonable indication of total expenditure, since food was not only by far the largest but also the most essential item of expenditure: only rent was anything like as essential, and this constituted a much smaller proportion of expenditure.

In order to compile a cost of living index for the Bristol region, it is necessary to extract all available price and wage data which can be securely dated at least to the year, and which can be compared because it consistently relates to the same commodity or service. It is recommended that each price and wage figure should initially be recorded on an index card for each year and filed in a series for each commodity or service, together with the amount of goods or services involved in the transaction being recorded, its place, date and source of the information, as follows;

Commodity Card:

CHEESE (cwt) 1685
17s 4d (2) Br.Inv. 1686/48 (24/11/1685: Horfield)
22s 6d (16) Br.Inv. 1685/34 (23/1/1684/5: Olveston)

Service Card:

MASON (day) 1556
1s 0d (13) (October: Bristol)
(*B.R.S.*, vol. 24 (1966), 24–5)

As with population tables (see chapter 3), 'Old Style' dates should be converted, for ease of comparison, into modern historical years beginning on January 1st. Once the data have been extracted from the sources, any clearly exceptional prices and wages can be eliminated, and a weighted average for each commodity and service calculated for each year. These results can be tabulated and expressed in the form of graphs to aid comprehension and also comparison with other economic and social series, such as agricultural or industrial production figures if available, annual baptism and burial figures (see chapter 3), trade statistics (see chapter 5), poor-relief returns (see chapter 8) etc. Construction of 11 year moving averages from the annual figures will also enable long-term historical trends to be isolated from short-term fluctuations caused by wars, disease, bad harvests and so forth: because of these short-term fluctuations, long-term comparisons should never be made between one year and another, since either or both may be exceptional and therefore not a true basis for comparison, which should be restricted either to decadal averages or to the moving average figures. Also as a result of these short-term fluctuations, the prices of some goods most sensitive to them (e.g. cereals varying considerably in price before and after the harvest) may need to be recorded on a monthly basis, and many kinds of labour had a 'summer' (high) and 'winter' (low) wage-rate, both of which must be recorded.

Price and wage data can be extracted from two types of documents: the first consist of accounts and bills recording actual payments, and these present no problems provided that the unit of weight or volume (for commodities) and of time (for services) is clearly stated; composite totals for more than one commodity must be ignored unless the unit price for each commodity is stated separately. The second type comprises price or wage statistics compiled by a contemporary authority (e.g. the cereal prices in the Bristol 'Assize of Bread' market returns) in order to ascertain the usual level of prices prevailing in the local market. These can also be used, as can inventory-type documents, provided that they can be checked against enough figures derived from accounts and bills to ensure that they are realistic. Local historians should ensure that data from the second class of record refer to estimated actual prices and wages, not to regulated maximum wages or minimum prices. In practice, there will not be sufficient data from most rural parishes to construct long annual series, but a combination of data from the whole region should enable this to be achieved. In the medieval period the most useful source is undoubtedly manorial account-rolls, though these became less useful after the later 14th century when demesnes were no longer being operated by their lords. In the early modern period, probate inventories are the most valuable source down to *c* 1720, but they must be supplemented and continued by other evidence, especially accounts of estates, households, towns, and institutions such as hospitals and, in the 19th century, Poor Law Unions. In the 20th century, newspaper advertisements and any available private household accounts will be the basis of local compilation, and the results can be compared with official cost of living indices. Some long series of assessed average prices also exist, notably the 'Assize of Bread' cereal price series for Bristol, which is virtually continuous from 1653 to 1825. It is important to concentrate attention on the products and services in most demand: foodstuffs, drink, clothing, fuel, lighting, rents, unskilled and skilled labour wage-rates: an index of the prices of, say, satins and velvets which only the privileged few could afford to buy before the 20th century would be valueless for local history.

Once annual price and wage series have been constructed, it is necessary to 'weight' the price series to allow for the greater importance of some goods in the ordinary household budget. The existing basis for this weighting is given in the articles by Phelps-Brown and Hopkins, but local historians should search for and record any similar budgetary information preserved in, for example, household accounts or social surveys. With regard to wages, it is unlikely that series of earnings as opposed to wage-rates will ever be available before the mid-20th century, but allowance should be made where possible for the number of days per year worked, which can be obtained from manorial, estate and business accounts. Although it is equally desirable, it is unlikely that any allowance can be made for the level of employment before the 20th century unless parish and poor-law union records are sufficiently detailed for this to be possible (see chapter 8). But matters such as these, and the length of the working day, the nature of the employment, work-discipline and so on are all important factors in the local standard of living; and any information on them in, for example, 'Blue Books', local newspapers, and descriptions by outsiders such as F.M. Eden, travellers etc. should be recorded and utilised. Both inside and outside the home, the quality of life is an intangible thing, but one as important if not more so than the more obvious and easily quantifiable aspects of life in the local community.

Generally speaking, it is unlikely that the level of prices and wages will vary greatly within the Avon county area at any one time, though the truth of this supposition will only emerge in the course of further work. Assuming this to be the case, the study of the cost of living in the area ought to be made on a regional basis, with local groups and individuals working in collaboration. A start has already been made on the extraction of price-data from the local probate inventories, and with help from other interested workers other sources could be exploited more quickly: offers of help are welcomed!

8

Local Administration and Politics

J.S. MOORE and M. WILLIAMS

Most of the previous chapters have been concerned mainly with the actions of individuals within the local community; we must now consider the ways in which that community acted collectively to deal with matters of common concern, the administration and government of the area. Here again the local historian of a parish or town cannot afford to be parochial, since the civil parish usually formed only a tithing of a larger medieval unit, the hundred, and both hundred and tithing in turn formed part of the county or shire (see Appendix). The hundred and tithing remained important in the countryside down to the 19th century, since even where the hundred court had vanished, hundred and tithing remained important administrative units for fiscal, judicial and military purposes. The increased powers of the county J.P.s from Tudor times onwards were also reflected in the growth, first informally, later formally, of Petty Sessional districts, which originally consisted in most cases of groups of hundreds. But the growing power of the J.P.s was paralleled, also from the 16th century, by the increasing use made by the central government of the civil parish as an administrative unit for mending roads and administering poor relief, and the increasing duties thrust on parish officials—churchwardens, overseers of the poor and surveyors of highways (waywardens). Petty constables, previously manorial or hundredal officers, often became responsible to the parish instead. The hundred and tithing were never formally abolished, but by the middle of the 19th century had withered away: when local government was reorganized in 1894, the new Urban and Rural Districts, like the earlier Poor Law Unions and Sanitary Authorities, comprised groups of civil parishes. The position of the boroughs in relation to the county was increasingly anomalous: borough courts often superseded hundred courts (e.g. in Bristol in the 12th–13th centuries) and grants of privileges by the Crown and landlords from the 12th century onwards led to a growing separation of some boroughs from their surrounding areas for judicial and administrative purposes, and some more important boroughs acquired separate commissions of the peace. In Avon only Bristol achieved independent county status in 1373, though Bath obtained its own commission of the peace with incorporation in 1590. Many nominal boroughs were merely urban appendages to the rural manors out of which they had arisen (e.g. Chipping Sodbury, Thornbury and Wickwar) and little or no powers of self-government accrued to them: real authority remained with the lord or his representatives in the manorial or borough courts, and additional powers tended to accumulate in the hands of shadowy oligarchies: town feoffees or trustees. These units provided the framework within which local administration operated: political action, in so far as this can be documented before the 19th century, tended to focus either on the county and Bristol and Bath, the only boroughs having the right to elect M.P.s, so far as the upper classes were concerned, or at a largely incoherent village level so far as their inferiors were concerned. From the 19th century onwards, successive extensions of the franchise and consequent reductions in the area of constituencies make local politics a more meaningful subject of study, and at the same time the necessary source materials, the archives of local political organizations, more frequently survive. The articulation of political ideas and the expression of public opinion also become much easier to trace through the local press (see chapter 12).

Early Political Units

The earliest known political divisions in our area are those of the Celtic tribes recorded in classical sources and their own coins, but since little is known of their internal history, their existence is only important to the local historian to the extent that their boundaries (and those of their constituent estates) may have survived into later periods (see chapter 2). Political divisions assumed greater importance in the Anglo-Saxon period, when eventually Gloucestershire formed part of the Mercian sub-kingdom of the Hwicce whose frontiers were preserved till the 16th century as the area of Worcester diocese. South Gloucestershire, however, was not originally part of this kingdom, but comprised a West Saxon province formed after the battle of Dyrham in 577, whose sense of separate identity was long preserved in local dialect and in the institution known down to the 13th century as the 'Seven Hundreds of Grumbalds Ash'. It would be interesting to discover if similar 'early groups of hundreds' ever existed in North Somerset. Somerset itself, in Saxon times part of Wessex, remained a separate county until 1973, with its own diocese, though it must be remembered that Bath Forum hundred, north of the Avon, was part of Mercia until the 9th or 10th century and therefore probably until then was included in south Gloucestershire. The western part of Wansdyke was probably built to be the northern defensive frontier of Somerset, though whether by post-Roman Britons or Anglo-Saxons is still disputed by archaeologists.

Hundred and Manor

Whatever the origins of the hundred as an institution, it is first generally recognized in the late 10th century and is fully displayed in

Domesday Book. In addition to being a useful unit of local administration, the hundred developed its own judicial organization with its own court-rolls which, when they survive, will enable an assessment to be made of its functions as a local centre for justice (the view of frankpledge) and the settlement of civil disputes, especially in small debt cases, down to *c*.1800. But though the hundred, like the shire, had originally been a unit of royal government, it was very liable to lose part or all of its powers to some of the manors within its area, so that the records of manor courts, where these survive (see chapter 4), are also important sources for local government and justice particularly in the medieval period. The extent to which manors acquired these hundredal powers and the reasons why they did so are important topics to which local historians can make a large contribution. They should note that although in theory jurisdiction was recorded in court leets or views of frankpledge whilst the normal manorial business of agricultural regulation and land registration was recorded in courts baron and courts customary, in practice all varieties of business may well occur indiscriminately whatever the name of the court. In addition to analysing the business of the hundredal and manorial courts, the local historian should also try to determine the effects of lordship. Was the lord resident or not? Was there more than one manor in the same village? Were the local officials and jurors a fairly random selection from the local population, serving by lot or in rotation, or were they mainly the larger and richer landholders and tenants? He should also remember that cases were frequently reviewed by higher courts (*Curia Regis*, King's Bench, Common Pleas, Assizes and Itinerant Justices, later Star Chamber and the Court of Requests, often also Chancery and Exchequer), and should investigate the available printed editions of and indexes to the records of these courts. This factor remains true in the early modern period, though the major local courts are, then and later, the Quarter Sessions and Petty Sessions. Why, finally, did manor and hundred disappear? Allegations in the 18th century of corruption, inefficiency and partiality in the conduct of business can be offset by protests at the abolition in 1839 of their powers to settle small debt cases because of their convenient proximity for the poorer local inhabitants—to reclaim a debt of 40 shillings in a court usually held in the local pub was both cheaper and easier than travelling to either county town. Another possibility is that the break up of estates, the local tendency in the early modern period to substitute leaseholds for lives in place of copyholds, and the enclosure of open fields deprived manorial courts of their basic functions of agricultural regulation and land-registration, and that manorial lords were no longer prepared to hold courts to transact judicial business from which they derived little or no profit. Increasingly, also, the administration of justice by private courts was thought to be inappropriate and potentially dangerous to the country as a whole (compare, in Scotland, the deliberate abolition of 'heritable jurisdictions' after 1745), though one major private court, that of the Honour of Gloucester, continued in business at Thornbury down to the 19th century.

The Civil Parish

The decline of feudalism and of the private administration of justice was accompanied by a deliberate revival under the Tudors of the shire as a unit and Quarter Sessions as the main local court at the higher level, and the transformation of the parish, till then a purely ecclesiastical institution (see chapter 9), into the major local unit of administration at the lower level, whilst Petty Sessions filled the vacuum created by the decline of hundredal and manorial courts. The role of the parish as a civil unit is well documented throughout Avon (see Gray and Ralph, and King, though both now need revision) and by its nature is a subject which the local historian is well qualified to study provided he remembers that the system he is studying was part of a national framework set up by the central government: his main concerns should be with the extent to which national regulations were enforced locally, and with exceptions to or innovations in the national system at a local level. Sometimes, as with the Bristol Incorporation of the Poor, these local innovations are the model for later improvements on a national scale—the 'Gilbert' unions in the 18th century and the Poor Law Unions in the 19th century. Though the churchwardens were basically concerned with church affairs (see chapter 9), they also became involved to some extent in local secular government, as *ex officio* overseers of the poor and with special responsibility for dealing with poor migrants, later the 'non-settled poor': their accounts, and the vestry minutes of the parish 'assembled in vestry' are therefore of some importance for this subject. The earliest civil responsibilities of the parish were the local highways under an act of 1555, but the accounts of the surveyors or waywardens rarely survive before the latter part of the 18th century. But the major new parish officials were the overseers of the poor, whose accounts form the essential documentation for the relief of poverty from 1572 to 1836—thereafter the overseers were merely rate-collectors for Poor Law Unions. Precisely because no parish was an island, the movement of paupers created special problems which affected some parishes much more than others, leading to the institution of the Law of Settlement in 1662. This created new sets of local records of great importance, not only for local government, but also for ascertaining economic and social conditions locally, since prosperous parishes might well experience an inflow of people in search of work from poorer parishes with a surplus of unemployed. These records include removal orders whereby paupers were returned to their parish of settlement; settlement certificates from their parish of settlement to their parish of residence, and examinations of paupers and vagrants. Bastardy created similar sets of records. The care of pauper children frequently resulted in apprenticeship indentures to provide for their technical training; more rarely, such children might be sent to local schools, resulting in bills for their schooling and maintenance. Less commonly, at any rate in Avon, parishes disposed of their poor *en masse* either to northern factories or by assisted emigration to the colonies. It is comparatively rare for detailed workhouse or poorhouse records to survive before 1834, and such records should always be carefully examined. Any of the above accounting series may be supported by detailed bills and vouchers which may add much informative detail, whilst churchwardens, overseers and surveyors all raised the bulk of their income by means of parish rates: these necessitated rate-books, which varied from a bare list of names with sums levied, to detailed assessments giving names of owners and occupiers, names and details of properties, gross rentals and assessed values, occasionally with detailed parish maps commissioned for the purpose. Much rarer and very valuable records, where they survive, are parish censuses, pauper inventories, and tithe-accounts, though these are mainly significant for population history (see chapter 3), agriculture (see chapter 4) and the standard of living (chapter 7). In addition to looking at how the parish officials raised and spent their money on communal concerns, the local historian should also consider the officials themselves and by whom they were chosen. Was the vestry an assembly of all adult males, or all householders, or a much smaller and more oligarchical 'select vestry' (especially after the Sturges-Bourne act of 1818)? Did it meet regularly or was it content to leave its officials mainly to their devices apart from annual auditing of accounts? Questions such as these can only be answered if the vestry minutes and main accounts survive; but even if these do not, the names and descriptions of the officials should be recoverable from settlement records and apprentice indentures, and the former at least may survive outside the parish, in the parishes to which paupers were returned; accounts and settlement records are also often to be found in the archives of Quarter Sessions as a result of appeals to or review by that court. Once it is known who the officials were, it should be possible also to determine what they were (see chapter 3), and whether they were drawn from the whole or only the upper ranks of local society, and also whether there was an annual turnover of officials or long periods of continuity. The answers to these questions may throw light on the quality and effectiveness of local administration.

Quarter Sessions

From the 16th century, the records of Quarter Sessions are of great utility, since the operations of that court influenced not only the administration of justice but also local government in all the parishes of the county. These include records of the court's judicial business (sessions rolls, order books and minutes), records generated by that business (presentments, indictments, recognizances and lists of J.P.s and juries), and records of county administration (licensing records, treasurers' accounts, vouchers, rating assessments, gaol records, and registration records of various kinds). The records of Quarter Sessions are especially important as the main local source of information on crime and punishment since the 16th century. Cases can be traced from information, presentment or indictment through to the final acquittal or sentence, and an analysis of the types of crime committed by various sections of the population can be fruitful in determining local attitudes to law and order, particularly before the establishment of permanent, paid police-forces in the mid-19th century. No local history can be complete without use of these records, since they show how far in practice legislation was actually enforced, as well as throwing much light on the conditions of life locally.

Modern Politics

Increasingly in the 19th century, local government, which had in the main been local, begins to become more remote from the local community, more professional and also more influenced by party-politics. The transfer of most poor-law responsibilities from the parish to the Poor Law Unions in 1836, the establishment of Rural Sanitary Authorities and other statutory bodies later in the Victorian period as a result of growing central government concern with social welfare and economic regulation, the creation of County Councils in 1889 and the Urban and Rural Districts in 1896, stripped the parish of virtually all its civil powers. After 1894 vestry minutes, where they survive, are concerned purely with church affairs, and the Parish Councils became and remain chiefly consultative representative bodies with little executive or financial power. In many parishes indeed, all civil records come to an end in 1834, with the result that at local level the latter part of the 19th century is in some respects the least well documented period since early Stuart times. Again, the records of all these new bodies ought to be examined since despite their length and formality much local information of value can on occasion be extracted from them—for example, the Frampton Cotterell Parish Council minutes include a most detailed and useful survey of the housing in the parish on the eve of the first World War. Local historians should also remember that in the period 1509–1660 and again after the 1780s central government was much involved in regulation and enforcement at local level, and that consequently reports on local affairs will be found for the earlier period in the State Papers Domestic and the papers of ministers such as the Hatfield MSS, and for the later period in the files of various ministries and government departments and in reports based on these files or independent enquiries, the 'Blue Books'. Before the extensions of the franchise after 1832, local politics were mainly decided by the aristocracy and gentry who alone exercised political power: the only exception to this in Avon was Bristol, where all burgesses had the vote. To what extent non-voters were involved in politics at this level is largely unknown, and is a prime subject for investigation by local historians, as is the extent to which, before the 19th century, political divisions at upper social levels were reflected in similar divisions at parish level. The starting point for such investigations must be the poll-books in which all votes cast by each voter were recorded from the early 18th century down to the Secret Ballot Act of 1872, very often with the occupation and residence of each voter. The correspondence of the major local families, e.g. the Berkeleys and Beauforts in Northavon, will also repay investigation. In the 19th and 20th centuries, the files of local political parties also need to be examined, where these survive: the archives of the Labour Party in Northavon before the 1960s appear to be lost, whilst the records of the locally important Independent Labour Party are not freely available to all historians. Records of voting divisions in vestries and Parish Councils, even when not explicitly along party-political lines, may well be so if the affiliations of the voters can be determined from other sources. Below all this overt activity is the often barely articulate voice of the bulk of the local population throughout history (see chapter 12) which may only reveal its discontent in the form of riot, revolt, and certain forms of crime, especially poaching; though this group did not achieve direct political representation until within the last hundred years upper-class fear of violence from the lower orders if pushed too far was an effective constraint on political action.

Bristol

A separate account of the administration and government of Bristol from 1373 is called for, both as the principal borough within the county of Avon and because from then until 1974 it was wholly independent of its neighbouring counties Gloucestershire and Somerset. The charter which granted this independence established a basic pattern of government that consolidated several centuries of borough privileges, and at the same time bestowed the supreme accolade, that of county status. It incorporated the mayor, henceforward a justice of the peace, sheriff and 40 of the worthiest men of the town into a Council with authority to act on behalf of the community in all legal affairs. It established county courts—a court of assize, court of sessions and court of mayor and sheriff—while the powers of existing courts were more clearly defined. These included the Tolzey Court, the Staple Court, two fair courts and a Court of Orphans. In all they exercised comprehensive jurisdiction over the variety of civil and criminal cases that arose and needed to be tried in an important commercial and industrial centre that was also a county.

The Council's responsibility for the good government of the town was wide-ranging. It framed rules for the registration of burgesses and for the regulation of the numerous craft guilds, markets and fairs, as well as for the maintenance of general order; it arranged for the collection of the town-customs at the port and the payment therefrom of the town-farm and other royal dues; it was responsible for the gaol and for the upkeep of the walls and quays; it had control, through the Mayor, over the price of bread and ale, and it sent two representatives to Parliament, invariably chosen from among the wealthy burgesses.

In the 15th century Bristol became the second richest town in England, with cloth the principal staple and wine the major import. Significantly the richer burgesses formed an increasing majority on the Council. By 1499 the movement towards an oligarchic system of government was complete when Henry VII gave his approval to a Council that was self-elected, and established a body of six Aldermen, chosen by the Mayor and Council, who were to be justices of the peace. The Recorder, as one Alderman, was a lawyer of some distinction, while the remaining Aldermen each had responsibility for one of the five wards into which the town was then divided for administrative purposes. Further, the Sheriff's criminal jurisdiction was transferred to the Mayor and two Aldermen; henceforward there were to be two Sheriffs who combined the office with that of the two Bailiffs and thereby acquired in addition their jurisdiction in civil cases, notably those tried in the Tolzey Court.

The pattern of Bristol's municipal administration is altogether much better documented from the 16th century, largely due to the efforts of the Chamberlain and the Town Clerk, two offices which were now firmly established. The Chamberlain was responsible for all corporate funds and estates. He paid the fees of officers from the Mayor to the Raker and had control of all public works; among other duties he was in charge of the admission of burgesses and the administration of the apprenticeship system. His accounts survive from 1532, registers of apprentices from the same date and registers of burgesses from 1558. The Town Clerk was the Corporation's legal adviser and by virtue of his office was primarily concerned with the administration of justice. He was Clerk of the Peace, Steward of the Corporation's manorial courts and assessor to several municipal courts. As Clerk to the Council, his record of its proceedings survive from 1598.

The bond between municipal and judicial administration, already close, became inextricably interwoven as more and more duties were placed on the Aldermen in their role as justices of the peace, notably when they became responsible for the administration of the Poor Law. By this time the number of Aldermen had increased to 12 and the city was divided into 11 wards, a twelfth ward being created when the Castle became part of the city. While the wards were important divisions for police purposes, it was the 17 parishes and the Castle Precincts that became the principal units of administration within Bristol, as the fine series of taxation and rating records, from 1662 and 1696 respectively, clearly demonstrate. In 1696 these units joined forces to form a Union for the relief of the poor, known as the Incorporation of the Poor, under the management of the Mayor, Aldermen and 48 guardians.

Other statutory bodies, such as the Bridge Trustees, Turnpike Trustees and Paving Commissioners were set up subsequently as the need arose. The Council was always well represented on these bodies, but it never considered that its own affairs were a matter for public concern, let alone participation. Its income, from the numerous estates which it owned in the city and surrounding country, from its markets and from the dues on shipping, had increased considerably, but at no time did it consider that this was part of the public purse. It is true that it had to contend with interference from the Crown, particularly in the 17th Century, but it maintained its autonomy. Mounting criticism led to the formation of a Chamber of Commerce in 1823, to fight for the reduction of dues collected by the Corporation; in 1831 riots broke out in favour of reform, and in the following year parliamentary franchise, hitherto the exclusive prerogative of the burgesses, was extended. General dissatisfaction was not assuaged, however, until the whole system of local government in Bristol was reformed.

The Municipal Corporations Act of 1835 effected the fundamental changes that were required. Under it the borough courts were allowed to continue, but the Aldermen were no longer to be justices of the peace, so that the Council lost the control which it previously exercised over the judiciary in Bristol. The Mayor, an *ex officio* justice of the peace, presided over a Council of 16 Aldermen and 48 Councillors who were elected by the ratepayers; the boundaries were extended to include the population in the suburbs, and there were now 16 wards. Only one Sheriff was allowed to be appointed.

The assets of the Corporation were declared public, and if insufficient to meet the needs of administration, provision was made for the levying of rates, provided that they were for the benefit of the community. Within a year management of the numerous charities which the Corporation had administered for centuries was transferred to a newly created body known as the Bristol Municipal Charity Trustees. The Chamberlain was transformed into the City Treasurer while the office of Town Clerk remained, in name if not in form, for his judicial functions were severely curtailed.

A noticeable feature of 19th-century government was the increasing recognition of the need for public services. The first duty of the Corporation after reform was the establishment of a police force. Other services followed, among them libraries, open spaces and electricity, all under the authority of Acts of Parliament, the supply of gas and water for example being left to private companies. The major concern, however, was the appalling lack of public health provision, and the adoption of the necessary powers by the Council to enable it to carry out improvements meant the creation of a whole new set of administrative machinery. A Local Board of Health was established, with responsibility for roads, drains, sewers, lighting, scavenging, removal of nuisances and regulation of slaughterhouses. Its powers were widened when it was recast in 1872 to become the Urban Sanitary Authority. Similarly, in 1870 the Council set up a separate Board to administer the education service, the Incorporation of the Poor in the meantime having become a regular Board of Guardians. Gradually these functions were absorbed in the work of the Council, which also assumed the functions of those local authorities in areas which were transferred from neighbouring counties to the city from 1895 onwards.

On the eve of local government reorganisation in 1974, the city was divided into 28 wards with a Council of 112 members and was represented by six Members of Parliament. It had made notable strides forward during the 20th century in the provision of new services such as housing, planning and an airport, the underlying theme being to provide a co-ordinated approach to the various needs of the community. This has led to a co-ordination of some services at national level, with health, electricity and gas coming under central government control; in

1971 the only surviving borough court, Tolzey, was abolished along with Quarter Sessions, in favour of a nationwide Crown Court system.

9

Church and Chapel

R.W. DUNNING

It is easier for historians to study institutions than to study people, and Church historians have been no exception. From academic works on diocesan administration to most church guides, emphasis has almost inevitably been placed on organs of government and physical remains, to the exclusion of a proper emphasis on the people who, preachers never cease saying, are the Church.

Local historians, attempting to write a Church guide, must understand at least some of the technical jargon; they must know the difference between a rectory, a vicarage, and a perpetual curacy, or between a deacon in Church and a deacon in Chapel; and they must use to the full the architectural and archaeological implications of the surviving fabric. But if they forget that churches and chapels were built and used by past and present generations for the worship of God, then they might as well write of country houses as if people never lived in them.

The emphasis on people makes the task more difficult, for the formal records of the Church were not kept for the historian. Yet the people of the Church also lived outside it, and using records of parish and estate, of town and court of law, it is possible to show how man has expressed his belief in God in each generation; how the Gospel first spread and then became the centre of medieval life; how uniformity was challenged, and how diversity of practice has come out of different sections of society at different times.

The Diocese

The medieval dioceses of Worcester and of Bath and Wells shared the area that is Avon between them. Thus for nearly a thousand years Bristol, one of the largest towns in England, lay at the fringes of church government, a problem recognised by at least two bishops of Worcester, Godfrey Giffard (1268–1302) and John Carpenter (1444–76), who sought to make Westbury-on-Trym a second headqaurters. Demands for more efficient administration and control led to the division of some of the larger dioceses and the formation of new sees based on populous centres. Gloucester diocese was thus founded in 1541 and Bristol in 1542. Gloucester and Bristol were briefly reunited between 1836 and 1897.

At first the bishop's role was pastoral, involving the care of clergy and people and the spread of the Faith. The gradual emergence of legal rights in a more complex society, however, demanded a formal system of administration. The registers, which are the written records of the bishops and their officers, often seen simply as quarries for the names of past rectors and vicars, bear witness also to the more unusual precedents which were the cause of their inclusion. The growing power of the bishops through their courts and officers and the shortcomings of clergy and laity are evident in the registers, along with the petty details which prove so important, like the way the bathers at Bath in the 1440s had their clothing held to ransom by the locals. The survival from the 15th century of the records of church courts adds a further dimension in terms of spiritual discipline and probate jurisdiction, revealing the Church as judge of the living and guardian of the dead. Among the complicated records of these courts are the presentments of churchwardens at visitations of archbishop, bishop or archdeacon. As a general guide to the religious views and practices of clergy and people alike (at least in the eyes of the wardens), they can be used to chart the progress of a parish through the currents of the Reformation or, less easily, through the Commonwealth experiment with Presbyterianism. By the 18th century, however, their increasing formality is a reflection of looser control by diocesan authorities as well as an indication of Anglican malaise. 19th century religious revival is automatically followed by a proliferation of records of visitations, boards and committees, and national legislation in the 20th century has added its weight of paper production, leaving the historian of the contemporary Church with a formidable task.

A further series of records, not exclusively diocesan or parochial, concern clerical incomes. From the national taxation records of 1291 (*Taxatio . . . Papae Nicholai IV*) and 1535 (*Valor Ecclesiasticus*) to the 18th century published lists of benefices and their values produced by Ecton (*Liber Valorum*, 1711) and Bacon (*Liber Regis*, 1786) the relative values of livings can be discovered. Glebe terriers among the diocesan records and the much rarer tithe or Easter books among parish collections often provide necessary correctives, illustrating well the difficult position of the tithe-claiming parson to be found in the pages of John Skinner's *Diary*. Probate inventories (see Chapter 3) which were compiled on the death of clergy as well as lay people, are also valuable: apart from the other uses of such inventories, they may contain lists of the parson's books, throwing some light on his level of learning. Occasionally, clerical diaries and account books may survive among parish records or elsewhere, as for Didmarton (in Lambeth Palace Library).

The Parish

The records of the parish, beginning much later than those of the diocese, are of equal importance, especially accounts of churchwardens, which complement the diocesan records, and the evidence of the churches themselves. Registers of christenings, marriages and burials compiled by informative incumbents can be so much more than simply lists of parishioners; and Registers of Services from the mid 19th century onwards are an invaluable continuation of the information found in the Ecclesiastical Census of 1851 in their record of the pattern of worship and the changes in attendance over the last hundred years. Diocesan handbooks, by whatever name, record details of Sunday schools, mission halls, hymn books, clergy movements and alterations to fabric and ornaments, as well as the essential background of church government from the late 19th century to the present day.

The Monasteries

Standing apart from the main-stream of the Church in the world were the religious houses, whose records have often more bearing on monks as landlords than on the spirituality of their lives. As landlords in the vanguard of agricultural advance, the larger monastic houses could afford to be pioneers, and historical accident has ensured better survival of their records than of those from secular estates. Domestic and internal records are rare, and the criticisms of bishops at visitations, notably at Keynsham in 1447, 1451 and 1455, necessarily critical. The dissolution of the monasteries and the dispersal of the monks might usefully be studied on a local basis. How many religious like Thomas Powell, formerly a monk of Bath, went into parochial life, and how many are never heard of again, perhaps practising in private those devotions which had been the centre of their lives for almost as long as they could remember?

The New Denominations

The churches which emerged from the 16th century onwards, first as movements forced underground by Anglican legislation and later as minorities tolerated with differing degrees of enthusiasm, created their own records as circumstances required or permitted; and they are often traced initially in the papers of Church or State which the hostile legislation produced.

The early Roman Catholics appear more regularly and more precisely as offenders in recusant rolls, visitation papers and the records of Quarter Sessions than in the later and much more personal memoirs of individual members. Increasing informal toleration allowed the growth of certain centres of influence, notably at Bath; and formal toleration in 1829 was followed by the establishment of the diocese of Clifton in 1851.

Records of Protestant Nonconformity include those of the Society of Friends (Quakers) whose distinctive way of life and language were designed to mark them out from the World they so abhorred, and yet to whose economic life they made, and continue to make, such a contribution. The establishment of places of worship for them and for Baptists, Independents, Presbyterians, Unitarians and others, each requiring a licence from bishop or magistrate requested by named and often identifiable people, and the trust deeds of each chapel complete with the occupations and addresses of leading members, throw light both on the changing (and often bewildering) theological views of each congregation, and on the economic and social status of its members. Rare domestic records of such congregations are of the utmost value in the same direction. The archives of Methodists, of special importance in the Bristol area, are arranged in a slightly different way, but still allow the spread of societies to be traced both in country and town in the wake of Wesley's own travels.

Origins

The beginnings of Christianity in any area must be a prime question for the historian. After the meagre traces of Roman Christianity have been pieced together and archaeologists have tried to suggest some possible survivals in orientated graves in pagan cemeteries, there remains a gap before reliable written sources indicate Christian Saxons in the countryside. And these are not individuals but institutions, centres of religious life founded by Christian kings from which preachers and teachers ventured into the pagan hinterland to spread the Faith. Sometimes they were religious communities in an obvious monastic sense like Bath, a convent of nuns founded *c* 676 on the boundary between Wessex and Mercia. Westbury-on-Trym, founded *c* 716, was a similar centre. Others, less prominent at an early date, are known as minsters, communities of secular clergy with an obvious missionary intent. Such centres can be recognised by their names or by the survival of links with the churches they founded: Bedminster's name seems to reveal its origin, Yate was early described as a minster, and Keynsham's beginnings are strongly suggested by the number of its daughter chapels—Queen Charlton, Publow, Felton in Whitchurch, Chewton Keynsham and St. Anne's.

Bitton was still remembered in the 16th century as the 'mother church' of Oldland and Hanham. It gave its name to a medieval rural deanery, and it possesses an important piece of Saxon sculpture, all features suggesting early origins. Similarly, Thornbury was the 'mother church' of Oldbury, Falfield and Rangeworthy, a group which together make an 'original' parish. 'Field' churches established by individual bishops or landowners in the later Saxon period are almost impossible to identify from any but archaeological evidence, but the process of foundation continued even later, perhaps as late as the 13th century, and individual churches can still be traced back to their 'family' origins. So Dundry was established from Chew Magna and never managed to obtain independence; Chipping Sodbury and Pensford were two late foundations, both the results of new settlements at market centres away from the original villages of Old Sodbury and Publow. Tracing these patterns in a number of parishes can lead to useful and far-reaching conclusions about settlements and their origins.

The ancient parish and deanery boundaries can show with even

greater clarity a large minster parish with its later divisions within a
continuous outer limit, or, as in the case of Chew Stoke for instance, can
outline the manor of Stoke Abbatis, the property of Keynsham Abbey, in
the lands on which tithes were payable after the Dissolution (much to the
chagrin of the rector of the parish) to the vicar of Chew Magna.

Urban churches and monasteries disturb this general pattern. The
formation of tiny parishes in Bath and Bristol, often the work of
prominent urban families, has an important bearing on the early
development of those cities and their suburbs. The establishment of
monasteries also calls for detailed study not only from the institutional,
but also from the topographical point of view. The fascinating possibility
of the site of St. Augustine's, Bristol, as a place of religious significance
associated with the Apostle of the English may not be repeated
elsewhere, but the choice and effect of the sites of Bath, Keynsham,
Westbury or Woodspring deserve closer study.

The Standards of the Clergy

Lists of rectors and vicars are only the beginning of another profitable
parish study. In the diocese of Bath and Wells most of the lists begin early
in the 14th century; in Worcester diocese they start in the 13th. The dates
depend on when the bishops' registers begin. Some individual parishes
can go back further, perhaps as much as a hundred years; one or two, like
Keynsham or Kingston Seymour, had priests at the time of the
Domesday Survey. And surely some of the 210 priests who gathered at
Westbury-on-Trym in 824 came from our area. Yet what have we, in the
end, but a list of names?

In fact, much more can be done. A systematic use of bishops' registers
and the records of the universities will go a long way to answer questions,
such as: did the parish attract good and learned men, and if so, was this
because of its good income or a powerful or interested patron? Was the
parish used as a sinecure for important clergy and left to the care of
curates? Did it suffer from such absenteeism?

Kingston Seymour was in the Middle Ages a moderately rich living
(worth 20 marks in 1291). Thomas, Earl of Lancaster, first cousin of the
King and the most prominent politician of his day, appointed William de
Melbourne in 1321. Melbourne was a Doctor of Civil Law of Oxford
University and already held two livings elsewhere. How long he held
Kingston is unknown, though he was still rector in January 1322. But the
following May he went abroad as Lancaster's representative at the Papal
Court, and it seems quite likely that he never set foot in the parish. The
King appointed Richard de la More as his successor in 1324, but the
bishop immediately licensed him to be absent for two years for study and
to seek minor orders. Thus at the time of his appointment he was still not
sufficiently educated, and was not able to say Mass nor carry out any of
the other functions of a priest. Nicholas de Bromlegh, appointed to
succeed in 1332, was similarly not in Holy Orders, and although made a
subdeacon in the following year, he was still not a deacon in 1335 and had

meanwhile collected the rectory of Greinton in addition. After him came Aylmer le Botiller, another man not in Holy Orders, who thereafter spent at least two years at Oxford. After that all is silence until 1349 when there was a dispute between him and the patron; in 1350 he refused to pay a debt of £5 to Thomas de Berkeley; and in 1351 he had to appeal to Rome against action by the bishop. He stayed at Kingston at least until 1370.

In the 16th century the rectors of Kingston were distinguished for other reasons. There was James FitzJames, DD, rector from 1528–41, son of a Chief Justice and nephew of a Bishop of London, who also held the rectory of North Cadbury and the Chancellorship of Wells Cathedral. After him the King appointed Walter Cretyng, LLD, a royal chaplain, archdeacon of Bath, vicar-general of the diocese, and incumbent at the same time of East Brent and Huntspill. In 1589 Robert Godwin was appointed by his father, Bishop Godwin, married his predecessor's widow, and lived in the parish until his death in 1613. He was followed by his brother Francis, a very able man who, besides holding Kingston Seymour, was a canon of Wells and Bishop of Llandaff (and later also of Hereford).

Kingston Seymour was chosen at random and can serve as an example of the interplay of prominent patrons and a reasonable income, all revealed from bishops' registers and the archives of Oxford University. The effect on the parish during these years cannot be assumed to have been necessarily bad, though a study of the visitation complaints would bring out specific problems. It remained true that until the 1830s a few prominent clergy were holding many of the best livings, leaving ill-paid and hard-worked curates like James Woodforde to care as best they might for several parishes at once.

The Beliefs of the People

The universal acceptance of the teachings from the medieval Church was rudely shaken by the Lollards, and from the late 14th century there was a steady stream of opposition, notably in Bristol's suburbs, through the influence of such men as William Smith and John Yonge in the 1440s, and of Richard Gryg of Wrington in the 1470s. These and a few others were bold enough to declare their unorthodox views on the Eucharist, confessions, images and the like. One of the central problems of the Reformation is the small number of people in that much wider movement whose views are known. There were those few Protestant martyrs under Mary; the much larger number of clergy who lost their livings, if only temporarily, for taking wives; there were a few individuals, including a Somerset servant girl whose protest at Chedzoy showed she had grasped some of the Lutheran theology; and there were the Catholic martyrs and the Puritan extremists of Elizabeth's reign. Prominent individuals might publish their beliefs for others to read; testators might at least indicate their views of the hereafter if the scribe taking down their last wills and testaments would permit them, but for

most other people, unless they were brought before a church court for
their misdeeds, their actions and opinions on one of the most
far-reaching movements in our history will remain unknown.

Polarisation of attitudes in the 17th century, strengthening the legal
measures used by whichever party was in power, provides the historian
with more information. From the fines and other measures taken against
Recusants, Catholic families can be traced with some success. Puritanism
within the Established Church may be followed in the practices of the
clergy, in their long and frequent sermons, lectures and exercises, in
their objection to the traditional parish jollifications like perambulations,
church ales and maypoles. Laudianism is recognised by insistence on
order and decency, on railed altars and proper vestments, on tradition as
opposed to liberty of conscience.

The emergence of nonconformist sects produced savage legislation
used effectively against the Quakers, whose sufferings were chronicled
in detail by their fellows. Forthcoming work on Somerset Quakers is
breaking new and important ground in attempting to analyse the social
background of the Society of Friends in the 17th century, a subject much
more difficult to study, though no less important to attempt, in other
denominations at the time and later. Records of individual
congregations, used in conjunction with secular material, may go a long
way to answer an important problem in religious history and may
establish whether, for example, the social background of Methodism in
Bristol in the late 18th century was typical of nonconformity in general in
the city, and how it compared with Dissent in the countryside. The
problem is still of importance in the 19th century, not only where it can
indicate causes for the growth or decline of a particular sect, but also
where it can shed light on the attraction of particular doctrines and
practices.

The social and political importance of nonconformity in the 18th and
19th centuries is of crucial interest, locally as well as nationally, in the
whole history of religious revival. The contrast between 'high church'
Uphill and 'low church' Weston-Super-Mare could be seen in dress as
well as in liturgy: the high churchman preferred soft hats, straight collars
and long coats, as well as 'short sermons, having the prayers chanted, and
the east end the cardinal point for the creed'. The origins of such
differing traditions there and in Clevedon, Clifton and Bath, and their
effect on parish life would prove a fascinating study.

Duty and Devotion

From as early as 1349 and with increasing frequency from the mid
15th century onwards we can begin to glimpse what individual people
thought of their parish church. Wills may be poor criteria, for the request
for holy burial, the few pence for tithes forgotten, and even a gift of
goods or money to church funds might be seen only as part of an
insurance for the hereafter; but a different picture is presented in the
day-to-day accounts of churchwardens, whose activities were at the

centre of parish life. These accounts, essential for tracing the changes in worship and ritual during the confusing years of the Reformation, are for an earlier period essential to show how lavishly people spent their money on fabric, decoration and ornaments. St. Ewen's, Bristol, for instance, had some 24 service books in 1455, and the wardens listed large quantities of vestments, jewels and ornaments, together with the names of donors. The complete list shows that services at St. Ewen's, as at most other churches at the time, were colourful and even noisy affairs. The great silver cross with images of the saints, the chalices, censers, painted retable, embroidered vestments, hangings and banners, the clothed images and the rood, rochets for the choirmen and serving boys, the bells and organ—all contributed to the magnificence of worship in a prosperous town parish. And when in 1493 a new church house was built in Broad Street, 16 people between them produced most of the cash, including a lady who paid 2d. a week during the building; wood, sand and other materials came from a dozen others.

The experience of St. Ewen's is unusual only in the detail and continuity of the surviving accounts. Most, either from country or town (Bath St. Michael from 1349, Yatton from 1445, St. Ewen's from 1454, all printed; Bristol All Saints from 1407, Bristol St. John from 1469, Banwell from 1516, Bristol Christ Church from 1531 and others still in manuscript), will make clear how much the church meant to individual people. The contrast with Post-Reformation accounts is extraordinary. Gifts to the church, so commonplace before, become rare; the fabric, the bells and the bellringers a constant charge. Income from property, seat rents, and payments of dues by householders and communicants are recorded by rote as if they were a charge to be grudged and avoided. Anglican 'decency and order' in worship had supplanted devotion by duty. The black cap and gown, liberal application of limewash, and the rubrics of the Book of Common Prayer were the order of the day. The only glory of many 17th century churches was the pulpit, whose tasseled cushion was so often worn out by the exertions of the preacher; and it was the pulpit which was the focus of nonconformist devotion.

There were still devout and devoted Anglicans, but with few exceptions Anglican records become formalised, and churchwardens' accounts little more than catalogues of repairs to the fabric, the purchase of State prayers, gifts of alms to travellers, and payment of the cost of visitation dinners. The picture of worship in country parishes drawn by 'Church-Goer' in the 1840s of droning parson, raucous parish clerk, inexpert musical accompaniment and largely silent congregation must have been common for two centuries, very unlike the enthusiasm created by Wesley and Whitefield. The loyalty of early Quakers to the Truth and to each other in face of fierce persecution or the ridicule borne by the first Methodists is evidence of a devotion unmatched in the Anglican Church as a whole until revival in the 19th century.

But revival came and devotion returned; and although devotion is most easily seen thereafter in the fabric rather than in the record, yet the contrast between the descriptions of 'Church-Goer' in the 1840s and 'Church Rambler' in the 1870s is surely sufficient testimony to devotion

in the Anglican church. Registers of services and parish diaries deserve
wider study for the wealth of material they contain, and they can be
complemented in many areas by Methodist circuit records to reveal a
splendid picture of the Church in the countryside.

The Fabric of the Faith

Parish churches by reason of their age have for long been studied for
the archaeology they contain, for the examples of architectural genius or
artistic merit preserved from the past. Yet they were built both as
expressions of religious devotion and as places for the exercise of that
devotion in its outward form. So the fabric of church and chapel, and
even more their furnishing, are themselves sources of information.
Fragments of medieval glass, traces of paintwork on wall or screen,
figures on pulpit, bench-end or tower, are continuing witness to the
colour and imagery of medieval religion. Secondary piscinas in even the
smallest churches, evidence of more than one altar, are enough to
indicate the importance of the Mass as the focal point of public worship,
though the number of medieval pulpits shows that preaching and
reading in public was not neglected.

The contrast with the Post-Reformation church is perhaps more
apparent than real. Large-scale rebuilding in the late 15th and early 16th
centuries, so noticeable in this part of the country, destroyed churches of
an earlier period. Any wholesale rebuilding on a similar scale after the
Reformation would have done the same, but people then had other
concerns and other priorities, and unless disaster struck (as at Keynsham
where the tower fell down and had to be rebuilt) or unless a wealthy
family wanted a more fashionable view from their mansion (Great
Badminton, Dodington, Redland Court) devotion was expressed in
different ways, and duty involved no more than patching the old fabric.

Furnishings were a different matter. The Puritan pulpit came to
dominate the parish church in the 17th century, though surviving
examples of untouched interiors are rare, best seen at Camely in Avon,
but better still just over the Somerset border at Holcombe Old Church or
Hardington. The arrangement of pews and pulpit is itself significant, a
two- or three-decker pulpit raising the parson high above his people, the
squire regarding his private pew as an extension of his parlour, the
farmers closeted in their boxes, half of them with their backs to parson
and communion table, and the labouring poor squeezed in on benches at
the back or in the gallery.

Pulpits were central to chapels too, where the focus was on the Word
or the preacher, and scale alone marks out a village chapel from an
imposing town tabernacle, where galleries almost surround a central
pulpit, and where the prominence of the organ denotes the importance
of hymn-singing in nonconformist worship. Anglicans adopted this
architectural tradition in their proprietary chapels in Bath, where the
minister's livelihood depended not on endowments but on the number
of regular hearers he could attract.

Anglican revival brought in its train a concern that the patched and crumbling churches were no fit places to attract the thousands lost either to nonconformity or to ignorance; that new churches were needed where the people were living; that proper worship demanded proper, and usually Gothic, surroundings. Victorian restoration has been blamed for much destruction, but it was as much required by the neglect of the past as by the hopes for the future. In 1851 a census was taken to record church and chapel attendances. This year was by no means the high water mark of revival, but is still a great contrast to the strength of Church and Chapel in the 1970s. The change has yet to be documented in detail, but local historians might usefully begin with a census of their own. If the subsequent story is of contraction and decay, it will not be for the first time; and if the practice of religion seems to be losing out to humanism and atheism, that, too, is the local historian's theme.

10

Education

R.B. HOPE

The Avon area can boast the provision of a rich variety of educational institutions over a long period of time, reflecting the growth and development of educational facilities in the country as a whole.

Growth of Schools

Schools of one kind or another had existed in Bristol, Bath, Westbury-on-Trym and Old Sodbury, for instance, in late medieval times. In addition to these schools, individual teachers also existed, sometimes laymen but more often unemployed or underemployed clergy, such as curates, chaplains and, in particular, chantry priests. The existence of the latter, frequently with some reference to their teaching, is well documented in the Chantry Certificates of 1547-8. But it was not until the 16th and 17th centuries that the first major educational impact was made with the emergence of two endowed Grammar Schools in Bristol—the Grammar School and the Cathedral School; the King Edward VI School in Bath; and other endowed schools at Thornbury, Wickwar, Henbury and Chipping Sodbury. Launched largely by private benevolence, these local centres of learning provided a classical education for the sons of the more prosperous families in town and country, and, through their foundation awards, for a small number of local poor boys as well.

Voluntary effort, inspired mainly by the religious zeal of the established Church in the post-Reformation period, was further responsible for other more philanthropic educational foundations on behalf of poor and deprived children. In 1590 Queen Elizabeth's Hospital was opened in Bristol, followed by the Red Maids' School for poor girls in 1634, and Edward Colston's boarding School in 1710. Then, following on the launching of the Society for the Propagation of Christian Knowledge in 1698, Charity schools were established in considerable numbers throughout the country during the 18th century. This region was no exception, and there is evidence to show the existence of many Charity schools in several parts of Bristol, in Bath, and at Dyrham, Henbury and Pucklechurch, amongst other places.

Even so, in this pre-industrial post-Reformation era educational opportunities were very restricted; indeed they were not deemed necessary at all in any large measure for ordinary folk. Only the wealthy, privileged classes of society were expected to enjoy the advantages of an extended education, either at home at the hands of private tutors, or at private fee-paying schools, or one of the older Universities. Most of the labouring poor before 1800 remained uneducated unless they were fortunate enough to find a free place at the local grammar school or a cheap dame school, or unfortunate enough to qualify for local charity. Consequently, the amount of educational provision that was available through voluntary effort and private philanthropy, by and large, sufficed until the closing decades of the 18th century.

All this then changed with the coming of modern industrial development, which brought a transition from a rural to an urban society during the 19th century. Concomitant with this was the large and rapid growth of population, with an ever-increasing number of children to be educated. The religious bodies valiantly tried to cope with the incipient problems of mass education as cheaply as possible between 1780 and 1830, first by introducing Sunday Schools and then monitorial schools. But voluntary effort and religious zeal (e.g. that of Hannah More) were no longer enough. The State was compelled to intervene.

In 1833 a first government grant of £20,000 was passed by Parliament to assist the National (Church of England) and British and Foreign (Nonconformist) School societies to build schoolhouses for the poor. By this measure a foundation for further State intervention had been laid. The annual government grant for educational purposes steadily increased throughout the 19th century; the influence of the religious bodies and the necessity for private philanthropy correspondingly declined; and by the end of the century, as a result of a series of Education Acts, a national system of compulsory and free elementary education for boys and girls had been established, embracing both the State and voluntary (Church) schools.

By the Forster Education Act of 1870, School Boards, the first local public bodies responsible for the day-to-day running of elementary education, had been set up. In 1902 the Balfour Education Act removed the School Boards and replaced them with statutory Local Education Authorities. Under these new L.E.A.s the range of local educational provision was considerably extended to Secondary and Further Education during the 20th century, resulting in the extensive and varied pattern of public education that we have today, supplemented by schools in the private sector.

This remarkable national development of mass elementary education during the 19th century is clearly substantiated locally. By 1800 a flourishing Sunday School movement was well under way, especially in the more populous Bristol and Bath districts. During the next 70 years a large number of elementary schools for the poorer classes were established throughout Avon by the Church of England authorities, and to a much lesser extent by the Nonconformists and Catholics. The needs of adults were also not ignored, as is testified by the formation of Adult Schools and Mechanics' Institutions in Bristol and Bath, together, at a later stage, with the Bristol Merchant Venturers' Technical College.

Further 'gap-filling' in educational provision continued after 1870 with the establishment of both urban and rural School Boards in many parts of Avon, including Bristol, Bath, Twerton, Radstock, Chew Magna, Weston-super-Mare, Kingswood, Bitton and Oldland. Indeed, so successful was this late Victorian popular education movement, that by the end of the 19th century an elementary school place was available for every child both locally and nationally.

Other types of schools, such as Ragged Schools, Industrial Schools and Special Schools for physically handicapped children, emerged during the 19th century, mostly in Bristol, as a result of both philanthropic and public effort. Nor was private enterprise on behalf of the growing numbers of the professional middle classes to be outdone, as witnessed by the emergence of many élitist boarding schools in this area, such as Kingswood (the Methodist Public School transferred from Bristol to Bath in 1852), the Royal School for daughters of Army Officers at Bath, Prior Park College, Monkton Combe and Clifton College; together with Clifton and Bath High Schools for Girls and Colston's and Redland High School for Girls, which largely catered for day pupils. The foundation of a University College at Bristol in 1876 was also a significant landmark.

Studies already undertaken

There is clearly plenty of scope for the educational historian in Avon, and some significant contributions to the history of education in the area have already been made.

Many histories of old schools in Bristol and Bath have been written, and these account for much of the limited amount of published material that is available. The Gloucestershire County Council also published in 1954 an historical survey of local educational facilities. A good deal of unpublished work, however, has been further carried out in recent years by students working for diplomas and higher degrees of the University of Bristol.

A large number of these University research studies concern educational developments in Bristol, mainly in the 19th and 20th centuries. Apart from a broad survey by Larcombe in 1924 of educational provision in the City before 1875, most of them concentrate on more specific themes such as the National Society's work in Bristol, 1811–1870; Roman Catholic elementary schools, 1847–1902; the implementation of the 1870 Education Act in Bristol; the work of the British School Board; adult education facilities in the 19th century; the Society of Merchant Venturers' contribution to the development of education in Bristol, and the beginnings of municipal secondary education in the City and county of Bristol from 1895 to 1919.

A smaller number of research studies have been concerned with Bath, and, as a result, the following topics have been examined in varying degrees of depth: educational developments in the City of Bath, 1830–1902, in relation to social and economic change; Bath elementary schools, 1862–1902; elementary education in Bath, 1902–1926, and the history of the Bath Home Economics College, 1892–1945. Other parts of

Avon outside Bristol and Bath have also attracted attention. Amongst a further group of recent studies can thus be found theses dealing with educational provision in North-West Somerset, 1750–1850; the effects of parliamentary and local government legislation upon Bitton Oldland Common C.E. Primary School, 1900–1939; elementary education in Nailsea, 1784–1944; educational provision in the Gordano Valley, 1870–1970, and the development of elementary education in Gloucestershire, 1698–1846.

Some interesting work has also been carried out under the auspices of the Bristol Archives classes run over many years by the Extra-Mural Department of Bristol University. In 1959 such studies included papers on 'The Certified Industrial School in Park Row, Bristol', and 'Schools and School Teachers in Bristol, 1870–1900', which entailed the use of school log books and School Board and L.E,A. records. Then again in 1960 similar studies were undertaken concerning elementary education in Bristol in the early 19th Century, with special reference to Clifton; and the Wills of Bristol Diocese, 1661–1670, which throws some light on the prevailing standards of literacy.

In addition, a number of more 'unofficial' investigations into local educational facilities have undoubtedly been carried out from time to time in various parts of the country by enthusiastic individuals. Certainly this has been the case at Weston-super-Mare, Nailsea and Thornbury, where examples of such work can be found in the local public libraries. Similar work has perhaps been done elsewhere, but these sporadic efforts are often not too well publicised and need a certain amount of 'digging out' with the help of a local librarian.

Some Sources and Topics for Further Study

Although a significant amount of research concerning various aspects of educational development in Avon has certainly been undertaken, mainly relating to Bristol and Bath, much obviously remains to be done. A complete picture of the history of education in Avon as a whole has by no means yet emerged, and it is only by knowing what was happening in all the different localities that this can be achieved. There appears to be plenty of scope, therefore, for both individuals and local history groups to look into the educational story of their own towns and villages, after it has been established, of course, that no such histories already exist.

Schools of one kind or another have played an important part in local affairs in Avon, as elsewhere, over many years; consequently a study of their growth and development must surely be a major concern of the local educational historian. The history of many local schools still needs to be written or re-assessed, and for the local historian interested in such a task there is a varied and substantial amount of source material to explore, the starting point invariably being the school itself if it is still functioning.

For the history of public elementary education in the 19th century school log books are a main source of information, especially after 1862 when the Revised Code made the keeping of them obligatory by all schools in receipt of a State grant. Many of these old log books, often containing a good deal of interesting information about the day-to-day activities of children and their teachers, are still retained by some Avon primary schools today others are to be found in the County Record Offices at Gloucester and Taunton and the City Record Offices at Bristol and Bath, along with some admission registers and minutes of Managers' meetings. Further useful sources of information are the Minutes, triennial reports and other records of the local School Boards, especially those in the Bristol and Bath districts. From 1903 onwards much additional L.E.A. material relating to both elementary and secondary schools, and technical education, becomes available and can be examined in the appropriate local Record and Education Offices.

Much information of interest to the local historian can also be gleaned from the many Parliamentary Papers on Education. Three of these deserve special mention.

Firstly, there are the Charity Commission Reports between 1819 and 1837: these reports throw considerable light on the state of local educational charities and help to supplement other surviving source material on 18th and 19th century Charity schools in Avon; secondly, the Minutes and Annual Reports of the Committee of Council on Education, 1839–1899, which give a lot of miscellaneous information about local schools, including H.M.I.s' reports; and thirdly, the Schools Inquiry Commission, 1868–9, which ran to 21 volumes and is a mine of information on Secondary schools.

Other Central Government records such as the files on individual schools kept at the Public Record Office, and the decennial Census Reports since 1801, including the very detailed 1851 Education Census, are further very helpful sources of information. These Census Reports, in particular, could provide interesting source material for local group studies. For instance, such groups might investigate the growth of population in specific parts of Avon in relation to local school provision; or examine such topics as the drift of population in certain parts of the county and its effects on schooling provision, as instanced by the shift of the woollen industry from Gloucestershire to Yorkshire, which apparently led to the decline of population and hence Grammar Schools at places like Wickwar.

Church records are another major source, which is not surprising in view of the long-standing interest of the religious bodies in education. The archives of the National Society, the Methodist Education Committee and the S.P.C.K. in London, for example, include extensive collections of School records. Diocesan archives also often contain valuable records such as Diocesan Education Board Minutes, Diocesan Inspectors' Reports, and licences and testimonials issued by the Church authorities to schoolmasters from the 16th century onwards, qualifying them to teach. It should not be forgotten that until well into the 19th century the individual teacher still played an important part in local education, arguably the major part before 1800. Some were full-time, others part-timers such as parsons, parish-clerks or farmers. Evidence of their work, apart from the system of episcopal licensing, is rare and should be noted where it survives, for example in census enumerators' books after 1841, references in newspapers and 'Blue Books' and in wills and inventories. The inventory of Robert Lawford of Stoke Gifford in May, 1641, for example, shows that he combined teaching and farming, with farming taking first place: 'the skole house chamber' was used to store oats and wheat, 'the lower roome in the skoole house' accommodating 'packe saddeles and other furniture and other impellments'. Their own records are even less likely to survive: one example in Avon is the account book of a rector of Iron Acton who kept a private school early in the 18th century, now preserved in the parish records.

Local newspapers, directories, guide books and periodicals can prove useful, though sometimes unreliable, sources of information, but they are particularly helpful regarding private schools. A great variety of these schools has undoubtedly flourished in considerable numbers throughout Avon during the last 200 years, but they were mostly short-lived, leaving few, if any, records. It is often only through advertisements in newspapers and guide books that the existence of many of these private schools can be brought to light and some sort of local picture of them created. Newspapers, directories and guide books also give much miscellaneous information about other types of schools; annual reports of schools and learned societies; advertisements for private tutors; School Board business, and details of local educational issues and controversies. When other primary source material is missing they can be especially valuable, and offer plenty of scope for imaginative group studies.

The basic matter of literacy also lends itself well to group effort. Literacy is very difficult to assess with any degree of accuracy before the second half of the 19th century, and estimates for earlier periods have usually been based on whether people actually signed their name, or made their mark, on official documents. Documents such as wills, inventories, leases, administration bonds, petitions, oaths, presentments of jurors and licences of various kinds, where they exist, can in fact still be used as some sort of yardstick for this purpose. But it seems generally agreed that probably the best locally available sources for making some approximate assessment of literacy before the 19th century are the marriage registers, which from 1754 onwards, in the Anglican Church at least, required the signature of both parties and two witnesses. By a careful study of local parish registers, therefore, much light could be thrown on standards of literacy prevailing amongst men and women in certain parts of Avon at different times. If sampling was carried out on a sufficiently wide scale, some local groups might even be able to consider questions such as contrasts between town and country districts in Avon; a comparison of Avon with other parts of the country; and the extent of the local improvement in literacy during the 19th century in relation to the expansion of popular education.

Several other possibilities are also worthy of attention by local groups. Topics for consideration might include an investigation into the early

Adult Education movement in the Avon area, centring around the growth of the Mechanics' Institute movement in towns and villages in the early 19th century, a field where apparently more such regional studies are urgently needed. Studying developments and changes in school architecture and design might also have some appeal. Old school buildings can still be seen standing in many parts of the county, waiting to be photographed, and architects' plans for many 19th century Avon schools can be seen at the Bristol, Gloucester and Taunton Record Offices. Tape-recording old people's reminiscences of their schooldays 60 or 70 years ago can also be very informative, interesting, rewarding and amusing; whilst for the more practically bent the assembling of a small-scale history of education exhibition or museum on the model of the very extensive one at Leeds University could prove stimulating.

11

Leisure and Recreation

J.H. BETTEY

This is a subject on which much work remains to be done, and is one which could well repay the attention of local historians. It is not, however, an easy topic on which to find material, since the evidence is scattered among many different documentary sources. There is an important difference between organised sports, games, spectacles, concerts and similar events for which evidence is likely to be forthcoming, and private diversions and amusements which are much less likely to have given rise to written records. Moreover for most people the opportunities for leisure were limited, and the historian will be led to ask questions about hours of work and holidays, and about the different sorts of people who were able to participate in various recreations. (For details of sources on these topics see Chapters 6 and 7.) Some useful general books are listed in the bibliography, but there is little which relates specifically to Avon.

For the Middle Ages comparatively little evidence is likely to be found on any kind of leisure activity. What time could be spent by most people upon recreations was almost entirely centred upon the social life of the parish church, and evidence is most likely to be found in church records. Surviving churchwardens' accounts, for example those for St Michael's, Bath, for Yatton or for some of the Bristol churches contain incidental references to parish feasts, Christmas, Easter, Whitsun and other festivities, to annual ceremonies and processions such as at the feast of Corpus Christi or the Rogationtide beating of the parish bounds, mummers' plays, and above all to church ales which were the main social, as well as money-raising, activities in most parishes. Churchwardens' accounts also contain information about the building of 'church houses' which were provided by many west-country parishes and where church ales and other parochial activities could take place. Examples are to be found in the Yatton churchwardens' accounts, and in the Church Book of St. Ewen's, Bristol. The latter contains the complete account of building a church house in Broad Street, Bristol in 1493. A good example of a surviving church house dated 1512 can be seen at Chew Magna (the Old Schoolroom), and others await recognition. The other most fruitful source of evidence for medieval leisure activities in local communities is also to be found in ecclesiastical records, in court cases, presentments and visitation records, since these have information on offences such as brawls, drunkenness, defamation, and similar disputes which may have arisen out of social activities and which often give valuable incidental information.

More material on leisure-time activities is available for the 16th and 17th centuries. The church continued to be an important focus of social life, and the more numerous churchwardens' accounts which survive for this period often contain useful evidence for social as well as religious life in the parish. The church's part in supervising morals also produces copious evidence in churchwardens' presentments and ecclesiastical court papers. These records will be found in the appropriate diocesan record offices, and although they are not easy to use, they well repay any labour spent on them. Useful printed examples of the sort of cases which can be found are contained in F.D. Price (ed.), *The Commissions for Ecclesiastical Causes within the Dioceses of Bristol and Gloucester, 1574* (BGAS, Rec.Sec., 1972).

The 17th century series of churchwardens' presentments in the Bristol Diocesan Record Office (EP/V/3) contain material about persons playing at ball in St. Mary Redcliffe churchyard, failure to attend church, drinking during the time of divine service, unlicensed alehouses, and various examples of lapses from the path of moral rectitude. The playing of 'fives' and other games in churchyards was common; John Aubrey, the 17th century Wiltshire antiquarian, provides interesting information about 'stobball-play' which he claimed was very popular around Bath, particularly on Colerne Down. The game consisted of striking a hard leather ball with a staff. Puritan attempts to suppress church ales during the 17th century also provide much incidental evidence for these important social occasions—an example of other use which can be made of this will be found in the article by T.G. Barnes listed in the Bibliography.

Records of cases in the secular courts will also yield good material for the 16th and 17th centuries. For example the Proceedings in the Court of Star Chamber relating to Somerset during the reigns of Henry VII and Henry VIII, which have been printed by the Somerset Record Society, contain an account of hunting by night by various men from the Chew Valley in the Bishop's park at Banwell. They killed 20 of the deer and set their heads on the pales of the park in defiance of the bishop. *The Letters and Papers of Henry VIII*, vol. 8 (ed. J. Gairdner), tell the story of William Meryck, a weaver of Kingswood, and other men from the same locality who were indicted in 1535 for poaching in various parks in south Gloucestershire, including deer parks at Alveston, Siston, Sodbury, Thornbury, Yate and Stoke Gifford. The records of the assize courts and of quarter sessions are an even more fruitful source of evidence about leisure activities. For example the quarter sessions records, many of which have been printed by the Record Societies, contain much material on alehouse tippling, drunkenness, gaming, church ales, bull-baiting and other similar activities. It is, of course, necessary to beware of supposing that those incidents which came before the courts were necessarily typical of the majority of occasions which passed off peaceably, attracted no attention and have left no record.

Another useful source of information can be found in the corporation records. For example *Ricart's Kalendar* (ed. L.T. Smith) is a mine of information about medieval Bristol and includes material on plays, mummers, civic festivities and other recreations. The Bath Chamberlains' Accounts (printed by Somerset Record Society) contain many references to market and fairs in the city, and to festivities on midsummer night, to bearwards and tumblers in the city and to visits by various companies of players and payments for plays. Similarly the Bristol corporation records refer to pageants and plays, such as the pageant to welcome Henry VII to the city in 1496 which included 'an Olifaunte with a Castell on his bakk, curiously wroughte...'; or the elaborate festivities with which Queen Elizabeth was greeted when she visited the city in 1574. John Latimer in his *Annals* and other works on Bristol also records all kinds of civic sports including drinking, wrestling, archery, bull-baiting, and the Mayor and his brethren playing at dice and going fishing in the river Frome. There are also references in the corporation records to bearwards, tumblers, players, etc., and to numerous civic occasions which provided an opportunity for feasting and merry-making. The records of markets and fairs, such as St. James' Fair in Bristol or the many other markets and fairs which were held in towns and villages throughout the area, will also provide evidence for the sort of entertainments which accompanied the more serious business. These will include spectacles of various kinds, circuses, freaks, trials of strength, and many similar diversions.

Maps such as estate or tithe maps can also provide useful evidence in the form of field and place names. For example, Millard's map of Bristol in 1673 shows bowling greens prominent within the city, and is a reminder of the popularity of this sport, particularly among the gentry during the 17th century. Field and place names will also record pastimes such as archery, bull-baiting, dancing, etc.; examples can be found in many places, for instance Chulrenhulle (Children's Hill) in Mangotsfield, Plythorn (tree where sport took place) in Thornbury, or Bull-pit in Paulton. Evidence of upper-class recreations particularly in Bristol and Bath can be obtained from the accounts of the increasing number of travellers, journalists and diarists who visited the area from the 17th century onwards and described what they saw and did, such as Pepys, Peter Mundy, Celia Fiennes, Defoe and many others. For informative local diaries in print which contain much information about the more private amusements such as cards, games, music etc., see the journal of Dr. Claver Morris of Wells (ed. E. Hobhouse) or the journal of the Rev. John Skinner of Camerton (ed. H. Coombs and A.N. Bax).

At all times drinking has been among the most popular of leisure activities and licences for alehouses, which from 1552 were granted by Justices of the Peace, provide a valuable source of local history. For example, the Gloucestershire Alehouse Recognizances for 1755 cover most of the county, including that part now in Avon, and give the names of the licensees and often also the names or signs of the inns. For later periods, directories provide information on inns and alehouses as well as on other facilities for recreation. Friendly Societies also played an important part in leisure activities and social life, including their weekly meetings, which were often held in pubs, and their annual 'club-walks': the earliest reference to the Feltmakers' Friendly Society at Frampton Cotterell is a newspaper mention of its annual procession in May 1761. (For references to this important topic see the works by Margaret Fuller and J.H. Bettey listed in the Bibliography).

From the 18th century onwards there were, for some members of society at least, greater opportunities for leisure and more organised, commercial activities available. Newspaper advertisements provide a valuable source of information for the sort of possibilities which existed for the pleasure-seeker. For the 19th century the work of Helen Meller describes in detail the range of organised activities, and also demonstrates how a variety of sources can be used to study the provision for leisure; her work also shows the importance of institutions and societies such as public libraries, art galleries, museums, temperance groups, the Y.M.C.A. and many others, including professional football teams. Theatres and music halls also played an increasingly important part in popular entertainment, and works on these subjects will be found in the Bibliography, particularly those by Kathleen Barker and Arnold Hare. Many of the multitude of Parliamentary Reports and Papers are useful for the study of leisure-time activities in the 19th century, and although the sheer mass of such Reports and their lack of adequate indexing makes them difficult to use, they well repay time spent upon them. Much helpful material will, for example, be found in the *Report from the Select Committee on the Observance of the Sabbath Day*, 1831-2, or the *Report of the Commissioners for Inquiring into Large Towns and Populous Districts*, 1844, and many others. A difficulty which has to be faced in any research with this subject is that often the most unlikely sources can provide valuable evidence. For example the accounts of building the new house at Dyrham early in the 18th century, which are in the G.R.O., contain references to the workmen absenting themselves in order to attend Colerne revel. The Gloucestershire Quarter Sessions Order Books, which are also in the G.R.O., contain several references to parish feasts and revels during the 18th century. An announcement in the *Bath Chronicle* for 1776 provides additional evidence; the magistrates of the Bath Forum division gave notice that all revels in the locality were to be suppressed on the grounds that

'the Custom of Keeping Revels in the several parishes within the division aforesaid hath occasioned idleness, drunkenness, riots, gaming, and all manner of vice, immorality, and profaneness amongst the lowest class of people, to the evil example of others, and the great disturbance, damage, and terror of the well-disposed, as well as tending greatly to the increase of the poor...'

Such items, as well as the much more numerous 19th century newspaper reports of garden parties, church bazaars, chapel tea-treats, Sunday school outings, or pig-club suppers, all provide valuable material for the historian. The work of B.M. Willmott-Dobbie on Batheaston shows what can be discovered with careful research, both documentary and oral, about pastimes in a rural community.

Only detailed local research, both among documentary sources and from local memories, can also reveal how much of the older tradition of entertainment survived until the early 20th century, including Christmas, Spring-time and Midsummer festivities, the sort of mummers' play which still exists at Marshfield, or the unamiable rural custom of the 'Skimmington' in which persons who had offended against the communal sense of propriety were publicly mocked. Researchers must always remember that beneath the organized public activities, about which it is fairly easy to find information, existed the leisure-time diversions of the majority of the population which have left few records. It is only possible to find out about such home entertainment as songs, plays, games, cards, private reading, folk-customs, etc., through the chance survival of diaries, letters or memories. Such material will only be found and preserved through the dedicated work of local historians, and it is in this field that their role is indispensable and can make an important contribution to historical knowledge.

12

Public Opinion and Popular Beliefs

J.S. MOORE

Most of the previous chapters have been concerned mainly with what people did in their localities in the past, and necessarily so: what they did is much more plentifully documented than what they said or thought. Yet their opinions and beliefs are an important historical topic not to be neglected: the great historian Maitland once said that the final goal of social history would be the recovery of 'the common thoughts of common men'. We should not assume that because most people in the past were illiterate (see chapter 10) they were inarticulate, or that because for most of the past they were politically, economically and socially dependent on the ruling minority, they could not hold opinions widely different from those of their masters. What, then, did the ordinary person in the past think and feel about his world?

Nevertheless, much of their thoughts on, for example, agriculture, can only be inferred from their actions—it is rarely that we can hear the past speaking to posterity. But the question is worth pursuing, and not simply for the last few generations through the recording of oral memory; important though the latter is, it should not be elevated to unimpeachable authority. Certainly, the memories of old people should be explored and recorded, but this requires patience, sympathy and a knowledge of interviewing techniques, to ensure that the answer given is genuine and not simply what it was thought the interviewer expected. Any facts and dates elicited should be checked thoroughly, since this will give some indication of how reliable information may be on matters that cannot be checked. In the writer's experience, old people are often more accurate on matters of opinion than matters of fact, and more reliable on the earlier than the later parts of their lives, though often chronologically imprecise; their views of the past are invaluable, but are only one source which should not be taken as gospel truth, even when sincere. Nevertheless, such memories are the most perishable of all historical evidence, and should be recorded as soon as possible: death comes to all of us, but records (especially in record offices) survive for our successors to work on.

Before the range of present oral memory, the local historian is dependent on written and printed records, and the latter should not be overlooked. In the last 150 years, many antiquarians and anthropologists have studied local folklore and dialect, and such studies both confirm and greatly augment the range of information obtained from oral memories, which can now go back no further than the late Victorian period. It will be clear from such studies how much of the spectrum of popular belief has been lost in the last hundred years as a result of migration, social mobility and education: for example the widespread local custom of 'skimmington', serenading those considered guilty of anti-social offences, especially adultery, with a cacophonous beating of pots, pans and dustbin-lids. Public opinion during this modern period can also be approached through local newspapers, both the 'news' sections and the correspondence columns, a task which, though laborious in the absence of indexes, will undoubtedly prove rewarding, not only for this subject, but for many other local history topics. In using newspapers we have to remember that, then as now, the 'news' may be politically biassed, whilst the individual letter-writer may be an atypical egotist; despite these disadvantages, newspapers are often the best or only source for many local events and views. This problem of individual egotism, or at least eccentricity, also affects what might otherwise seem the most obviously individualist records from the past, namely diaries and autobiographies. In any case, most such records before the 20th century were not compiled by members of the lower classes who, even if increasingly literate after 1850, were not habitual writers. In addition, autobiographies were not contemporary records but usually selective and partial recollections written in self-justification, whilst the diarist also is likely to be in some sense abnormal. Correspondence, though again rarely extant except for the gentry and above, is less likely to be deliberately tendentious or misleading and is therefore also a valuable source not to be ignored. Nonetheless, any surviving letters, diaries or autobiographies, particularly of working-class people, should be preserved and utilised on account of their rarity: at best, they may be an invaluable corrective to the views expressed by socially predominant contemporaries, throwing light on the life and opinions of the classes least well documented by archives. Unfortunately, however, the existing lists of diaries and autobiographies are outdated, incomplete and not topographically indexed, though the local historian is more likely by diligent enquiry to discover previously unknown examples than anyone else. A further guide to the formation of public opinion, besides the content of syllabuses in the developing education system (see chapter 10), may be found in any surviving library records, as for example, those of the Iron Acton Reading Society, showing the books provided and those most in demand by users. A further approach to popular aspirations may be made through the study of surviving records of local friendly societies, trade-union branches and political party records, though none of those are common and, where they exist, often difficult of access. Here again, local knowledge and contacts are the best means of discovering what if anything exists.

Before the 19th century, the thoughts, like the actions, of most people are chiefly documented in records produced for other purposes by

official bodies of various kinds, mainly of a judicial nature. Records of
the common law courts are not of great value for this purpose, since in
general indictments and witnesses' statements tend to be summarized in
a fairly standard form, even where the substance originated in a verbal
statement, for example in riot cases. On the other hand, in the courts
which had a Roman or Civil law background, such as the ecclesiastical
courts, the Courts of Chancery and Exchequer, and the 'prerogative
courts' of Requests and Star Chamber, the practice prevailed that
indictments ('allegations') and witnesses' statements ('depositions')
should preserve direct speech verbatim, so that the records of these
courts are the principal source for this subject in the early modern
period. They are therefore the nearest approach we have to the speech
and thoughts of our ancestors, particularly those of the ecclesiastical
courts which, until the 19th century, were the chief bodies dealing with
cases of slander and defamation of character at local level. Down to the
18th century, wills are also a valuable guide to the thoughts and
aspirations of our ancestors: these can reveal much of their world, both
in material and in mental and emotional aspects. Most wills were written
for local testators by local scribes and mirrored quite closely the patterns
of thought and expression of the local community. After the middle
decades of the 18th century, and earlier in the case of the upper classes,
most wills are less useful in this respect, reflecting in the main the
stereotyped phraseology of the lawyers who drew them up, though the
nature and destination of bequests may still be illuminating. The
ecclesiastical court and probate records are with the other records of the
appropriate diocese, and the records of all the other, national, courts are
in the P.R.O.

Some other national government records are also important for the
study of this subject. In periods of crisis, English governments tried
deliberately to keep themselves informed on the state of public opinion,
since they normally had insufficient armed forces at their disposal to
suppress outbreaks of rebellion without great difficulty, and therefore
wished to defuse potentially dangerous situations before they escalated
to the point of rebellion. As a result, in the Tudor and early Stuart
period, the Privy Council made great efforts to keep its finger on the
pulse of public opinion, and the information it obtained is preserved in
the State Papers Domestic in the P.R.O. and in various ministerial
collections, notably those of the Cecil family (Lansdowne MSS. in the
British Library and the Salisbury MSS. at Hatfield). Again during the
period of the Revolutionary and Napoleonic wars and their aftermath
(c1790–c1830), similar reports were made which concentrated
particularly on working-class agitation: these are now among the Home
Office Papers in the P.R.O. Another approach to the problem utilising
the government's knowledge of public opinion is to analyse the
preambles in Acts of Parliament, proclamations and other official
pronouncements (e.g. minsterial speeches in Parliament), in which the
ostensible reasons for policies are stated. That is not of course to assume
that the reasons given are necessarily the real reasons for government
action, either in 1578 or 1978, but they will be reasons, however

insincere, which governments thought the populace would find at least plausible. In the very modern period, other official reports (e.g. to the Home Intelligence Directorate during World War II) may be supplemented by semi-official or private surveys of public opinion where these survive (e.g. the Mass Observation archives now in the University of Sussex Library), though the present use of small scientifically designed representative samples means that local information may never have been collected, and in printed summaries (e.g. the *P.E.P. Reports*) specifically local information has usually been aggregated to provide a national picture. With care, conclusions can also be drawn from literature (novels and plays) and memoirs, though it is often difficult to be sure what is drawn from life and what from the creative imagination. But no history of modern Gloucestershire, for example, could afford to ignore the insights of John Moore's novels and Laurie Lee's *Cider with Rosie*.

Finally, in the more remote and undocumented past, the evidence of place-names should not be neglected for the light thrown on aspects of popular belief, which in total may only become fully documented much later in history (see Keith Thomas' work). The long survival of pagan beliefs of different kinds is evidenced in such names as Grimsbury in Bitton ('Grim's Hill'), Wansdyke in north Somerset ('Woden's Ditch'), and the numerous holy wells (e.g. Pennywell in east Bristol and St. Aldhelm's well in Pucklechurch) as much as in the numerous pagan sites deliberately converted by St. Augustine and his successors on Pope Gregory's advice into centres of Christian worship, as at Oldbury-on-Severn and Stanton Drew, for example. Such evidence in turn links up with traditional practices and customs which have survived into the very modern period, to be recorded by folklore students and remembered by that great fount of popular tradition, the 'ancientest inhabitants'.

APPENDIX
Local Administrative Units in Avon
J.S. MOORE

The local historian will need to know in what administrative units below county and diocese level his parish was included in the past. He should not assume that manors were identical in area with parishes of the same name: some parishes contained more than one manor, and some manors spread into more than one parish. The best sources here are manorial maps, surveys and rentals and, where available, inclosure awards.

For judicial, financial and administrative purposes the counties were divided into hundreds and the hundreds into tithings: the latter were often but not always equivalent to parishes. In the Middle Ages the best guide to the allocation of places within hundreds is to be found for 1086 in Domesday Book (new translation in progress for Gloucestershire (ed. J.S. Moore) and Somerset (ed. C. Thorn), to be published by Phillimore) and in the 'Nomina Villarum' of 1316 and other returns printed in *Feudal Aids*, vol. 2 (H.M.S.O., 1900), pp. 234–302 (Gloucestershire) and vol. 4 (H.M.S.O., 1906), pp. 272–440 (Somerset). In the modern period, 18th and 19th century county maps and early Victorian county directories are the best guides. For south Gloucestershire the composition of each hundred from 1086 onwards is detailed in A.H. Smith, *The Place Names of Gloucestershire*, vol. 3 (English Place Names Society, 1964) at the start of the section for each hundred. The 19th century county directories are the best guides to Petty Sessional and County Court districts—originally these were often based on groups of hundreds—to Poor Law Unions (1834–1929) and other *ad hoc* statutory bodies, e.g. Sanitary Authorities, and to Urban and Rural District Councils (1894–1973).

For ecclesiastical purposes, south Gloucestershire was within Worcester diocese until 1541, thereafter Bristol and Gloucester dioceses; north Somerset, apart from Abbot's Leigh which was in Bristol diocese from 1542, was in Bath and Wells diocese. The dioceses were divided into archdeaconries and rural deaneries: in the medieval period, the parishes can be located in the 1291 *Taxatio Ecclesiastica... Papae Nicholai IV* (Rec. Comm, 1802), pp. 196–205 (Bath and Wells), 216–40 (Worcester) and in the 1535 *Valor Ecclesiasticus*, vol. 1 (Rec. Comm, 1810), pp. 121–226 (Bath and Wells); vol. 2 (Rec. Comm, 1814), pp.

409–503 (Bristol and Gloucester). Few changes took place before the 19th century when many new 'ecclesiastical parishes' (more correctly, chapelries and ecclesiastical districts) were established by Order in Council: these are printed in the *London Gazette*, and copies are also to be found in diocesan archives. Changes in the composition of modern archdeaconries and deaneries can be traced through surveys in diocesan archives, in Crockford's *Clerical Directory*, diocesan yearbooks, county directories and, for Bristol and Gloucester dioceses, in the indexes to I.F. Kirby's catalogues of the diocesan archives.

Bibliography: I
Books and Articles

Like all bibliographies, this is both selective and already out-of-date: the selectivity can be remedied by consulting the two standard bibliographical series for English history, the *Bibliographical Handbooks* produced by the American Conference on British Studies (M. Altschul, *Anglo-Norman England, 1066–1154* (Cambridge, 1969); D.J. Guth, *Late-Medieval England, 1377–1485* (Cambridge, 1976); M. Levine, *Tudor England, 1485–1603* (Cambridge, 1968); W.L. Sachse, *Restoration England, 1660–89* (Cambridge, 1971); J.F. Altholz, *Victorian England, 1837–1901* (Cambridge, 1970): other volumes are being prepared) and the more elaborate series by the Royal Historical Society (E.B. Graves (ed), *Bibliography of English History to 1485* (Oxford, 1975); C. Read (ed), *Bibliography of British History. . . 1485-1603* (Oxford, 2nd ed., 1959); G. Davies, M.F. Keeler (ed), *Bibliography of British History. . . 1603-1714* (Oxford, 2nd ed., 1970); S.J. Pargellis, D.J. Medley (ed), *Bibliography of British History. . . 1714–1789* (Oxford, 1951); L.M. Brown, I.R. Christie (ed), *Bibliography of British History. . . 1789-1851* (Oxford, 1977); H.J. Hanham (ed), *Bibliography of British History. . . 1851-1914* (Oxford, 1976).).

The standard local bibliographies, all decades out-of-date, are, for Gloucestershire, F.A. Hyett, W. Bazeley (ed), *Bibliographer's Manual of Gloucestershire Literature*, **1, 2** (Gloucestershire, 1895–6) and R.F. Austin, *Catalogue of the Gloucestershire Collection* (Gloucester, 1928); for Bristol, F.A. Hyett, W. Bazeley (ed), *Bibliographer's Manual of Gloucestershire Literature*, **3** (Gloucester, 1897) and E.R.N. Matthews, *Bristol Bibliography* (Bristol, 1916); and for Somerset, E. Green, *Bibliotheca Somersetensis* (Taunton, 3 vols, 1902). Supplementary card indexes for later works are maintained in the respective central libraries of Gloucester, Bristol and Taunton. Also useful is J.C. Rowles (ed), *Library Resources in S.W. England and the Channel Islands* (2nd ed., 1978). The local historian can keep in touch with new work as it appears by consulting the annual lists in the *Economic History Review*, *History*, and *Agricultural History Review*, and the annual volume of the *British Humanities Index*, *Regional List* for the area.

For books, the place of publication is stated only when it is not London, and the country only when it is not Great Britain. The titles of journals and record series have been abbreviated as follows:

AgHR: *Agricultural History Review*; *ArchJ*: *Archaeological Journal*; *BG*: *Transactions of the Bristol and Gloucestershire Archaeological Society*; *BGC*: J. Cannon, P.V. McGrath (ed), *Essays in Bristol and Gloucestershire History*

(Bristol, 1976); *BGRS: Bristol and Gloucestershire Archaeological Society Records Section; BIAS: Journal of the Bristol Industrial Archaeology Society; BIHR: Bulletin of the Institute of Historical Research; BRS: Bristol Record Society Publications; CQR: Church Quarterly Review; EcHR: Economic History Review; EngHR: English Historical Review; EPNS: English Place-Names Society Publications; IL: Index Library (British Records Society); JBAA: Journal of the British Architectural Association; JTH: Journal of Transport History; LH: Local Historian* (previously *Amateur Historian); LPS: Local Population Studies; MA: Medieval Archaeology; MM: Mariner's Mirror; PP: Past and Present; SA: Somerset Archaeology and Natural History* (previously *Proceedings of the Somerset Archaeological and Natural History Society); SCH: Studies in Church History; SRS: Somerset Record Society; TAMS: Transactions of the Ancient Monuments Society; TIBG: Transactions of the Institute of British Geographers; TRHS: Transactions of the Royal Historical Society; VCH: Victoria County History.* (All these are journal and series whose future publications should be checked for additions to this bibliography.)

The figure in heavy type following the journal or record society abbreviation is the volume number; the arabic numerals in ordinary type following the journal or part number are the inclusive page references. Other abbreviations used are as follows: ed: edition; (ed): editor(s); NS: New Series; repr: reprinted; ser: series.

Books, journals or record series not available in your local library can be obtained through the Inter-Library Loan Service: for access to this facility and for any further help, consult your local library or, in case of difficulty, the Avon Central Library.

Chapter 1

Local History: End and Means

Sources and Methods

The best basic introductions are F. Celoria, *Teach Yourself Local History* (1958) and R.W. Dunning, *Local Sources for the Young Historian* (1973). More advanced guides include R.B. Pugh, *How to write a parish history* (1954); J. West, *Village Records* (1962), and in particular W.G. Hoskins, *Local History in England* (2nd ed, 1972); A. Rogers, *Approaches to Local History* (1977: 2nd ed. of *This was their world* (1972).) and A. MacFarlane, S. Harrison, C. Jardine, *Reconstructing historical communities* (1977). Two works by D. Iredale are especially useful for the methods of studying local history: *Enjoying Archives* (Newton Abbot, 1973) and *Local History Research and Writing* (Leeds, 1974). The essential advanced guide to sources is W.B. Stephens, *Sources for English Local History* (Manchester, 1972) which can be supplemented by references in W.H. Chaloner, R.C. Richardson (ed), *British Economic and Social History: a bibliographical guide* (1976). Other useful works include L.J. Redstone, F.W. Steer, *Local Records* (1953); W.G. Hoskins, *Provincial England* (1963) and *Fieldwork in Local History* (1967); F.G. Emmison, D.W. Humphreys, *Local History for Students* (1966); F.G. Emmison, *Archives and Local History* (Chichester, 2nd ed. 1978) and *Introduction to Archives* (Chicester, 1978); J.L. Hobbs, *Local History and the Library* (2nd ed, 1973); J. Fines, *The History Student's Guide to the Library* (Chichester, 1973); R. Storey, L. Madden, *Primary Sources for Victorian Studies* (Chichester, 1977) and W.B. Stephens, *Teaching Local History* (Manchester, 1977). The value of collaborative effort is stressed in A. Rogers (ed), *Group Projects in Local History* (Folkestone, 1977). All these general works contain chapters relevant to the subjects covered in later chapter bibliographies, but specific references have been excluded to save space and money. A useful glossary of historical terms is given in J. Richardson, *The Local Historian's Encyclopaedia* (New Barnet, 1974), though some entries need to be chekced with specialist authorities. Other valuable guides to sources of value to local historians include G.R. Elton, *Sources of History: England 1200–1640* (1969); J.J. Bagley, *Historical Interpretation* (2 vols, 1965, 1971, repr. 1972); L.M. Munby (ed), *Short guides to records* (1972); W.R. Powell, *Local history from Blue Books* (1962); J. Thirsk (ed), *Land, Church and People* (1970); and G.K. Clark, *Guide for Research Students working on Historical Subjects* (Cambridge, 1958). All the above books have good bibliographies: F.W. Kuhlicke, F.G. Emmison, *English Local History Handlist* (4th ed, 1969) is very useful. The objectives of local history are discussed in detail in H.P.R. Finberg, *Approaches to History* (1962), chapter 5; W.R. Powell, 'Local History in Theory and Practice', *BIHR*, **31**, 41–8; W.G. Hoskins, *English Local History: the past and the future* (Leicester, 1966); H.P.R. Finberg, V.H.T. Skipp (ed), *Local History: Objective and Pursuit* (Newton Abbot, 1967); A. Rogers, 'New Horizons in Local History', *LH*, **12**, 67–73; and in two books by A.M. Everitt, *New Avenues in English Local History* (Leicester, 1970) and *Ways and Means in Local History* (1971). The problems of publication are considered in W.G. Hoskins, *Local History in England* (2nd ed, 1972), chapter 12, and A. Rogers (ed), *Group Projects in Local History* (Folkestone, 1977), chapter 12: some possible solutions are outlined in I. Waters, 'The Chepstow Society and local history publication', *LH*, **2**, 212–4; B. Garside, 'A twenty years' local history project', *LH*, **3**, 183–4; and H.E. Priestly, 'A new venture: a parish history in parts', *LH*, **4**, 120–5.

Handwriting

L.C. Hector, *The Handwriting of English Documents* (2nd ed, 1966), H.E.P. Grieve, *Examples of English Handwriting, 1150–1750* (Chelmsford, 4th ed, 1974) and D. Iredale, *Enjoying Archives* (Newton Abbot, 1973), chapters 13–14, cover the whole range of scripts. For the medieval period, A. Rycraft, *English Medieval Handwriting* (York, 1972) and K.C. Newton, *Medieval Local Records: a reading aid* (1971) are valuable guides. For the later period, consult F.G. Emmison, *How to read local archives, 1550–1700* (1967); G.E. Dawson, L. Kennedy-Skipton, *Elizabethan Handwriting, 1550–1650* (1968); A. Rycraft, *Sixteenth and Seventeenth Century Handwriting* (York, 2 vols, 2nd ed, 1969); and W.S. Buck, *Examples of Handwriting, 1550–1650* (1973). Common contractions and abbreviations are explained in C.T. Martin, *The Record Interpreter* (2nd ed, 1910, repr. Horsham, 1976), which also has a good list of the Latin equivalents of English christian names: L. Maidbury, 'English Christian names in Latin', *LH*, **1**, 312–4, and L. Maidbury, 'English surnames in Latin', *LH*, **1**, 368–71, can also be consulted.

Chronology

C.R. Cheney, *Handbook of dates for students of English history* (3rd ed, 1970) is the standard guide to the old and new style calendars and the use of regnal years and Christian festivals for dating purposes; F.M. Powicke, E.B. Fryde, *Handbook of British Chronology* (2nd ed, 1961), provides additional information, including the dates of bishops of the church in England.

Language

E.A. Gooder, *Latin for Local History* (2nd ed, 1978) and R.F. Glover, R.W. Harris, *Latin for Historians* (Oxford, 3rd ed, 1963) are good introductions to medieval Latin; the standard dictionary is R.E. Latham, *Revised Medieval Latin Word List* (Oxford, 1965), but this excludes words which remained unchanged in meaning and spelling from classical times: for these, consult any standard Latin dictionary, e.g. Cassell's or Smith's, or in case of difficulty, C.T. Lewis, C. Short, *A Latin Dictionary*

(Oxford, 1879, repr. 1966). There are no good guides to Old or Middle English or to Norman-French: for these, specialist help should be sought through A.L.H.A. Local English dialect terms can, however, be checked in J. Wright, *The English Dialect Dictionary* (6 vols, 1898–1905), supplemented by the glossary by C.J. Spittal included in J.S. Moore (ed), *The Goods and Chattels of Our Forefathers* (Chichester, 1976).

General Historical Background

The elementary *Penguin* and the more advanced *Oxford Histories of England* provide an adequate general background to English history; for economic and social history, the following are particularly recommended: M.M. Postan, *Medieval Economy and Society* (1972); S. Pollard, D.W. Crossley, *The Wealth of Britain* (1968); L.A. Clarkson, *The Preindustrial Economy of England* (1971); P. Mathias, *The First Industrial Nation* (1969); H.J. Perkin, *The Origins of Modern English Society, 1780–1880* (1969); J. Ryder, H. Silver, *Modern English Society: History and Structure, 1850–1970* (2nd ed, 1977); A.H. Halsey (ed), *Trends in British Society since 1900* (1972). For rural local history, H.P.R. Finberg (ed), *Agrarian History of England and Wales* (Cambridge, 1967–, in progress) is essential reading. W.G. Hoskins, *The Midland Peasant* (1957) is the classic example of a village history by the *doyen* of English local history.

History of Avon

H.P.R. Finberg, *Gloucestershire: the history of the landscape* (2nd ed, 1975); H.P.R. Finberg (ed), *Gloucestershire Studies* (Leicester, 1957); A.H. Smith (ed), *The Place-Names of Gloucestershire, 4* (*EPNS, 41*), introduction; F. Walker, *The Bristol Region* (1972), chapters 7–10; C, A.M. Hadfield, *The Cotswolds: a new study* (Newton Abbot, 1973); R. Atthill, *Old Mendip* (Dawlish, 1964); B.S. Smith, E. Ralph, *History of Bristol and Gloucestershire* (Beaconsfield, 1972); R.H. Hilton, *A Medieval Society* (1966); R.H. Hilton, *The English Peasantry in the later Middle Ages* (Oxford, 1975); J.H. Bettey, *Rural Life in Wessex, 1500–1800* (Bradford-on-Avon, 1977); C.M. MacInnes, *Bristol: a Gateway of Empire* (Bristol, 1939, repr. Newton Abbot, 1968); C.M. MacInnes, W.F. Whittard (ed), *Bristol and its adjoining counties* (1955, repr. Wakefield, 1973), part 2; B. Little, *The City and County of Bristol* (1954); R.A. Buchanan, N. Cossons, *Industrial Archaeology of the Bristol Region* (Newton Abbot, 1969), J.S. Moore (ed), *The Goods and Chattels of Our Forefathers* (Chichester, 1976), introduction; *Victoria County History of Gloucestershire, 2* (1907); *Victoria County History of Somerset, 1, 2* (1906, 1911). The quality of the above is variable: some are only partly historical, others are rather poor but not yet replaced by anything better. Much valuable work exists in the form of unprinted university theses and dissertations: for these see R. Bilboul, F.R. Kent (ed), *Retrospective Index to theses of Great Britain and Ireland, 1716–1950, 1* (*Social Sciences and Humanities*) (Santa Barbara (U.S.A.), 1975); ASLIB, *Index to theses accepted for higher degrees in the universities of Great Britain and Ireland* [from 1950] (1953 to date); and the *BIHR Theses Supplement* (1933 to date).

The bibliographies to chapters 2–12 are arranged in three sections: 'General' (introductory works at national level); 'Sources and Methods' (books and articles dealing specifically with the evidence and how to use it, though many of the works in the first section also consider these topics); and 'Local Sources and Studies' (books and articles dealing mainly with the Avon area or the earlier units out of which it was formed, though where no good local works have yet appeared examples have been drawn from further afield.

Chapter 2

The Rural and Urban Landscape

See also bibliographies to chapters 4 (agriculture), 5 (trade, transport and communications), 6 (industry) and 7 (housing).

General

W.G. Hoskins, *The Making of the English Landscape* (1955, repr, 1970); W.G. Hoskins, *Fieldwork in Local History* (1967); O.G.S. Crawford, *Archaeology in the Field* (1953); P.J. Fowler, *Approaches to Archaeology* (1977); M. Aston, T. Rowley, *Landscape Archaeology* (Newton Abbot, 1975); M. Aston, J. Bond, *The Landscape of Towns* (1976); D.P. Dymond, *Archaeology for the Historian* (1967); D.P. Dymond, *Archaeology and History* (1974); J. Finberg, *Exploring Villages* (1958); M.W. Beresford, *History on the Ground* (1957); H.C. Darby (ed), *Historical Geography of England before 1800* (Cambridge, 5th ed., 1963); H.C. Darby (ed), *New Historical Geography of England* (Cambridge, 1973); C.C. Taylor, *Fields in the English Landscape* (1975); T. Rowley (ed), *Anglo-Saxon Settlement and the Landscape* (Oxford, 1974); H.C. Bowen, *Ancient Fields* (1962); J. Thirsk, 'The Beginning of the Village', *LH,* **6,** 166–9; B. Roberts, 'The Study of Village Plans', *LH* **9,** 233–41; M.W. Beresford, J.K. St. Joseph, *Medieval England: an aerial survey* (Cambridge, 1958); M.W. Beresford, *The Lost Villages of England* (1954); K.J. Allison, *Deserted Villages* (1970); M.W. Beresford, J.G. Hurst (ed), *Deserted Medieval Villages: Studies* (1971), chapters 1–6; M.W. Beresford, *New Towns in the Middle Ages* (1967); N. Fairbrother, *New Lives, New Landscapes* (1970); A.R.H. Baker, J.B. Harley, *Man made the Land* (Newton Abbot, 1973); R.H. Best, J.T. Coppock, *The Changing Use of Land in Britain* (1962); J. Haddon, *Local Geography in Rural Areas* (1964); W.G. Hoskins, L.D. Stamp, *The Common Lands of England and Wales* (1963); J.A. Steers, *The Coastline of England and Wales* (Cambridge, 2nd ed., 1964); W. Savage, *The Making of Our Towns* (1952); A. Everitt, 'Urban Growth, 1570–1770', *LH,* **8,** 118–25; H.J. Dyos (ed), *The Study of Urban History* (1968); E. Johns *British Townscapes* (1965); T.D. Atkinson, *Local Style in English Architecture*

(1947); A. Clifton-Taylor, *The Pattern of English Building* (1972); J. Haddon, *Local Geography in Towns* (2nd ed., 1975); J. Haddon, *Discovering Towns* (1970); E. Shirley, *English Deer Parks* (1867); J.C. Cox, *Royal Forests of England* (1905); J. Reynolds, *Windmills and Watermills* (1970); R.J. Brown, *Windmills of England* (1976).

Sources and Methods

J. Haddon, *Fieldwork in Geography* (1974); Ordnance Survey, *Field Archaeology: some notes for beginners* (4th ed., 1963); A. Rogers, T. Rowley, *Landscapes and Documents* (1974); J.K. St. Joseph, *The Uses of Air Photography* (2nd ed, 1977); D.R. Wilson (ed), *Aerial reconnaissance for archaeology* (1975); C.C. Taylor, *Fieldwork in Medieval Archaeology* (1974); Council for British Archaeology, *British archaeology: a booklist* (1960); J.M. Coles, *Field Archaeology in Britain* (1972); M.D. Hooper, *Hedges and Local History* (1971); G.E. Fussell, *The Exploration of England: a select bibliography of travel and topography 1570–1815* (1935); E. Moir, *The Discovery of Britain* (1964); J.E. Vaughan, 'Early guide books as sources of local history', *LH*, **5**, 183–8; L.B. Mayne, 'Tourists of the past', *LH*, **3**, 20–5; L.B. Mayne, 'Select bibliography of tours in... England!, *LH*, **3**, 26–31, 114; G.W.A. Nunn, *British Sources of Photographs and Pictures* (1952); M.W. Barley, *A Guide to British Topographical Collections* (1974); J. Wall, *Directory of British Photographic Collections* (1978); M.V.J. Seaborne, 'Pictorial Records', *LH*, **5**, 151–4; E.J. Priestly, 'Illustrating Local History', *LH*, **7**, 59–62; A. Sutcliffe, 'Nineteenth Century Cities: a study of visual evidence', *LH*, **9**, 400–6; J. Batley, 'Pictures as a source of local history', *LH*, **10**, 355–60; N. McCord, 'Photographs as historical evidence', *LH*, **13**, 23–36; J.B. Harley, *Maps for the Local Historian* (1972); J.B. Harley, C.W. Phillips, *The Historian's Guide to Ordnance Survey Maps* (1964); 'Historicus', 'Topography and Maps', *LH*, **3**, 115–20; R. Douch, 'Geography and the Local Historian', *LH*, **3**, 286–91; A.R.H. Baker, 'Local History in Early Estate Maps', *LH*, **5**, 66–71; J.H. Andrews, J.B. Harley, P. Laxton, *The Interpretation of Early Maps* (Folkestone, 1978); M. Gelling, *Signposts to the Past: Place-Names and the History of England* (1978); J. Field, *English Field-Names: a Dictionary* (Newton Abbot, 1972); E. Ekwall, *English River-Names* (1928); P.H. Reaney, *The Origin of English Place Names* (1960); E. Ekwall, *Concise Oxford Dictionary of English Place-Names* (Oxford, 4th ed., 1960); A.H. Smith (ed), *English Place-Name Elements* (*EPNS*, **25, 26**); P.H. Sawyer, *Anglo-Saxon Charters: an annotated list* (1968); F.M. Stenton, 'The Historical Bearing of place-name studies', *TRHS*, 4th ser, **22**, 1–22; **23**, 1–24; **24**, 1–24; **25**, 1–13; M. Gelling, 'Pre-Conquest Local History: evidence from Anglo-Saxon charters', *LH*, **1**, 241–5; M. Gelling (ed), *The Place-Names of Berkshire*, **7** (*EPNS*, **51**), part 2, introduction; M. Gelling, 'Recent work on English place-names', *LH*, **11**, 3–7; M. Gelling, 'Topographical settlement-names', *LH*, **12**, 273–7; G.D. Johnston, 'Boundaries', *LH*, **4**, 67–72; J.D. Jackson, 'Fossil field boundaries', *LH*, **4**, 73–7; J. Porter, 'Encroachment as an element in the rural landscape', *LH*, **11**, 141–7; R.H. Reid, 'Tracing Roman roads', *LH*, **4**, 282–90; D. Hooke, 'The reconstruction of ancient trackways', *LH*, **12**,

212-20; P.H. Sawyer (ed), *Medieval Settlement: continuity and change* (1976); P.J. Fowler (ed), *Recent Work in Rural Archaeology* (Bradford-on-Avon, 1975); D.M. Wilson (ed), *Archaeology of Anglo-Saxon England* (1976), chapters 1-3.

Local Sources and Studies

D. Hinton, *Alfred's Kingdom: Wessex and the South, 800-1500* (1977); H.P.R. Finberg, *Gloucestershire: the history of the landscape* (2nd ed., 1975); A.H. Smith (ed), *The Place-Names of Gloucestershire*, **3, 4** (*EPNS*, **40, 41**); F. Walker, *The Bristol Region* (1972), chapters 2-4; P.J. Fowler (ed), *Archaeology and the Landscape* (1972), chapters 7-8; D. Bonney, 'Pagan Saxon Burials and boundaries in Wiltshire', *Wiltshire Archaeological Magazine*, **61**, 25-30; H.P.R. Finberg, *Early Charters of the West Midlands* (Leicester, 1961), chapter 1 (Gloucestershire); H.P.R. Finberg, *Early Charters of Wessex* (Leicester, 1964), chapter 3 (Somerset); G.B. Grundy, *Saxon Charters and Field Names of Gloucestershire* (Gloucester, 2 vols, 1935-6); G.B. Grundy, *Saxon Charters and Field Names of Somerset* (Taunton, 1935); J.S. Moore (ed), *Domesday Book: Gloucestershire* (Chichester, forthcoming); C. Thorn (ed), *Domesday Book: Somerset* (Chichester, forthcoming); C.S. Taylor, *An Analysis of the Domesday Survey of Gloucestershire* (Bristol, 1889); R.W. Eyton, *Domesday Studies: Somerset* (2 vols, 1880); T.W. Whale, *Analysis of Somerset Domesday* (Bath, 1902); H.C. Darby, I.B. Terrett, *Domesday Geography of Midland England* (Cambridge, 2nd ed., 1971), chapter 1 (Gloucestershire); H.C. Darby, R.W. Finn, *Domesday Geography of S.W. England* (Cambridge, 1967), chapter 3 (Somerset); M. Williams, *The Draining of the Somerset Levels* (Cambridge, 1970); D. Sylvester, *The Rural Landscape of the Welsh Borderland* (1969); J. Finberg, *The Cotswolds* (1977); H.P.R. Finberg (ed) *Gloucestershire Studies* (Leicester, 1957); R.H. Leech, *Small Medieval Towns in Avon* (Bristol, 1975); W. Savage, 'Somerset Towns', *SA*, **99/100**, 49-74; R. Atkyns, *The ancient and present state of Gloucestershire* (1712); J. Collinson, *The history and antiquities of the county of Somerset* (Bath, 3 vols, 1791); R. Warner, *A walk through some of the western counties of England* (Bath, 1800); Bristol and Gloucestershire Archaeological Society, *A Gloucestershire and Bristol Atlas* (Bristol, 1961); C.W. Chalklin, *The Provincial Towns of Georgian England* (1974); M.D. Label (ed), *Atlas of Historic Towns*, **2** (1976) [includes Bristol]. W.E. Tate, *Somerset Enclosure Acts and Awards* (Taunton, 1948); W.E. Tate, 'Gloucestershire Enclosure Acts and Awards', *BG*, **64**, 1-70; P. Abercrombie, B.F. Brueton, *Bristol and Bath Regional Planning Scheme* (Liverpool, 1930); G.E. Payne, *Gloucestershire: a physical, social and economic survey and plan* (Gloucester, 1945); Department of the Environment, *Severnside: a feasibility study* (1971). T. Stuart-Menteath, S.W.E. Vince (ed), *The Land of Britain: report of the land-utilization survey of Britain*, **67** (Gloucestershire), **86** (Somerset); A.F. Mutton (ed), *Second Land Utilization Survey of Great Britain, Map of Bristol East* (1975); D.C. Findley, *Soils of the Mendip District* (Harpenden, 1965); D.C. Findley, *Soils of the Southern Cotswolds* (Harpenden, 1976); Soil Survey of Great Britain, *Map of Soils of the County of Avon* (Harpenden, 1978). The following works by R. Winstone are a unique photographic record of a modern town whose medieval centre was largely destroyed in World War II: *Bristol's History* (Bristol, 2 vols, 1969, 1975); *Bristol in the 1850's* (Bristol, 2nd ed., 1978); *Bristol's Earliest Photographs* (Bristol, 2nd ed., 1974); *Bristol as it was, 1860–79* (Bristol, 3 vols, 1968, 1971, 1972); *Bristol in the 1880's, 1890's* (Bristol, 2 vols, 1973, 1978); *Bristol as it was, 1900–39* (Bristol, 3 vols, 1972, 1976, 1978); *Bristol in the 1920's* (Bristol, 2nd ed., 1977); *Bristol Blitzed* (Bristol, 1976); *Bristol in the 1940's* (Bristol, 2nd ed., 1970); *Bristol as it was, 1950–9* (Bristol, 3 vols, 1969, 1970, 1972); *Bristol old and new* (1974); *Bristol today* (Bristol, 4th ed., 1971); *Bristol's pictorial past* (Bristol, 1978); *History of Bristol's Suburbs* (Bristol, 1977); *Bristol's Suburbs in the 1920's and 1930's* (Bristol, 1977). D. Bromwich, R.W. Dunning, *Victorian and Edwardian Somerset from old photographs* (1977) is also valuable.

Chapter 3
Population and the Structure of Local Society

General

J.C. Russell, *British Medieval Population* (Albuquerque (U.S.A.), 1948); J.D. Chambers, *Population, Economy and Society in Preindustrial England* (Oxford, 1972); M.W. Flinn, *British Population Growth, 1700–1850* (1970); H.J. Habakkuk, *Population Growth and Economic Development since 1750* (Leicester, 1974); N.L. Tranter, *Population since the Industrial Revolution* (1974); E.A. Wrigley, *Population and History* (1969); M. Drake (ed), *Population in Industrialization* (1969); D.V. Glass, R. Revelle, *Population and Social Change* (1972); T. McKeown, *The Modern Rise of Population* (1976); P. Laslett, *The World we have lost* (2nd ed., 1971); P. Laslett, R. Wall (ed), *Household and Family in Past Time* (Cambridge, 1972); J. Goody, J. Thirsk, E.P. Thompson (ed), *Family and Inheritance: Rural Society in Western Europe, 1200–1800* (Cambridge, 1978); A.S. Wohl (ed), *The Victorian Family* (1978); E.A. Wrigley (ed), *Nineteenth Century Society* (Cambridge, 1972); A. Redford, *Labour Migration in England, 1800–1850* (Manchester, 3rd ed., 1976); R. Mitchison, *British Population Change since 1860* (1977); D.C. Marsh, *The Changing Social Structure of England and Wales, 1871–1961* (2nd ed., repr. 1971).

Sources and Methods

T.H. Hollingsworth, *Historical Demography* (1969); E.A. Wrigley (ed), *Introduction to English Historical Demography* (1966); M.W. Beresford, *Lay Subsidies (1290–1334) and Poll Taxes (1377, 1379 and 1381)* (Chichester, 1964); J.Z. Titow, *English Rural Society, 1200–1350* (1969); J. Thirsk, *Sources of Information on Population, 1500–1760* (Chichester, 1965); M. Drake, *Historical Demography: problems and projects* (Milton Keynes, 1974); M. Drake, P. Hammerton, *Exercises in Historical Sociology* (Milton Keynes, 1974); E.A. Wrigley, 'Parish Registers and Population History', *LH*, **6**, 146–150, 198–203; J.A. Johnston, 'Family Reconstitution and the local historian', *LH*, **9**, 9–15; R.W. Ambler, 'Non-Parochial Registers and the local historian', *LH*, **10**, 59–64; M.W. Beresford, *The unprinted census returns of 1841, 1851 and 1861 for England and Wales* (Chichester, 1966); L. Bradley, *A Glossary for Local Population Studies* (Torquay, 1971). No attempt has been made to list the many useful articles in *Local Population Studies*, the main journal for the study of sources and methods in local population history.

Local Sources and Studies

J. MacLean, 'Chantry Certificates, Gloucestershire', *BG*, **8**, 229–308;
E. Green (ed), *Somerset Chantry Certificates, SRS*, **2;** J. Gairdner (ed),
'Bishop Hooper's Visitation of Gloucester Diocese, 1551', *Eng.HR*, **19**,
98-121; D. Walker, W.J. Shiels; J. Kent (ed), *An Ecclesiastical Miscellany*
(*BGRS*, **11**), pt. 2; J. Smith, *Men and Armour for Gloucestershire in 1608*
(1902); R.H., A.J. Tawney, 'An Occupational Census of the Seventeenth
Century', *EcHR*, **5**, 25–64; C.R. Elrington, 'The Survey of Church
Livings in Gloucestershire', *BG*, **83**, 85–98; P. Ripley, 'The Parish
Register Evidence for the Population of Gloucester', *BG*, **91,** 199–206;
J.S. Moore (ed), *The Goods and Chattels of Our Forefathers* (Chichester,
1976), introduction; E. Ralph, M.E. Williams (ed), *The Inhabitants of
Bristol in 1696, BRS*, **25**; R. Atkyns, *The Ancient and Present State of
Gloucestershire* (1712); S. Rudder, *A New History of Gloucestershire*
(Cirencester, 1779, repr. Dursley, 1977); A. Percival, 'Gloucestershire
Village Populations', *LPS*, **8**, 39–47; E. Grebenik, H.A. Shannon, *The
Population of Bristol* (Cambridge 1943). Nineteenth century population
figures are tabulated in *VCH Gloucestershire*, **2** and *VCH Somerset*, **2**. For
the role of the major local families, see bibliography to chapter 8.

Chapter 4
Agriculture

General

E.E. Kerridge, *The Farmers of Old England* (1973); N. Harvey, *History of Farm Buildings in England and Wales* (Newton Abbot, 1970); S. Applebaum, 'Agriculture in Roman Britain', *AgHR*, **6**, 66–86; S. Applebaum, 'The Pattern of Settlement in Roman Britain', *AgHR*, **11**, 1–14; D.M. Wilson, 'Anglo-Saxon Rural Economy: a survey of the archaeological evidence', *AgHR*, **10**, 65–79; R.V. Lennard, *Rural England, 1086–1135* (Oxford, 1959); H.L. Gray, *English Field Systems* (Cambridge (U.S.A.), 1915, repr. 1959); C.S. Orwin, *The Open Fields* (Oxford, 3rd ed., 1967); W.O. Ault, *Open Field Farming in Medieval England* (1972); J.Z. Titow, *English Rural Society, 1200–1350* (1969); R.C. Russell, *The Logic of Open Field Systems* (1974); J. Thirsk, 'The Common Fields', *PP*, **29**, 3–25; J. Thirsk, 'The origins of the common fields', *PP*, **33**, 142–7; H.C. Darby, *Historical Geography of England before 1800* (Cambridge, 1936); H.C. Darby, *A New Historical Geography of England* (Cambridge, 1973); F.G. Emmison, *Types of Open Field Parishes in the Midlands* (1937); N.J. Hone, *The Manor and Manorial Records* (3rd ed., 1925); H.S. Bennett, *Life on the English Manor* (Cambridge, 2nd ed., 1960); N. Denholm-Young, *Seignorial Administration in England* (Oxford, 2nd ed., 1963); A.E. Levett, *Studies in Manorial History* (repr, 1963); R.J. Faith, 'Peasant Families and Inheritance Customs in Medieval England', *AgHR*, **14**, 77–95; E.E. Kerridge, *Agrarian Problems in the Sixteenth Century and after* (1969); E.E. Kerridge, *The Agricultural Revolution* (1967); W.G. Hoskins, 'Harvest Fluctuations and English Economic History, 1480–1759', *AgHR*, **12**, 28–46; **16**, 15–31; C.J. Harrison, 'Grain Price Analysis and Harvest Qualities, 1465–1634', *AgHR*, **19**, 135–55; R.W. Sturgess, 'The Agricultural Revolution on the English Clays', *AgHR*, **14**, 104–21; **15**, 82–7; W.E. Tate, *The English Village Community and the Enclosure Movements* (1967); G.E. Mingay, *English Landed Society in the Eighteenth Century* (1963); J.D. Chambers, G.E. Mingay, *The Agricultural Revolution, 1750–1880* (1966); G.E. Mingay, *Enclosure and the Small Farmer in the Age of the Industrial Revolution* (1968); G.E. Mingay (ed), *The Agricultural Revolution* (1977); G.E. Mingay (ed), *Arthur Young and his times* (1976); E.L. Jones, *Agriculture and the Industrial Revolution* (Oxford 1974); F.M.L. Thompson, *English Landed Society in the Nineteenth Century* (2nd ed., 1971); E.L. Jones, *The Development of English Agriculture, 1815–73* (1968); E.J. Hobsbawm, G. Rudé, *Captain Swing* (1973); J.P. Dunbabin, *Rural Discontent in nineteenth century Britain* (1974); P. Horn, *Labouring*

Life in the Victorian Countryside (Dublin, 1977); G.E. Mingay, *Rural Life in Victorian England* (1977); R.H. Best, J.T. Coppock, *The Changing Use of Land in Britain* (1962); P.J. Perry, 'Where was the "Great Agricultural Depression"...?', *AgHR*, **20**, 30–45; I. Niall, *To speed the plough* (1977); P.J. Perry, *British Farming in the Great Depression, 1870–1914* (Newton Abbot, 1975); H.P.R. Finberg (ed), *Agrarian History of England and Wales* (Cambridge, 1967–, in progress).

Sources and Methods

R.H. Hilton, 'Content and Sources of English Agrarian History before 1500', *AgHR*, **3**, 3–19; J. Thirsk, 'Content and Sources of English agrarian history after 1500', *AgHR*, **3**, 66–79; J.L. Fisher, *Medieval Farming Glossary* (1968); T.B. Franklin, 'Domesday', *LH*, **1**, 261–4, 297–300, 344–7; R.E. Latham, 'Feet of Fines', *LH*, **1**, 5–9; H.B. Rodgers, 'Land-use in Tudor Lancashire: the evidence of the Final Concords', *TIBG*, **21**, 79–97; R.E. Latham, 'Inquisitions Post Mortem', *LH*, **1**, 77–81; M. McGuiness, 'Inquisitions Post Mortem', *LH*, **6**, 235–42; E. Kerridge, 'The manorial survey as a historical source', *LH* **7**, 2–7; L. Sherwood, 'The Court Baron', *LH*, **2**, 374–6; W.B. Johnson, 'Notes before reading court rolls', *LH*, **4**, 98–100; W.F. Mumford, 'Studying medieval court rolls', *LH*, **10**, 83–7; G.R.C. Davis, *Medieval Cartularies of Great Britain* (1958); H.C. Prince, 'Park-land in the English Landscape', *LH*, **3**, 332–49; **4**, 23–5; A.R.H. Baker, 'Local History in Early Estate Maps', *LH*, **5**, 66–71; A.A. Dibben, *Title Deeds, 13th–19th Centuries* (1968); B.C. Jones, 'Inventories of Goods and Chattels', *LH*, **2**, 76–9; O. Ashmore, 'Inventories as a source of Local History: Farmers' *LH*, **4**, 186–95; W.D. Rubenstein, D.H. Duman, 'Probate Valuations: a tool for the historian', *LH*, **11**, 68–71; S. Porter, 'The Making of Probate Inventories', *LH*, **12**, 36–7; P.J. Perry, J.R. Walton, 'A Source for agricultural history: newspaper advertisements', *LH*, **9**, 334–7; **10**, 271–6; R. Stanley-Morgan, 'Records of village mills', *LH*, **2**, 172–5; R. Wailes, *Windmills in England* (1948, repr. 1975); R.J. Brown, *Windmills of England* (1976); E.M. Gardner, 'On Mill Hunting', *LH*, **2**, 326–9; E.J. Evans, 'Tithing Customs and Disputes: the evidence of Glebe Terriers', *AgHR*, **18**, 17–35; P. Roebuck, 'Leases and Tenancy Agreements', *LH*, **10**, 7–12; M. Turner, 'Recent Progress in the study of parliamentary enclosure', *LH*, **12**, 18–25; S.W. Martin, 'The Farm Buildings of the Agricultural Revolution', *LH*, **12**, 407–15; D.B. Grigg, 'The Land Tax Returns', *AgHR*, **11**, 82–94; J.M. Martin, 'Landownership and the Land Tax Returns', *AgHR*, **14**, 96–103; D.B. Grigg, 'A Source on Landownership: the Land Tax Returns', *LH*, **6**, 152–6; D.B. Grigg, 'The Changing Agricultural Geography of England: a commentary on the sources available for the reconstruction of the agricultural geography of England, 1770–1850', *TIBG*, **41**, 73–96; A.F.J. Brown, 'Working-class movements in the countryside', *LH*, **3**, 49–54; H.C. Prince, 'The Tithe Surveys of the Mid-Nineteenth Century', *AgHR*, **7**, 14–26; R.J.P. Kain, 'Tithe Surveys and the study of land occupation', *LH*, **12**, 88–92; E.A. Cox, B.R. Dittmer, 'The Tithe Files of the Mid-Nineteenth Century', *AgHR*, **13**, 1–16; J.T. Coppock, 'The Agricultural Returns as a source for local history', *LH*, **4**, 49–55; J.D. Marshall, 'The People who left the land', *LH*, **3**, 185–9; J.T. Coppock, 'Changes in farm and field boundaries in the 19th century', *LH*, **3**, 292–8; R.J. Colyer, 'The use of estate home farm accounts as sources for nineteenth century agricultural history', *LH*, **11**, 406–13; P. Horn, 'Landowners and the agricultural trade union movement of the 1870's', *LH*, **11**, 134–40.

Local Sources and Studies

See Bibliographies to Chapter 2 for Anglo-Saxon charters and Domesday, Chapter 7 for rural housing and Chapter 12 for oral evidence.
A.S. Ellis, 'On the landholders of Gloucestershire named in Domesday Book', *BG*, **4**, 86–198; M. Hollings (ed), *The Red Book of Worcester* (*WHS*, **42**, pt. 4); B.A. Lees (ed), *Records of the Templars in England in the Twelfth Century* (Oxford, 1935); J.E. Jackson (ed), *An Inquisition of the Manors of Glastonbury for 1189* (*Roxburghe Club*, **108**); M.M. Postan, 'Glastonbury Estates in the Twelfth Century', *EcHR*, 2nd Ser, **5**, 358–67; **9**, 106–18; **28** 524–7; R.V. Lennard, 'The Demesnes of Glastonbury Abbey in the Twelfth Century', *EcHR*, 2nd Ser, **8**, 355–63; **28**, 517–523; E. Hobhouse (ed), *Rentalia et Custumaria* (*SRS*, **5**); S.J. Madge, E.A. Fry, E. Stokes (ed), *Abstracts of Inquisitions Postem for Gloucestershire* (*IL*, **30**, **40**, **47**); E.A. Fry, 'The Inquisitiones Post Mortem for Somerset, 1216–1649', *SA*, **44**, 79–148; **47**, 1–122; E. Green (ed), *Somerset Feet of Fines, 1196–1485* (*SRS*, **6**, **12**, **17**, **22**); J. MacLean, 'Gloucestershire Feet of Fines, 1199–1272, 1588–1612', *BG*, **16**, 167–95; **17**, 126–259; W.H. Hart (ed), *Historia et Cartularium Monasterii Sancti Petri Gloucestriae* (*RS*, **33**); W. Hunt (ed), *Two Chartularies of the priory of St. Peter at Bath* (*SRS*, **7**); A. Watkin (ed), *The Great Chartulary of Glastonbury* (*SRS*, **59**, **63**, **64**); C.D. Ross (ed), *Cartulary of St. Mark's Hospital, Bristol* (*BRS*, **21**); B.R. Kemp, D.M. Shorrocks (ed), *Medieval Deeds of Bath and District* (*SRS*, **73**); R.H. Hilton, *A Medieval Society: the West Midlands at the end of the thirteenth century* (1966); R.H. Hilton, *The English Peasantry in the later Middle Ages* (Oxford, 1975); E.S. Lindley, 'A Kingswood Abbey Rental', *BG*, **70**, 145–51; C.E. Watson, 'The Minchinhampton Custumal', *BG*, **54**, 203–384; J. Maclean, 'The Manor of Tockington', *BG*, **12**, 123–69; E.S. Lindley, 'Kingswood Abbey: its lands and mills', *BG*, **73**, 115–91; **74**, 36–59; **75**, 73–104; G. Beachcroft, A. Sabin (ed), *Two Compotus Rolls of St. Augustine's Abbey, 1491–2, 1511–2* (*BRS*, **9**); A. Sabin (ed), *Some Manorial Accounts of St. Augustine's Abbey, Bristol* (*BRS*, **22**); J.S. Moore (ed), *The Goods and Chattels of Our Forefathers* (Chichester, 1976); J.A. Yelling, 'Common Land and Enclosure in E. Worcestershire, 1540–1870', *TIBG*, **45**, 157–68; J.A. Yelling, 'Probate Inventories and the geography of livestock farming: a study of E. Worcestershire, 1540–1750', *TIBG*, **51**, 111–26; J.A. Yelling, 'The Combination and Rotation of Crops in E. Worcestershire, 1540–1660', *AgHR*, **17**, 24–43; J.A. Yelling, 'Changes in Crop Production in E. Worcestershire, 1549–1867', *AgHR*, **21**, 18–34; S.W. Harbin (ed), *Somerset Enrolled Deeds* (*SRS*, **51**); L.J.U. Way, 'The 1625 Survey of the Smaller Manor of Clifton', *BG*, **36**, 220–50; J.

Latimer, 'Clifton in 1746', *BG*, **23**, 312-22; D. Defoe, *Tour through England and Wales* (3 vols, 1724-6, repr. 1974); W.E. Tate, 'Gloucestershire Enclosure Acts and Awards', *BG*, **64**, 1-70; W.E. Tate, *Somerset Enclosure Acts and Awards* (Frome, 1948); W. Marshall, *The Rural Economy of Gloucestershire* (Gloucester, 2 vols, 1789); W. Marshall, *The Rural Economy of the West of England* (2 vols, 1796, repr. Newton Abbot, 1970); A. Young (ed), *Annals of Agriculture* (46 vols, 1784-1815); W. Cobbett, *Rural Rides* (2 vols, 1830, repr. 1973); W.R. Powell, *Local History from Blue Books* (1962); W.E. Minchinton, 'Agriculture in Gloucestershire during the Napoleonic Wars', *BG*, **68**, 165-83; M. Williams, 'The 1801 Crop Returns for Somerset', *SA*, **113**, 69-85; J. Billingsley, *General View of the Agriculture of the County of Somerset* (1795, 2nd ed., Bath, 1798); G. Turner, *General Review of agriculture of the country of Gloucester* (1794); T. Rudge, *General view of the agriculture of the country of Gloucester* (1807); W. Marshall, *Review and Abstract of the county reports to the Board of Agriculture*, **2**, **5**, (York, 1818, repr. Newton Abbot, 1968); *Journal of the Royal Agricultural Society of England* (1839–, in progress); J. Caird, *English Agriculture in 1851* (2nd ed, 1852); T.D. Acland, W. Sturge, *The Farming of Somersetshire* (1851); G.P. Davis, *Social and Economic Change in a Somerset Village: Newton St. Loe* (Unpublished M.Sc. thesis, University of Bath, 1975); G.P. Davis, *The Langtons at Newton Park* (Bath, 1976); H. Rider Haggard, *Rural England* (2 vols, 1902); R. Jefferies, *Hodge and his Masters* (1880, repr. 2 vols, 1966).

Chapter 5
Trade, Transport and Communications

General

I.D. Margary, *Roman Roads in Britain* (3rd ed., 1973); S. Reynolds, *Introduction to the history of medieval English towns* (1977); I. Starsmore, *English Fairs* (1975); T.H. Lloyd, *The English Wool Trade in the Middle Ages* (Cambridge, 1977); P.J. Bowden, *The Wool Trade in Tudor and Stuart England* (1962); J.E.V. Crofts, *Packhorse, Wagon and Cart: Land Carriage and Communications under the Tudors and Stuarts* (1967); J. Thirsk, *Economic Policy and Projects: the development of a consumer society in early modern England* (Oxford, 1978); T.S. Willan, *The Inland Trade* (Manchester, 1977); S.M. Jack, *Trade and Industry in Tudor and Stuart England* (1977); W. Albert, *The Turnpike Road System in England, 1663–1840* (Cambridge, 1972); J. Copeland, *Roads and their traffic, 1750–1850* (Newton Abbot, 1968); E. Pawson, *Transport and economy: the turnpike roads of eighteenth century Britain* (1977); P.S. Bagwell, *The Transport Revolution from 1770* (1974); M.J.T. Lewis, *Early Wooden Railways* (1970); T.C. Barker, C.J. Savage, *An Economic History of Transport in Britain* (3rd ed., 1974); H.J. Dyos, D.H. Aldcroft (ed), *British Transport: an economic survey from the seventeenth century to the twentieth* (Leicester, 1969); D.H. Aldcroft, *British Transport since 1914* (Newton Abbot, 1975); W.H. Chaloner, B.M. Ratcliffe (ed), *Trade and Transport* (Manchester, 1978); C. Hadfield, *British Canals* (Newton Abbot, 5th ed., 1974); T.S. Willan, *River Navigation in England, 1600–1750* (Manchester, 2nd ed., 1964); K.J. Bonser, *The Drovers* (1970); H. Pollins, *Britain's Railways: an industrial history* (Newton Abbot, 1971); J. Simmons, *Railways in Britain* (2nd ed, 1968); J.R. Kellett, *The Impact of Railways on Victorian Cities* (1969); D. Davies, *A History of Shopping* (1966); A. Adburgham, *Shops and Shopping, 1800–1914* (1964); J.B. Jeffery, *Retail Trading in Britain, 1850–1950* (1954); P. Mathias, *The Retailing Revolution* (1967).

Sources and Methods

J.S. Moore, 'The History of English Roads', *Queen's Highway*, **5**, 18–9; **6**, 16–9; **8**, 26–9; **10**, 14–6; C. Hadfield, 'Sources for the History of British Canals', *JTH*, **2**, 80–9; B.F. Duckham, 'Inland Waterways: some sources for their history', *LH*, **6**, 8–10; R.C. Jarvis, 'Sources for the history of ports', *JTH*, **3**, 76–93; R.C. Jarvis, 'Sources for the history of ships and shipping', *JTH*, **3**, 212–34; M. Robbins, *Points and signals: a* *railway historian at work* (1967); J. Simmons, *Railway history in English local records* (Leicester, 1954).

Local Sources and Studies

G.B. Grundy, 'The Ancient Highways and Tracks of Wiltshire, Berkshire and Hampshire...', *Arch.J.*, **75**, 69–194; G.B. Grundy, 'The Ancient Highways of Worcestershire and the Middle Severn basin', *Arch.J.*, **91**, 66–96, 241–68; **92**, 98–141; G.B. Grundy, 'The Ancient Highways of Dorset, Somerset and the West Country', *Arch.J.*, **94**, 257–90; **95**, 174–223; W.F. Grimes (ed), *Aspects of Archaeology in Britain and Beyond* (1951), chapter 10; H.W. Timperley, E. Brill, *Ancient Trackways of Wessex* (1965); P.G. Hughes, *Wales and the Drovers* (1943); H.P.R. Finberg (ed), *Gloucestershire Studies* (Leicester, 1957), chapter 3; N.F. Hulbert, I.F.H. Jones, 'A survey of Somerset Fairs', *SA*, **82**, 83–157; **84**, 171–2; **91**, 71–81; D. Walker, *Bristol in the early Middle Ages* (Bristol, 1971); J.W. Sherborne, *The Port of Bristol in the Middle Ages* (Bristol, 1971); E.M. Carus-Wilson (ed), *The Overseas Trade of Bristol in the later Middle Ages* (*BRS*, **7**); E.M. Carus-Wilson, *The Merchant Adventurers of Bristol in the fifteenth century* (Bristol, 1962); E.M. Carus-Wilson, O. Coleman, *England's Export Trade, 1275–1547* (1963); D.B. Quinn, *Sebastian Cabot and Bristol Exploration* (Bristol, 1962); D.B. Quinn, *England and the discovery of America, 1481–1620* (1974); E.M. Carus-Wilson (ed), *Medieval Merchant Venturers* (2nd ed, 1967), chapter 1; W. Childs, *Anglo-Castilian Trade in the later Middle Ages* (Manchester, 1977); G.P. Harrison, *Bristol Cream* (1955); F.W. Potto-Hicks, 'Robert Sturmy of Bristol', *BG*, **60**, 169–79; P.V. McGrath, 'The Wills of Bristol Merchants in the Great Orphan Books', *BG*, **68**, 91–109; E.E. Rich (ed), *The Staple Court Books of Bristol* (*BRS*, **5**); J. Vanes (ed), *The Ledger of John Smyth, 1538–50* (*BRS*, **28**); J.W. Damer-Powell, 'Lists of Bristol Ships, 1571–2', *BG* **52**, 117–22; J. Vanes, *The Port of Bristol in the Sixteenth Century* (Bristol, 1977); T.S. Willan, 'River navigation and trade of the Severn Valley, 1600–1750', *EcHR*, **7**, 68–79; P.V. McGrath, *The Merchant Venturers of Bristol* (Bristol, 1975); P.V. McGrath (ed), *Records relating to the Society of Merchant Venturers in the seventeenth century* (*BRS*, **17**); P.V. McGrath (ed), *Merchants and Merchandise in seventeenth century Bristol* (*BRS*, **19**); P.V. McGrath, *John Whitson and the merchant community of Bristol* (Bristol, 1970); W.B. Stephens, 'Trade Trends at Bristol, 1600–1700', *BG*, **93**, 156–61; H.E. Nott, E. Ralph (ed), *The Deposition Books of Bristol, 1643–54* (*BRS*, **6,13**); J.P. Wilton, 'Gloucestershire tokens of the 17th, 18th and 19th Centuries', *BG*, **13**, 130–45; W. Bidgood, 'Somerset Trade Tokens', *SA*, **32**, 115–54; H. Symons, H. Gray, 'Somerset Trade Tokens, 17th Century', *SA*, **61**, 115–27; J.H. Hamer, 'Trading at St. White Down Fair, 1637–49', *SA*, **112**, 61–70; W.E. Minchinton (ed), *The Trade of Bristol in the eighteenth century* (*BRS*, **20**); W.E. Minchinton, *The Port of Bristol in the eighteenth century* (Bristol, 1962); W.E. Minchinton (ed), *Politics and the port of Bristol in the eighteenth century* (*BRS*, **23**); C.M. MacInnes, *Bristol and the Slave Trade* (Bristol, 1963); P. Marshall, *The anti-slave trade movement in Bristol* (Bristol, 1968);

P. Marshall, *Bristol and the abolition of slavery* (Bristol, 1976); W.E. Minchinton, 'Bristol—metropolis of the west in the eighteenth century', *TRHS*, 5th ser., **4**, 69–89; P.T. Marcy, 'Bristol's Roads and Communications on the eve of the industrial revolution', *BG*, **87**, 149–72; N. Cossons, S.A. Rees, 'Turnpike roads of the Bristol Region', *BIAS*, **1**, 6–16; **5**, 19–24; A.F. Williams, 'Bristol Port Plans and improvement schemes of the eighteenth century', *BG*, **81**, 138–88; R.A. Buchanan, 'The Construction of the Floating Harbour', *BG*, **88**, 184–204; C.F.W. Dening, *Old Inns of Bristol* (Bristol, 4th ed, 1949); J.F. Meehan, *A few of the famous inns of Bath and district* (Bath, 1913); N.D. Harding, W.D. Bowman (ed), *Bristol and America* (Bristol, 1929); J. Press, *The merchant seamen of Bristol, 1746–1789* (Bristol, 1976); J.W. Damer-Powell, *Bristol Privateers and ships of war* (Bristol, 1930); C. Hadfield, *The Canals of south-west England* (Newton Abbot, 1967); K.R. Clew, *The Somersetshire Coal Canal and Railways* (Newton Abbot, 1971); K.R. Clew, *The Kennet and Avon Canal* (Newton Abbot, 1968); K.R. Clew, *The Dorset and Somerset Canal* (Newton Abbot, 1971); A. Elton, 'The prehistory of railways', *SA*, **107**, 31–59; D.St.J. Thomas, *Regional History of the railways of Great Britain*, **1** (1960); J. Simmons (ed), *The Birth of the Great Western Railway* (Bath, 1971); E.T. MacDermott, *History of the Great Western Railway* (2 vols, 2nd ed, 1964); C.G. Maggs, *The Bristol and Gloucester and Avon and Gloucesterhire Railway* (Lingfield, 1969); R. Atthill, *The Somerset and Dorset Railway* (Newton Abbot, 1967); R. Winstone, *Bristol's Trams* (Bristol, 1975); P.W. Gentry, *The tramways of the West of England* (2nd ed., 1960); H. Bush, *Bristol Town Dues* (Bristol, 1828); C.H. Cave, *A History of Banking in Bristol from 1750 to 1899* (Bristol, 1899); B.W. Alford, 'The economic development of Bristol in the nineteenth century: an enigma?' *BGC*, 252–83; C. Wells, *A short history of the port of Bristol* (Bristol, 1909); R.A. Buchanan, *Nineteenth century engineers in the port of Bristol* (Bristol, 1971); R.A. Buchanan, 'Brunel in Bristol', *BGC*, 217–51; G.E. Farr, *The Steamship Great Western* (Bristol, 1963); G.E. Farr, *The Steamship Great Britain* (Bristol, 2nd ed., 1965); E. Corlett, *The Iron Ship* (Bradford on Avon, 1975); J.C.G. Hill, *Shipshape and Bristol Fashion* (Liverpool, 1951); W.G. Neale, *At the port of Bristol* (Bristol, 2 vols, 1968, 1970); G.E. Farr, *Shipbuilding in the port of Bristol* (1977); G.E. Farr (ed), *Records of Bristol ships, 1800–1838* (*BRS*, **15**); G.E. Farr, *Bristol shipbuilding in the nineteenth century* (Bristol, 1971); G.E. Farr, 'Bristol Channel pilotage, historical notes on its administration and craft', *MM*, **39**, 27–44; P. Stuckey, *The sailing pilots of the Bristol Channel* (Newton Abbott, 1977); R.C. Tombs, *The Bristol Royal Mail* (Bristol, 1899); H.L. Matthews, 'The sea fish and fisheries of the Bristol district' (*Proceedings of the Bristol National History Society*, **1933**, 442–62); C. Jordan, *Severn Enterprise* (1977); Bristol Omnibus Co., *The people's carriage, 1874–1974* (Bristol, 1974); J. Pudney, *Bristol fashion: some account of the earlier days of Bristol aviation* (1960); C.H. Barnes, *Bristol Aircraft since 1910* (1964).

Chapter 6
Industry

General

S. Kramer, *The English Craft Gilds* (New York (U.S.A.), 1927); J. Thirsk, 'Industries in the Countryside' (in F.J. Fisher (ed.), *Essays in the Economic and Social History of Tudor and Stuart England* (Cambridge, 1961).); D.C. Coleman, *Industry in Tudor and Stuart England* (1975); S.M. Jack, *Trade and Industry in Tudor and Stuart England* (1977); T.H. Lloyd, *The English Wool Trade in the Middle Ages* (Cambridge, 1977); S. Reynolds, *Introduction to the History of English Medieval Towns* (1977); P.J. Bowden, *The Wool Trade in Tudor and Stuart England* (1962); J. Thirsk, *Economic Policy and Projects: the development of a consumer society in early modern England* (Oxford, 1978); J.U. Nef, *The Rise of the British Coal Industry* (2 vols, 1932, repr. 1966); B. Lewis, *Coalmining in the eighteenth and nineteenth centuries* (1971); H. Hamilton, *The English Brass and Copper Industries to 1800* (1926, repr. 1967); R. Gentle, R. Feild, *English Domestic Brass, 1680–1810* (1975); J. Hatcher, T.C. Barker, *A History of British Pewter* (1975); E.J. Cocks, B. Walters, *A History of the Zinc Smelting Industry in Britain* (1968); C. Singer (ed) *A History of Technology* (Oxford, 5 vols, 1954–8); N.B. Harte, K. Ponting (ed), *Textile History and Economic History* (Manchester, 1973); T.S. Ashton, *The Industrial Revolution, 1760–1830* (Oxford, 2nd ed., 1968); J.D. Chambers, *The Workshop of the World, 1830–1850* (Oxford, 1961); R.M. Hartwell, *The Industrial Revolution in England* (1965); W.H.B. Court, *The Rise of the Midland Industries, 1600–1838* (Oxford, 1938); J.T. Ward, R.G. Wilson (ed), *Land and Industry: the landed estate and the industrial revolution* (Newton Abbot, 1971); A.A. Aspinall, *Early English Trade Unions* (1949); H.B. Pelling, *History of British Trade Unionism* (3rd ed, 1976); P.S. Bagwell, *Industrial Relations* (Dublin, 1975).

Sources and Methods

K. Hudson, *Industrial Archaeology: a new introduction* (3rd ed, 1976); K. Hudson, *Handbook for Industrial Archaeologists* (1967); M. Rix, *Industrial Archaeology* (1967); A. Raistrick, *Industrial Archaeology: an historical survey* (1972), R.A. Buchanan (ed), *Theory and Practice of Industrial Archaeology* (Bath, 1968); R.A. Buchanan, *Industrial Archaeology in Britain* (1972); J.P.M. Pannell, *Techniques of Industrial Archaeology* (Newton Abbot, 2nd ed, 1974); J.K. Major, *Fieldwork in Industrial Archaeology* (1975); T.C. Barker, *Business Records* (1960); L.M. Wulcko, 'Fire Insurance Policies as a source of Local History', *LH*, **9**, 3–8; H.A.L. Cockerell, E. Green, *The British Insurance Business, 1547–1970: an introduction and guide to* *historical records in the United Kingdom* (1976); Council for Small Industries in Rural Areas, *Select List of books and information sources on trades, crafts and small industries in rural areas* (1968); S. Pollard, 'Sources for Trade Union History', *LH*, **4**, 177–81; E.J. Hobsbawm, 'Records of the Trade Union Movement', *Archives*, **4**, 129–37; E. Frow, M. Katanka, *History of British Trade Unionism: a select bibliography* (1969); A.W. Gottschalk, T.G. Whittingham, N. Williams, *British Industrial Relations: an annotated bibliography* (Nottingham, 1969); Interdepartmental Committee on Social and Economic Research, *Labour Statistics (Guide to Official Sources, 1)* (2nd ed, 1950).

Local Sources and Studies

R.A. Buchanan, N. Cossons, *Industrial Archaeology of the Bristol Region* (Newton Abbot, 1969); R.A. Buchanan, N. Cossons, *Industrial History in Pictures—Bristol* (Newton Abbot, 1970); F. Walker, *The Bristol Region* (1972); *VCH Gloucestershire*, **2**; *VCH Somerset*, **2**; S.J. Jones, 'The Growth of Bristol', *TIBG*, **11**, 55–83; B.W.E. Alford, 'The Economic Development of Bristol in the nineteenth century: an enigma?', *BGC*, 252–83; R.A. Buchanan, *The Industrial Archaeology of Bath* (Bath, 1964); R.S. Neale, 'The Industries of the City of Bath in the first half of the 19th century', *SA*, **108**, 132–44; C.M. MacInnes, W.F. Whittard (ed), *Bristol and its adjoining counties* (Bristol, 1955); A.P. Woolrich, 'Notes on the Bibliography of Industrial Bristol', *BIAS*, **2**, 30–2; *Histories of famous firms: Bristol Survey* (2 vols, 1959–60); J. Anstie, *The Coalfields of Gloucestershire and Somerset* (1873, repr. Bath, 1969); H. Cossham, *The Bristol Coalfield* (Bath, 1876); C.G. Down, A.S. Warrington, *The History of the Somerset Coalfield* (Newton Abbot, n.d. [1971]); R.K. Bluhm, *Bibliography of the Somerset Coalfield* (1968); J.A. Bulley, ' "To Mendip for Coal": a study of the Somerset Coalfield before 1830', *SA*, **97**, 46–78; **98**, 17–54; W. Sanders, *Map of the Bristol coal fields and country adjacent* (Bristol, 19 sheets, 1862); K.H. Rogers, *The Newcomen Engine in the West of England* (Bradford on Avon, 1976); W.T. Saniger, *Leaves from a Barton Hill Notebook* (Bristol, 1954); G. Davis, 'Coalmining at Newton St. Loe', *BIAS*, **10**, 27–33; M.J.H. Southway, 'Kingswood Coal', *BIAS*, **4**, 28–31; **5**, 25–31; M.J.H. Southway, 'The Bedminster Connection', *BIAS*, **9**, 4–6; J. Day, *Bristol Brass—The history of the industry* (Newton Abbot, 1973); J.W. Gough, *The Mines of Mendip* (Newton Abbot, 2nd ed, 1967); J.W. Gough (ed), *Mendip Mining Laws* (*SRS*, **45**); C.J. Schmitz, 'An account of Mendip Calamine mining in the early 1870s', *SA*, **120**, 81–3; I. Blanchard, 'The Miner and the Agricultural Community in Later Medieval England', *AgHR*, **20**, 93–106; I. Blanchard 'Labour Productivity and Work Psychology in the English Mining Industry, 1400–1600', *EcHR*, 2nd ser, **31**, 1–24; H.B. Walters, 'The Gloucestershire Bell Foundries', *BG*, **34**, 111–9; **41**, 49–86; R. Jenkins, 'The copper works at Redbrook and at Bristol', *BG*, **63**, 145–67; F, G.B. Buckley, 'Clock and watchmakers of the 18th century in Gloucestershire and in Bristol', *BG*, **51**, 305–19; R. Atthill, *Old Mendip* (Newton Abbot, 1964); K. Hudson, *The Fashionable Stone* (Bath, 1971); W. Ison, *The Georgian Buildings of Bath* (1948, repr. Bath, 1969); W. Ison, *The*

Georgian Buildings of Bristol (1952, repr. Bath, 1978); C. Crick, *Victorian Buildings in Bristol* (Bristol, 1975); F.C. Jones, *Bristol's water-supply and its story* (Bristol, 1946); D.G. Tucker, 'The Beginnings of electricity supply in Bristol', *BIAS*, **5**, 11–18; F. Buckley, 'The early glasshouses of Bristol', *Transactions of the Society of Glass Technology*, **9**, 36–61; B.J. Greenhill, 'Nailsea Glass Works', *BIAS*, **4**, 26–7; A.C. Powell, 'Glassmaking in Bristol', *BG*, **47**, 211–58; Z. Josephs, 'The Jacobs of Bristol, glassmakers', *BG*, **95**, 98–101; H. Owen, *Two Centuries of Ceramic Art in Bristol* (Bristol, 1920); W.J. Pountney, *Old Bristol Potteries... between 1650 and 1850* (Bristol, 1920); R.H. Kinvig, 'The Historical Geography of the West Country Woollen Industry', *Geographical Teacher Reprints*, **10**; R. Perry, 'The Gloucestershire Woollen Industry, 1100–1690', *BG*, **66**, 49–137; K.G. Ponting, *History of the West of England Cloth Industry* (1957); J. de L. Mann, *The Cloth Industry in the West of England from 1640 to 1880* (Oxford, 1971); K.G. Ponting, *The Woollen Industry of South-West England* (Bath, 1971); J. Tann, *Gloucestershire Woollen Mills* (Newton Abbot, 1967); K.H. Rogers, *Wiltshire and Somerset Woollen Mills* (Edington, 1976); S.J. Jones, 'The Cotton Industry in Bristol', *TIBG*, **13**, 61–79; J.J. Simpson, 'The Wool Trade and Woolmen of Gloucestershire', *BG*, **53**, 65–98; J. Tann, 'Some Problems of Water Power: a study of mill siting in Gloucestershire', *BG*, **84**, 53–77; W.E. Minchinton, 'The beginnings of trade unionism in the Gloucestershire woollen industry', *BG*, **70**, 126–41; W.E. Minchinton, 'The petitions of the weavers and clothiers of Gloucestershire in 1756', *BG*, **73**, 216–27; J. Day, 'The last of the Dyewood Mills', *Industrial Archaeology*, **3**, 119–26; R. Stiles 'The Old Market Sugar Refinery, 1684–1908', *BIAS*, **2**, 10–17; I.V. Hall, 'Whitson Court Sugar House, Bristol, 1655–1824', *BG*, **53**, 65–98; I.V. Hall, 'John Knight, junior, Sugar Refiner' *BG*, **68**, 110–64; I.V. Hall, 'Temple Street Sugar House', *BG*, **76**, 118–40; I.V. Hall, 'The Garlicks', *BG*, **80**, 132–59; I.V. Hall, 'The Daubenys', *BG*, **84**, 113–40; **85**, 175–201; J.E. Pritchard, 'Tobacco Pipes of Bristol in the 17th century and their makers', *BG*, **45**, 165–92; B.W.E. Alford, *W.D. and H.O. Wills* (1973); I.C. Walker, *The Bristol Clay Tobacco-Pipe Industry* (Bristol, 1971); I.C. Walker, *Clay Tobacco Pipes, with particular reference to the Bristol Industry* (Ottawa (Canada), 1977); O. Ward, 'The Mills of the Bristol Frome', *BIAS*, **2**, 24–5; B. Attwood, 'The BIAS Paper Mills Survey', *BIAS*, **3**, 11–21; A.H. Shorter, 'Paper Mills in Gloucestershire', *BG*, **71**, 145–61; M. Watts, 'Windmills of Somerset', *BIAS*, **6**, 21–31; J. Bryant, 'Ropewalks and Ropemakers of Bristol', *BIAS*, **10**, 12–17; A.P. Woolrich, 'Swedish Travellers', *BIAS*, **4**, 28–31; M. Doughty, O. Ward, 'Shortwood Brickworks', *BIAS*, **8**, 11–13; H. Torrens, 'The Early Years of Stothert and Pitt', *BIAS*, **9**, 24–30; C.H. Barnes, 'Bristol and the Aircraft Industry', *BIAS*, **5**, 4–10; J. Pudney, *Bristol fashion: some account of the earlier days of Bristol aviation* (1960); E.J. Brill, *Cotswold Crafts* (1977); T. Nichols, H. Beynon, *Living with capitalism: class relations and the modern factory* [Avonmouth] (1977).

For works on port industries, shipbuildings, canals and railways, see bibliography to chapter 5.

Chapter 7
Housing and the Standard of Living

(a) Housing

General
M.W. Barley, *The English Farmhouse and Cottage* (1961); M.W. Barley, *The House and Home* (1963); S.O. Addy, *The Evolution of the English House* (2nd ed. 1933); P.S. Fry, *British Medieval Castles*, (Newton Abbot, 1975); O. Cook, *The English House through Seven Centuries* (1968); E. Mercer, *English Vernacular Houses* (1975); J. & J. Penoyre, *Houses in the Landscape: a regional study of vernacular building styles in England and Wales* (1978); A. Clifton-Taylor, *The Pattern of English Building* (2nd ed, 1972); A. Clifton-Taylor, R.W. Brunskill, *English Brickwork* (1977); D. Iredale, *This Old House* (Tring, 2nd ed, 1970); P. Eden, *Small Houses in England, 1520–1820* (1969); E. Mercer, 'The Houses of the Gentry', *PP*, **5**, 11–32; J. Summerson, *Architecture in Britain, 1530–1830* (5th ed, 1969); C.W. Chalklin, *The Provincial Towns of Georgian England* (1974); M. Girouard, *A Social History of the English Country House* (Yale (USA), 1977); M. Girouard, *The Victorian Country House* (Oxford, 1971); M.A. Simpson, T.H. Lloyd (ed), *Middle-Class Housing in Britain* [1750–1914] (Newton Abbot, 1977); M.I. Wilson, *The English country house and its furnishings* (1977); E.T. Joy, *English Furniture, 1800–1851* (1978); V. Parker, *The English House in the Nineteenth Century* (1970); M. Kaufmann, *Housing of the Working Classes and the Poor* (1907, Wakefield, repr. 1975); S.D. Chapman (ed), *The History of Working-Class Housing* (Newton Abbot, 1971); E. Gauldie, *Cruel Habitations: a history of working-class housing, 1780–1918* (1974); J.N. Tarn, *Working-Class Housing in Nineteenth Century Britain* (1971); J.N. Tarn, *Five per cent Philanthropy: an account of housing in urban areas between 1840 and 1914* (Cambridge, 1975); J. Burnett, *A Social History of Housing, 1815–1970* (Newton Abbot, 1978); D. Rubinstein, *Victorian Homes* (Newton Abbot, 1975); W. Harvey, *A History of Farm Buildings in England and Wales* (1970).

Sources and Methods
R. de Z. Hall, *A Bibliography of Vernacular Architecture* (Newton Abbot, 1972); T. West, *The Timber Frame House in England* (Newton Abbot, 1971); J.T. Smith, 'The Evolution of the English Peasant House to the late seventeenth century: the evidence of buildings', *JBAA*, 3rd ser, **33**,

122-47; J. Thompson, 'Investigating domestic buildings', *LH*, **7**, 126-32; R.W. Brunskill, *Illustrated Handbook of Vernacular Architecture* (1971); R.W. Brunskill, 'A Systematic Procedure for Recording English Vernacular Architecture', *TAMS*, NS, **13**, 43-126; C.F. Innocent, *The Development of English Building Construction* (Newton Abbot, 2nd ed, 1971); J. Sheppard, 'Vernacular Buildings in England and Wales', *TIBG*, **40**, 21-37; W.G. Hoskins, *Fieldwork in Local History* (1967), chapters 6-7; J.T. Smith, E.M. Yates, *On the dating of English houses from External Evidence* (Hampton-on-Thames, 1972); R.A. Cordingley, 'British Historical Roof-Types and their members: a classification', *TAMS*, NS, **9**, 73-130; M.W. Barley, 'Glossary of Names for rooms in houses of the sixteenth and seventeenth centuries' (in I.L. Foster, L. Alcock (ed), *Culture and Environment* (Cardiff, (1963), 480-1); Council for British Archaeology, *The Investigation of Smaller Domestic Buildings* (1955); W.A. Pantin, 'Monuments or Muniments: the interrelation of Material Remains and Documentary Sources', *MA*, **2**, 158-68; G.I. Meirion-Jones, 'The Use of Hearth Tax Returns and vernacular architecture in settlement studies', *TIBG*, **53**, 133-60; L.M. Wulcko, 'Fire Insurance Policies as a source for local history', *LH*, **9**, 3-8; H.A.L. Cockerell, E. Green, *The British Insurance Business, 1547-1970: an introduction and guide to historical records in the United Kingdom* (1976); J.H. Harvey, *Sources for the history of houses* (1974).

Articles in *Vernacular Architecture* have been excluded in the interests of economy: this journal is essential reading for everyone interested in the history of housing.

Local Sources and Studies

A.T. Broadbent, C.A. Minoprio, *The minor domestic architecture of Gloucestershire* (1931); W.G. Davie, E.G. Dawber, *Old cottages, farmhouses and other stone buildings in the Cotswold district* (1905); W.J. Robinson, *West Country Manors* (Bristol, 1930); E.A. Ruggles, *Small stone houses of the Cotswold district* (Cleveland (USA), 1931); A.D.K. Hayward, 'Thornbury Castle', *BG*, **95**, 51-8; J.S. Moore (ed), *The Goods and Chattels of Our Forefathers* (Chichester, 1976); R. Machin (ed), *Probate Inventories and Manorial Excepts of Chetnole, Leigh and Yetminster* (Bristol, 1976); A. Conyers (ed), *Wiltshire Extents for Debts (Wiltshire Records Society*, **28**); C. Dale (ed), *Wiltshire Apprentices and their Masters (Wiltshire Records Society*, **15**); C. Fox, F.R.S. Raglan, *Monmouthshire Houses* (Cardiff, 3 vols, 1951-4); D. Portman, *Exeter Houses, 1400-1700* (Exeter, 1966); R. Potts (ed), *A Calendar of Cornish Glebe Terriers, 1673-1735* (*Devon and Cornwall Rec. Soc.*, N.S., **19**); V.M., F.J. Chesher, *The Cornishman's House* (Truro, 1968); D.C. Verey, *The Buildings of England: Gloucestershire* (2 vols, 1970); N. Pevsner, *The Buildings of England: North Somerset and Bristol* (1958); W.A. Pantin, 'Medieval Priests' Houses in S.W. England', *MA*, **1**, 118-46; W.A. Pantin, 'Chantry Priests' Houses and other Medieval Lodgings', *MA*, **3**, 216-58; W.A. Pantin, 'Medieval Town-House Plans', *MA* **6/7**, 202-39; R.K. Field, 'Worcestershire peasant buildings, household goods and farming equipment in the later

Middle Ages', *MA*, **9**, 105–45; N.W. Alcock, 'The Medieval Cottages of Bishops Clyst, Devon', *MA*, **9**, 146–53; N.W. Alcock, M. Laithwaite, 'Medieval Houses in North Devon and their Modernization', *MA*, **17**, 100–25; R.H. Hilton, P. Rahtz, 'Upton, Gloucestershire', *BG*, **85**, 70–146; **88**, 74–126; P.J. Fowler, J. Bennett, 'Archaeology and the M5 Motorway', *BG*, **92**, 21–81, esp., 46–57; L.J. Walrond, 'Beacham's Cottage, Pitney', *SA*, **97**, 79–89; L.C. Hayward, R.W. McDowall, 'The George Hotel, Yeovil', *SA*, **109**, 84–97; L.J. Walrond, 'An Early Jointed Cruck Building at S. Bradon', *SA*, **114**, 68–73; R. de Z. Hall, C. Austin, 'A Cruck-Roofed House in N. Cadbury', *SA*, **114**, 63–8; R. de Z. Hall, C. Austin, 'The Medieval Houses of Stocklinch', *SA*, **116**, 86–100; **R.** Taylor, 'Castle House, Taunton Castle', *SA*, **118**, 25–7; E.H.D. Williams, 'Some Two-Unit Houses in Somerset', *SA*, **118**, 28–38; R.J.E. Buch, 'The Tudor Tavern, Fore Street, Taunton', *SA*, **119**, 15–21; M.B. MacDermott, 'Church House at Spaxton', *SA*, **119**, 15–21; C. Powell, R. Wilkes, 'Blindbacks for Brassworkers', *BIAS*, **8**, 26–8; K. Hudson, *The fashionable stone* (Bath, 1971); C.F.W. Dening, *The Eighteenth Century architecture of Bristol* (Bristol, 1923); W. Ison, *The Georgian Buildings of Bath* (1948, repr. Bath, 1966); W. Ison, *The Georgian Buildings of Bristol* (1952, repr, Bath, 1978); C. Crick, *Victorian Buildings in Bristol* (Bristol, 1975); B. Little, *Bath Portrait* (3rd ed,1972); P., R. Coard, *Vanishing Bath* (Bath, 3 vols, 1971–3); T. Edwards, *Bristol* (1951); T.H. Burrough, *Bristol* (1970); E.H.D. Williams, R.G. Gilson, 'Dating of the smaller Somerset Houses from external appearance', *SA*, **120**, 13–20.

(b) Standard and Cost of Living

General

J. Burnett, *History of the Cost of Living* (1969); J.E.T. Rogers, *Six Centuries of Work and Wages* (11th ed, 1912); J.C. Drummond, A. Wilbraham, *The Englishman's Food* (2nd ed, 1958); D. Hartley, *Food in England* (1954); P. Laslett, *The World We have lost* (2nd ed, 1971); E.P. Thompson, *The Making of the English Working Class* (1966); E. Shorter, *The Making of the Modern Family* (1976); P. Laslett, *Family Life and Illicit Love in Earlier Generations* (Cambridge, 1977); L. Stone, *The Family, Sex and Marriage in England, 1500–1800* (1977); G.E. Fussell, *The English Rural Labourer; his home, furniture, clothing and food from Tudor to Victorian times* (1949); A.S. Wohl (ed), *The Victorian Family* (1978).

Sources and Methods

E.V. Morgan, *The Study of Prices and the value of money* (1950); W.T. Layton, G. Crowther, *Introduction to the Study of Prices* (3rd ed, 1938); J.E.T. Rogers, *A History of Agriculture and Prices from 1259 to 1793* (Oxford, 7 vols, 1866–1902); W. Beveridge, *Prices and Wages in England* (1939); E.H. Phelps-Brown, S.V. Hopkins, 'Seven Centuries of Building Wages', *Economica*, NS, **22**, 195–206, and 'Seven Centuries of the Prices of Consumables Compared with Builders' Wage-Rates', *Economica*, N.S.,

23, 296–314; A. J. Taylor, *The Standard of Living in Britain in the Industrial Revolution* (1975); M.I. Thomis, *The Town Labourer and the Industrial Revolution* (1975).

Local Sources and Studies

M. Sharp (ed), *Bristol Constables' Accounts* (*BRS.*, forthcoming volume); E. Hobhouse (ed), *Churchwardens' Accounts of. . . Yatton* (*SRS*, **4**); C.B. Pearson (ed), 'The Churchwardens' Accounts of the Church and Parish of St. Michael within the North Gate, Bath, 1349–1575', *SA*, **23**, part 3; **24**, part 3; **25**, part 3; **26**, part 3; B.R. Masters, E. Ralph (ed), *The Church Book of St. Ewen's Bristol, 1454–1584* (*BGRS*, **6**); G. Beachcroft, A. Sabin (ed), *Two Compotus Rolls of St. Augustine's Abbey, Bristol, for 1491–2 and 1511–2* (*BRS.*, **9**); A. Sabin (ed), *Some Manorial Accounts of St. Augustine's Abbey, Bristol* (*BRS.*, **22**); D.M. Livock (ed), *City Chamberlain's Accounts in the Sixteenth and Seventeenth Centuries* (*BRS.*, **24**); J. Vanes (ed), *The Ledger of John Smythe, 1538–1550* (*BRS.*, **28**); J.S. Moore (ed), *The Goods and Chattels of Our Forefathers* (Chichester, 1976); F.D. Wardle (ed), *Accounts of the Chamberlains of the City of Bath, 1586–1602* (*SRS*, **38**); R.S. Neale, 'The Standard of Living, 1780–1814: a regional and class study' (Bath), *EcHR*, 2nd ser, **19**, 590–606.

Chapter 8

Local Government and Politics

General

J. Redlich, F.W. Hirst, *History of Local Government in England* (2nd ed., 1970); S. & B. Webb, *History of English Local Government* (11 vols, 1903–29, repr. 1963); A. Harding, *A Social History of English Law* (1966); N.J. Hone, *The Manor and Manorial Records* (2nd ed, 1912); H.M. Cam, *The Hundred and the Hundred Rolls* (1930); H.M. Cam, *Liberties and Communities in Medieval England* (Cambridge, 1944); C. Stephenson, *Borough and Town* (Cambridge (U.S.A.), 1933); J. Tait, *The Medieval English Borough* (Manchester, 1936); G.E. Mingay, *The Gentry: the rise and fall of a ruling class* (1977); W.E. Tate, *The Parish Chest* (Cambridge, 3rd ed, 1969); E. Moir, *The Justice of the Peace* (1969); J.H. Gleason, *Justices of the Peace in England, 1558–1640* (Oxford, 1969); J.H. Thomas, *Town Government in the Sixteenth Century* (1933, repr, New York (USA), 1969); W.K. Jordan, *The Charities of Rural England, 1480–1660* (1961); W.K. Jordan, *Philanthropy in England, 1480–1660* (1959); J. Pound, *Poverty and Vagrancy in Tudor England* (1971); G.W. Oxley, *Poor Relief in England and Wales, 1601–1834* (Newton Abbot, 1974); G. Taylor, *The Problem of Poverty, 1660–1834* (1969); D. Owen, *English Philanthropy, 1660–1960* (Oxford, 1965); M.E. Rose, *The English Poor Law, 1780–1930* (Newton Abbot, 1971); J.D. Marshall, *The Old Poor Law, 1795–1834* (1968); J. Roach, *Social Reform, 1780–1880* (1978) J.R. Hay, *The Development of the British Welfare State, 1880–1975* (1978); T. Hayter, *The Army and the Crowd in mid-Georgian England* (1978); E.P. Thompson, *Whigs and Hunters* (1975); D. Hay, P. Linebaugh, E.P. Thompson, *Albion's Fatal Tree: Crime and Society in Eighteenth Century England* (1975); F.W.S. Craig, *British Parliamentary Election Results, 1832–1970* (4 vols, 1969, 1971, 1974, 1977); J. Stephenson, R. Quinault, *Popular Protest and Public Order* (1975); M. Drake, *Introduction to Historical Psephology* (Milton Keynes, 1974); J.R. Vincent, *Pollbooks: how Victorians voted* (Cambridge, 1967); A. Aspinall (ed), *Early English Trade Unions* (1949); H.B. Pelling, *History of British Trade Unionism* (3rd ed, 1976); P.S. Bagwell, *Industrial Relations* (Dublin, 1975); A. Clinton, *The Trade Union Rank and File: Trades Councils in Britain, 1900–1940* (Manchester, 1978); E.J. Bristow, *Vice and Vigilance: purity movements in Britain since 1700* (Dublin, 1978); P.H.J.H. Gosden, *The Friendly Societies of England, 1815–75* (Manchester, 1961); J.J. Tobias, *Nineteenth Century Crime: Prevention and Punishment* (Newton Abbot, 1972); D. Philips, *Crime and Authority in Victorian England* (1978); J.J. Tobias, *Crime and Industrial Society in the Nineteenth Century* (1972); G. Sutherland (ed), *Studies in the Growth of Nineteenth Century Government*

(1971); B. Keith-Lucas, *English Local Government in the Nineteenth and Twentieth Centuries* (1977).

Sources and Methods

F.J.C. Hearnshaw, *Municipal Records* (1918); F.G. Emmison, I. Gray, *County Records* (4th ed, 1973); C. Gross, *A Bibliography of British Municipal History* (New York (U.S.A.), 1897, repr. Leicester, 1966); G.H. Martin, S. McIntyre (ed), *Bibliography of British and Irish Municipal History,* 1 (Leicester, 1972); Interdepartmental Committee on Economic and Social Research, *Local Government Statistics (Guides to Official Sources,* **3**) (1953).

Local Sources and Studies

N.D. Harding, H.A. Cronne, R.C. Latham (ed), *Bristol Charters 1155-1899* (*BRS*, **1**, **11-2**); E.W.W. Veale (ed), *The Great Red Book of Bristol* (*BRS*, **2, 4, 8, 16, 18**); L.T. Smith (ed), *The Maire of Bristowe is Kalendar* (Camden Society, N.S., **5**); E.E. Rich (ed), *The Staple Court Books of Bristol* (*BRS*, **5**); F.B. Bickley (ed), *The Little Red Book of Bristol* (Bristol, 2 vols, 1900); E. Ralph (ed), *The Great White Book of Bristol* (*BRS*, forthcoming volume); D. Douglas, 'Bristol under the Normans', *BGC*, 101-8; W. Maitland (ed), *Pleas of the Crown for the county of Gloucester. . . 1221* (1884); C.E. Chadwyck-Healey, L. Landon (ed), *Somerset Pleas. . . 1228-1280* (*SRS*, **11, 36, 41, 44**); J.B. Given, *Society and Homicide in Thirteenth Century England* (Stanford (USA), 1977) [includes Bristol]; E.A. Fuller, 'Pleas of the Crown at Bristol, 15 Edw. I', *BG*, **22**, 150-78; E.G. Kimball, 'Rolls of the Gloucestershire Sessions of the Peace, 1361-1398', *BG*, **62**; J. Latimer, 'On the Hundredal and Manorial Franchise of the Furcas, Tumbrel and Pillory in the County of Gloucester in the Middle Ages', *BG*, **12**, 114-22; W. Illingworth, J. Caley (ed), *Rotuli Hundredorum,* **1** (1812); W. Illingworth, J. Caley (ed), *Placita de Quo Warranto* (1818); E.A. Fuller, 'The Tallage of 6 Edw I and the Bristol Rebellion', *BG*, **19**, 171-228; E. Ralph, *The Government of Bristol, 1373-1973* (Bristol, 1973); J.T. Driver, 'Parliamentary Burgesses for Bristol and Gloucester, 1422-1437', *BG*, **74**, 60-127; D. Hollis (ed), *Calendar of the Bristol Apprentice Book, 1532-69* (*BRS*, **14**, forthcoming volumes); D.M. Livock (ed), *City Chamberlains' Accounts in the Sixteenth and Seventeenth Centuries* (*BRS,* **24**); F.D. Wardle (ed), *Accounts of the Chamberlains of the City of Bath, 1568-1602* (*SRS*, **38**); W.K. Jordan, *The Farming of the Charitable Institutions of the West of England* [1480-1660], *American Philosophical Society Transactions,* N.S, **50**; W.B. Willcox, *Gloucestershire: a study in local Government, 1590-1640* (New Haven (U.S.A.), 1940); G. Bradford (ed), *Proceedings in the Court of Star Chamber* (*SRS*, **27**); T.G. Barnes, *A County under the Personal Rule: Somerset, 1629-40* (Oxford, 1961); E.H. Bates-Harbin, M.C.B. Dawes (ed), *Quarter Sessions Records, 1607-39, 1646-60, 1666-77* (*SRS*, **23, 24, 28, 34**); T.G. Barnes, J.S. Cockburn (ed) *Somerset Assize Orders, 1629-59* (*SRS*, **65, 71**); I.F. Jones, 'Aspects of Poor Law Administration, 17th to 19th Centuries, from Trull Overseers' Accounts' *SA*, **95**, 72-105; W.R. Williams,

Parliamentary History of the County of Gloucester. . . from 1213 to 1898 (Hereford, 1898); E.E. Butcher (ed), *The Bristol Corporation of the Poor, 1696–1834* (BRS, **3**); E.E. Butcher, *Bristol Corporation of the Poor, 1696–1898* (Bristol, 1972); C.R. Hudleston, '[South] Gloucestershire Voters in 1710', *BG*, **58**, 195–205; P. Rogers, 'Daniel Defoe, John Oldmixon and the Bristol Riots of 1714', *BG*, **92**, 145–56; A.L. Browne, 'Penal Laws in Gloucestershire', *BG*, **61**, 287–93; J. Cannon, 'Bath Politics in the Eighteenth Century', *SA*, **105**, 87–105; J. Cannon, 'Gloucestershire Politics, 1750–1800', BG, **79**, 293-7; E. Moir (ed), *Local Government in Gloucestershire, 1775–1800 (BGRS,* **8**); J. Money, *Experience and Identity: Birmingham and the West Midlands, 1760–1800* (Manchester, 1978); J.R.S. Whiting, *Prison Reform in Gloucestershire, 1776–1820* (Chichester, 1975); E. Moir, 'The Gloucestershire Association for Parliamentary Reform, 1780', *BG*, **75**, 171–91; R.S. Neale, *Class and ideology in a provincial city: Bath, 1800–1850* (1966); G. Bush (ed), *Bristol and its municipal government, 1820–1851 (BRS,* **29**); J. Williams, 'Bristol in the General Elections of 1818 and 1820', *BG*, **87**, 173–201; I.P. Collis, 'The Struggle for Constabulary Reform in Bristol', *SA*, **99/100**, 75–104; S. Thomas, *The Bristol Riots* (Bristol, 1974); J. Cannon, *The Chartists in Bristol* (Bristol, 1964); R. Walters, *The Establishment of the Bristol Police Force* (Bristol, 1975); D. Large, F. Round, *Public Health in mid-Victorian Bristol* (Bristol, 1974); D. Large, R. Whitfield, *Bristol Trades Council, 1873–1973* (Bristol, 1973); S. Bryher [S. Bale], *An account of the Labour and Socialist movement in Bristol* (Bristol, 3 vols, 1929–31); E. Jackson, *A study in democracy: being an account of the rise and progress of industrial co-operation in Bristol* (Manchester, 1911); A. Bullock, *The Life and Times of Ernest Bevin,* **1** (1960), chapters 1–2; R.V. Clements, *Local notables and the city council* (1969); G. Elton, *Among Others* (1938), chapter 9; R.S. Milne, H.C. Mackenzie, *Straight Fight* [1951] (1954); R.S. Milne, H.C. Mackenzie, *Marginal Seat, 1955* (1958); F. Hyett, C. Wells, 'Members of Parliament for Gloucestershire and Bristol, 1900–20', *BG*, **51**, 321–60. Most Poll Books for Bristol will be found in Avon Central Reference Library and the Bristol Record Office, and for Bath in the Bath Reference Library: the *Bath Poll Book of 1855* has been reprinted (Milton Keynes, 1974).

The role of the major local families can be seen from some case studies: W. Bazeley, 'The Earls of Gloucester', *BG,* **3**, 368–89; D. Walker, 'Miles of Gloucester', *BG,* **77**, 66–84; D. Walker, 'The Honours of the Earls of Hereford in the Twelfth Century', *BG,* **79**, 174–211; R.B. Patterson (ed), *Earldom of Gloucester Charters* (Oxford, 1973); M. Altschul, *A baronial family in medieval England: the Clares, 1217–1314* (Baltimore (U.S.A.), 1965); J. Smith, *The Berkeley Manuscripts* (Gloucester, 3 vols, 1883–5); J.H. Cooke, 'The Great Berkeley Law Suit of the 15th and 16th Centuries', *BG,* **3**, 305–24; H. Barkley, 'The Earlier House of Berkeley', *BG,* **8**, 193–223; T. Veal, 'The Domestic Life of Berkeley Castle', *BG,* **19**, 85–104; H.S. Kennedy-Skipton, 'The Berkeleys of Yate', *BG,* **21**, 25–31; W.J. Smith, 'The Rise of the Berkeleys', *BG,* **70**, 64–80; **71**, 101–21; C. Rawcliffe, *The Staffords, Earls of Stafford and Dukes of Buckingham, 1394–1521* (Cambridge, 1977); J.N. Langston, 'The Staffords and

Howards of Thornbury', *BG*, **72**, 79–104; J.N. Langston, 'The Giffards of Brimpsfield', *BG*, **65**, 105–28; R.F. Butler, 'The Last of the Brimpsfield Giffards and the Rising of 1321-2', *BG*, **76**, 75–97; R. Austin, 'Notes on the family of Bradeston', *BG*, **47**, 279–86; F.J. Poynton, 'The Family of Haynes', *BG*, **9**, 277–9; **10**, 226–9; R.H. Codrington, 'Memoir of the Family of Codrington', *BG*, **21**, 301–45; L.J.U. Way, 'The Smyths of Ashton Court', *BG*, **31**, 244–60; J.N. Langston, 'The Pastons of Horton', *BG*, **77**, 97–126; B. Campbell, *The Badminton Tradition* (1978).

Chapter 9
Church and Chapel

General

W.O. Chadwick, *History of the Church: a select bibliography* (2nd ed, 1966); J.R.H. Moorman, *History of the Church in England* (2nd ed, 1967); M. Deanesly, *The Preconquest Church in England* (2nd ed, 1963); G.W.O. Addleshaw, *The Beginnings of the Parochial System* (York, 3rd ed, 1970); G.W.O. Addleshaw, *The Development of the Parochial System from Charlemagne (768–814) to Urban II (1088–99)* (York, 2nd ed, 1970); J. Godfrey, *The English Parish, 600–1300* (1969); G.H. Cook, *The Medieval English Parish Church* (1954); H.S. Braun, *Parish Churches: their architectural development* (1970); D. Knowles, R.N. Hadcock, *Medieval Religious Houses: England and Wales* (1953); K.L. Wood-Legh, *Perpetual Chantries in Britain* (Cambridge, 1965); R. Finucane, *Miracles and Pilgrims: Popular Beliefs in Medieval England* (1978); J.B. Russell, *Witchcraft in the Middle Ages* (Cornell (U.S.A.) 1975); C. Cross, *Church and People, 1450–1660* (1976); A.G. Dickens, *The English Reformation* (1964); F. Heal, R. O'Day (ed), *Church and Society in England: Henry VIII to James I* (1977); A.T. Hart, *The Country Clergy, 1558–1660* (1958); A. Morey, *The Catholic Subjects of Elizabeth I* (1978); J. Bossy, *The English Catholic Community, 1570–1850* (1975); M.R. Watts, *The Dissenters from the Reformation to the French Revolution* (Oxford, 1978); H. Davies, *The English Free Churches* (Oxford, 2nd ed, 1963); R.T. Jones, *Congregationalism in England, 1662–1962* (1962); D.M. Thompson, *Nonconformity in the nineteenth century* (1972); A. Armstrong, *The Church of England, the Methodists and Society, 1700–1850* (1973); A.D. Gilbert, *Religion and Society in Industrial England: Church, Chapel and Social Change, 1740–1914* (1976); E.R. Norman, *Church and Society in England, 1770–1970* (Oxford, 1976); S. Andrews, *Methodism and Society* (1970); R. Currie, *Methodism divided* (1968); W.J. Townsend, *A New History of Methodism* (2 vols, 1909); A.M. Smith, *The Established Church and Popular Religion, 1750–1850* (Harlow, 1972); W.R. Ward, *Religion and Society in England, 1790–1850* (1972); O. Chadwick, *The Victorian Church* (2 vols, 2nd ed, 1970, 1972); B. Heeney, *A Different Kind of Gentleman: Parish Clergy as Professional Men in Early and Mid-Victorian England* (Hamden (U.S.A.), 1977); K.S. Inglis, *The Churches and the Working Classes in Victorian England* (1963); H. MacLeod, *Class and Religion in the Late Victorian City* (1974); J.D. Gay, *The Geography of Religion in England* (1971); J.H. Briggs, I. Sellars, *Victorian Nonconformity* (1973); A.M. Everitt, *The Pattern of Rural Dissent: the 19th Century* (Leicester, 1972); R. Currie, A. Gilbert, L. Horsley, *Churches and churchgoers: patterns of church growth in the British Isles since 1700* (Oxford, 1977).

Sources and Methods

D. Baker (ed), *Materials, Sources and Methods of Ecclesiastical History* (Oxford, 1975); J.S. Purvis, *Introduction to Ecclesiastical Records* (York, 1953); F.R.H. Du Boulay, *Handbook of Medieval Ecclesiastical History* (1952); J.S. Purvis, *Dictionary of Ecclesiastical Terms* (1962); D.M. Owen, *The Records of the Established Church in England* (1970); W.E. Tate, *The Parish Chest* (Cambridge, 3rd ed. 1969); P. Hair, *Before the Bawdy Court* (1972); E.R.C. Brinkworth, *The Archdeacon's Court (Oxfordshire Records Society*, **23**); E.R.C. Brinkworth, 'The Records of the Clergy', *LH*, **2**, 82–6; E.R.C. Brinkworth, 'Records of the church courts', *LH*, **2**, 50–3; E.R.C. Brinkworth, 'The Records of bishops' and archdeacons' visitations', *LH*, **2**, 19–22; D.M. Owen, 'The use of ecclesiastical records for secular subjects', *LH*, **5**, 44–50; D.M. Owen, 'Sources for chuch history', *LH*, **9**, 65–74; F.H.A. Micklewright, 'The Reformation and the local historian', *LH*, **7**, 253–7; A. Davidson, 'Recusant History: a bibliographical article', *LH*, **9**, 283–9; W.R. Powell, 'Protestant Nonconformist Records and the Local Historian', *Archives*, **5**, 1–6; W.R. Powell, 'Sources for the History of Protestant nonconformist churches in England', *BIHR.*, **25**, 213–27; A.G. Matthews, *Calamy Revised* (Oxford, 1934); A.G. Matthews, *Walker Revised* (Oxford, 1948); G. Lyon Turner (ed), *Original Records of Early Nonconformity* (3 vols, 1911–14); A. Gordon, *Freedom after Ejection* (Manchester, 1917); C.E. Welch, 'Archives and Manuscripts in nonconformist libraries', *Archives*, **6**, 235–8; J. Smith, 'The Local Records of Nonconformity', *LH*, **8**, 131–4; K. Twinn, 'Dr. Williams' Library', *LH*, **9**, 115–20; F.H.A. Micklewright, 'The local history of Victorian secularism', *LH*, **8**, 221–7; W.F. Swift, T. Shaw, *How to write a local history of Methodism* (Leicester, 2nd ed, 1964).

Local Sources and Studies

For monastic cartularies, see bibliography to chapter 4. I.M. Kirby, (ed), *Diocese of Gloucester: Catalogue of the Records of the Bishop and Archdeacons* (Gloucester, 1968); I.M. Kirby (ed), *Diocese of Bristol: Catalogue of the Records of the Bishop and Archdeacons and of the Dean and Chapter* (Bristol, 1970); W.H. Bird, W.P. Baildon (ed), *Manuscripts of the Dean and Chapter of Wells* (2 vols, 1907, 1914); I. Gray, E. Ralph (ed), *Guide to the Parish Records of the City of Bristol and the County of Gloucester* (*BGRS*, **5**): J.E. King (ed), *Inventory of Parochial Documents in the Diocese of Bath and Wells and the County of Somerset* (Taunton, 1938); *VCH Gloucestershire*, **2** (1907), *VCH Somerset*, **2** (1911); W.J. Robinson, *West Country Churches* (Bristol, 4 vols, 1914–6); D.C. Verey, 'The Perpendicular Style in the Cotswolds', *BGC*, 127–46; D.C. Verey, *Cotswold Churches* (1976); A.K. Wickham, *Churches of Somerset* (Newton Abbot, 2nd ed, 1965); R.C.S. Walters, *Ancient wells, springs and holy wells of Gloucestershire* (Bristol, 1928); H.M. Porter, *The Celtic Church in Somerset* (Bath, 1971); C.A.R. Radford, 'The Church in Somerset down to 1100', *SA*, **106**, 28–45; R.W. Dunning (ed), *Christianity in Somerset* (Taunton, 1976); R.W. Dunning, 'The Minster at Crewkerne', *SA*, **120**, 63–7; *Registers of the Bishops of Bath and Wells, 1265–6, 1309–63, 1401–1559* (*SRS*, **1, 9, 10, 13, 29–32, 49–50,**

52, 54–5) *Registers of the Bishops of Worcester, 1268–1327, 1339–49, 1375–95* (*WHS*, **7, 15, 22, 39, 40;** N.S., **4, 7**); S. Ayscough, J. Caley (ed), *Taxatio... Papae Nicholai IV* (1802); G. Vanderzee, J. Caley (ed), *Nonarum Inquisitiones* (1807); J. Le Neve, B. Jones (ed), *Fasti Ecclesiae Anglicanae... 1066–1300*, **2** (1971), 99–109 (Worcester diocese); the volume for Bath and Wells diocese is in preparation; J. Le Neve, D.E. Greenaway (ed), *Fasti Ecclesiae Anglicanae... 1300–1541*, **4** (1963), 54–63 (Worcester), **8** (1964) (Bath and Wells); post-1541 volumes are in preparation; R.M. Haines, *The Administration of the Diocese of Worcester in the first half of the fourteenth century* (1965); C.S. Taylor, 'The Chronological Sequence of the Bristol Parish Churches', *BG*, **32**, 202–18; C.S. Taylor, 'The Parochial Boundaries of Bristol', *BG*, **33** 126–39; J.C. Dickinson, 'The Origins of St. Augustine's, Bristol', *BGC*, 109–26; M.Q. Smith, *The Medieval Churches of Bristol* (Bristol, 1970); R.H. Warren, 'The Medieval Chapels of Bristol', *BG*, **30**, 181–211; H.C. Maxwell-Lyte, 'Somerset Incumbents, 1354–1401', *SA*, **78**, 44–108; R.W. Dunning, 'Somerset Parochial Clergy, 1373–1404', *SA*, **114**, 91–5; F.W. Weaver (ed), *Somerset Incumbents* (Bristol, 1889); E. Hobhouse (ed), *Churchwardens' Accounts of... Yatton* (*SRS*, **4**); C.B. Pearson (ed), 'The Churchwardens' Accounts of St. Michael's Bath', *SA*, **23**, part 3; **24**, part 3; **25**, part 3; **26**, part 3; B.R. Masters, E. Ralph (ed), *The Church Book of St. Ewen's Bristol, 1454–1584* (*BGRS*, **6**); R.W. Dunning, *The Administration of the Diocese of Bath and Wells, 1401–91* (University of Bristol, Ph.D. thesis, 1963); A.F. Judd, *The Life of Thomas Bekynton* (Chichester, 1961); M.J. Morgan, *John Carpenter, Bishop of Worcester, 1444–76* (University of Birmingham, M.A. thesis, 1960); R.W. Dunning, 'The Wells Consistory Court in the 15th Century', *SA*, **106**, 46–61; R.W. Dunning, 'The Household of the Bishops of Bath and Wells in the later Middle Ages', *SA*, **110**, 24–39; J.A.F. Thomson, *The Later Lollards, 1414–1520* (Oxford, 1965); F.W. Weaver (ed), *Somerset Wills* (*SRS*, **16, 19, 21**); D.O. Shilton, R. Holworthy (ed), *Medieval Wills from Wells, 1534–46, 1554–6* (*SRS*, **40**); T.P. Wadley (ed), *Notes or abstracts of the wills contained in the Great Orphan Book of Wills* (Bristol, 1886); P.V. McGrath, M.E. Williams (ed), *Bristol Wills, 1546–1603* (Bristol, 2 vols, 1975, 1978); E.A. Fry, L.L. Duncan, W.P.W. Phillimore (ed), *Calendar of Wills proved in the consistory court of the Bishop of Gloucester, 1541–1650, 1660–1800* (*IL*, **12, 34**); E.A. Fry (ed), *Calendar of Wills proved in the Consistory Court (City and Deanery of Bristol Division) of the Diocese of Bristol, 1572–1792* (*IL*, **17**); L. Wilkinson, 'The Chantries of Westbury-on-Trym', *BG*, **19**, 374–93; E.E. Williams, *The Chantries of William Canynges in St. Mary Redcliffe* (Bristol, 1950); E.G.C.F. Atchley, 'The Halleway Chantry of the Parish Church of all Saints, Bristol', *BG*, **24**, 74–125; C.S. Taylor, 'The Religious Houses of Bristol and their dissolution', *BG*, **29**, 81–126; T.F. Palmer (ed), *Collectanea* (*SRS*, **39, 43**); J. Caley, J. Hunter (ed), *Valor Ecclesiasticus* (6 vols, 1810–34); P.M. Hembry, *The Bishops of Bath and Wells, 1540–1640* (Oxford, 1967); J. Maclean, 'Chantry Certificates, Gloucestershire', *BG*, **8**, 229–308; E. Green (ed), *Somerset Chantry Certificates* (*SRS*, **2**); F.W. Weaver, 'The Fate of the Dispossessed Monks and Nuns', *SA*, **38**, 327–46; G. Baskerville, 'The Dispossessed Religious of Gloucestershire', *BG*, **49**, 63–122; J. Gairdner, 'Bishop Hooper's Visitation of Gloucester Diocese, 1551', *EngHR*, **19**, 98–121; F.D. Price, 'Gloucester Diocese under Bishop Hooper, 1551–3' *BG*, **60**, 51–151; K.G. Powell, 'The Beginnings of Protestantism in Gloucestershire', *BG*, **90**, 141–57; K.G. Powell, 'The Social Background to the Reformation in Gloucestershire', *BG*, **92**, 96–120; K.G. Powell, *The Marian Martyrs and the Reformation in Bristol* (Bristol, 1972); V.J. Torr, 'Ecclesiastical Somerset in 1563', *Somerset and Dorset Notes and Queries*, **30**, 83–94; D. Walker, W.J. Sheils, J. Kent (ed), *An Ecclesiastical Miscellany (BGRS*, **11**); P. McGrath, 'Gloucestershire and the Counter-Reformation', *BG*, **88**, 5–28; F.S. Hockaday, 'The Consistory Court of the Diocese of Gloucester', *BG*, **46**, 195–287; R.H. Clutterbuck, 'State Papers respecting Bishop Cheyney and the Recusants of the Diocese of Gloucester', *BG*, **5**, 222–37; M.M.C. Calthrop, H. Bowler (ed), *Recusant Rolls 1 and 2* (*CRS*, **18, 57**); J.A. Williams, *Bath and Rome* (Bath, 1963); J.A. Williams (ed), *Catholicism in Bath* (*CRS*, **65–6**); F.D. Price, 'An Elizabethan Church Official: Thomas Powell, Chancellor of Gloucester Diocese', *CQR*, **138**, 94–112; F.D. Price, 'Elizabethan Apparitors in the Diocese of Gloucester', *CQR*, **134**, 37–55; F.D. Price, 'The Abuses of Excommunication and the decline of Ecclesiastical Discipline under Queen Elizabeth', *EngHR*, **57**, 106–15; F.D. Price, 'Bishop Bullingham and Chancellor Blackleech', *BG*, **91**, 175–98; F.D. Price (ed), *The Commission for Ecclesiastical Causes within the Dioceses of Bristol and Gloucester (BGRS*, **10**); G.I. Soden, *Geoffrey Goodman, Bishop of Gloucester, 1583–1656* (1953); A.E. Robinson (ed), *Life of Bishop Kidder* (*SRS*, **37**): H.A.L. Rice, *Thomas Ken, Bishop and Non-Juror* (1958); W.M. Marshall, *George Hooper, 1640–1727, Bishop of Bath and Wells* (Sherborne, 1976); C.R. Elrington, 'The Survey of Church Livings in Gloucestershire, 1650', *BG*, **83**, 85–98; D.S. Bailey (ed), *Wells Cathedral Chapter Act Book, 1663–83* (*SRS*, **72**); R.S. Mortimer, *Early Bristol Quakerism, 1654–1700* (Bristol, 1967); R.S. Mortimer (ed), *Minute Book of the Men's Meeting of the Society of Friends in Bristol, 1667–1700* (*BRS*, **26, 30**); S.C. Morland (ed), *Somerset Quarterly Meeting, 1668–99* (*SRS*, **75**); R. Hayden (ed), *The Records of a Church of Christ in Bristol, 1640–87 (BRS*, **27**); R.W. Dunning, 'Some Somerset Parishes in 1705', *SA*, **112**; 71–92; M.F. Stieg (ed), *The Diary of John Harrington* (*SRS*, **74**); E.A. Fry, 'The Autobiography of the Rev. Elias Rebotier, Rector of Axbridge', *SA*, **40**, 91–112; J. Ecton, *Liber Valorum et Decimarum* (1711); J. Bacon, *Liber Regis* (1786); H. Coombs, A.N. Bax (ed), *Journal of a Somerset Rector... parochial affairs of the parish of Camerton, 1822–32* (1930); G. Eayrs, *Wesley, Kingswood and the Free Churches* (Bristol, 1911); I. Jones, *Bristol Congregationalism* (Bristol, 1947); G.H. Wicks, *Whitefield's Legacy to Bristol and the Cotswolds* (Bristol, 1914); W. St. J. Kemm, *A Study of the Church of England in the Diocese of Bath and Wells, 1790–1840* (University of Birmingham, M.A. thesis, 1965); R.W. Dunning, 'Nineteenth Century Parochial Sources', *SCH*, **11**, 301–8; W.J. Barker, 'Henry Ryder of Gloucester, 1815–24: England's first evangelical bishop', *BG*, **89**, 130–44; J. Leech, *The Church Goer* (Bristol, 4 vols, 1845, 1850, 1851, 1888); H. Lewis, *The Church Rambler* (1876); G.H. Wicks, *Bristol's heathen neighbours* (Bristol, 1911);

Bath and Wells Diocesan Kalendar (1888–1906) and *Directory and Almanack* (1908 to date); *Bristol Diocesan Directory* (*Handbook*, 1950–9) (1897–1949, 1960 to date); *Gloucester* (*and Bristol*, 1869–96) *Diocesan Kalendar* (1869–1926) and *Yearbook* (1926 to date); *Gloucester Diocesan Magazine* (1906–46) and *Gazette* (1947 to date).

Chapter 10
Education

General

A.F. Leach, *The schools of medieval England* (2nd ed, 1916, repr. New York (U.S.A.), 1969); N. Orme, *English Schools in the Middle Ages* (1973); M.V.J. Seaborne, *The English School: its architecture and organization, 1370–1970* (2 vols, 1971); J. Lawson, H. Silver, *A social history of education in England* (1973); L. Stone, *The University in Society: Oxford and Cambridge from the 14th to the early 19th century* (1975); H. Kearney, *Scholars and Gentlemen: Universities and Society in Pre-Industrial Britain, 1500–1700* (1970); J. Simon, *Education and Society in Tudor England* (Cambridge, 1966); W.H.G. Armytage, *Four hundred years of British education* (Cambridge, 2nd. ed, 1970); H.C. Barnard, *A history of English education from 1760 to 1944* (2nd. ed, 1961); M.G. Jones, *The Charity School Movement* (Cambridge, 1938); B. Simon, *Studies in the history of education, 1780–1870* (1960); D. Wardle, *English popular education, 1780–1870* (Cambridge, 1970); T.W. Laqueur, *Religion and Respectability: Schools and Working Class Culture, 1780–1850* (Yale (USA), 1978); E.G. West, *Education and the Industrial Revolution* (1975); J. Musgrave, *Society and education in England since 1800* (1968); J.S. Hurt, *Education in evolution: Church, State, Society and Popular Education, 1800–1870* (1971); G. Sutherland, *Elementary education in the nineteenth century* (1971); P. Horn, *Education in Rural England, 1800–1914* (Dublin, 1978); T. Kelly, *History of Public Libraries in Great Britain, 1845–1975* (2nd. ed, 1977); T. Kelly, *Books for the People* (1977); M. Cruickshank, *Church and state in English education, 1870 to the present day* (1963).

Sources and Methods

G. Baron, *A bibliographical guide to the English educational system* (3rd. ed, 1965); C.W.J. Higson (ed), *Sources for the history of education* (1967); C.M. Cipolla, *Literacy and development in the West* (1969); R.S. Schofield, 'The Measurement of literacy in pre-industrial England' (in J. Goody (ed), *Literacy in traditional societies* (Cambridge, 1968), 311–25); W.P. Baker, *Parish registers and illiteracy in east Yorkshire* (Hull, 1961); L. Stone, 'Literacy and education in England, 1640–1900', *PP, 42*, 69–139; M. Sanderson, 'Literacy and social mobility in the Industrial Revolution in England', *PP, 56*, 75–104; *64*, 108–12; T.W. Laqueur, 'Literacy and social mobility in the Industrial Revolution in England', *PP, 64*, 96–107; R.B. Pugh, 'Sources for the history of English primary schools', *British Journal of Educational Studies, 1*, 43–51; C.M. Turner, 'Mechanics Institutes, a topic for local study', *LH, 7*, 63–5; M.V.J. Seaborne, *Recent education from local sources* (1967); A.B. Emden, *Biographical Register of the University of Oxford to 1500* (Oxford, 3 vols, 1957-9); A.B. Emden, *Biographical Register of the University of Oxford, 1501-40 (Oxford, 1974); A.B. Emden, Biographical Register of the University of Cambridge to 1500* (Cambridge, 1963); J.A. Venn, *Alumni Cantabrigenses* (Cambridge, 5 vols, 1922-7, 1940); J. Foster, *Alumni Oxonienses, 1500-1886* (Oxford, 8 vols, 1887-91); J. Foster (ed), *The Register of Admissions to Gray's Inn, 1521-1889* (1889); Lincoln's Inn, *The Records of the Honourable Society of Lincoln's Inn*, 1, *Admissions, 1420-1799* (1896); W.H. Cooke (ed), *Students admitted to the Inner Temple, 1547-1660* (1878); H.A.C. Sturgess (ed), *Register of Admissions to the Honourable Society of the Middle Temple from the fifteenth century to the year 1944* (3 vols, 1949); E. Williams, *Staple Inn* (1906), Appendix E.

Local sources and studies
VCH. Gloucestershire, 2, 313-448; *VCH. Somerset*, 2, 435-65; N. Orme, *Education in the West of England, 1548-1966* (Exeter, 1976); A.C. Percival, 'Gloucestershire grammar schools from the 16th to the 19th centuries', *BG*, 89, 109-22; J.R. Holman, 'Some aspects of higher education in Bristol and Gloucestershire, c.1650-1750', *BG*, 95, 86-97; A. Platts, G.H. Hainton, *Education in Gloucestershire: a short history* (Gloucester, 1954); H.J. Larcombe, *The Progress of education in Bristol: a sketch of the development of education in Bristol from early times to about the year 1875* (Typescript, 1924, in Avon Central Library); C.P. Hill, *The History of Bristol Grammar School* (1951); R.B. Hope, *Educational development in the City of Bath, 1830-1902* (Unpublished Ph.D. thesis, University of Bristol, 1970); W. Roberts (ed), *Memoirs of the life and correspondence of Mrs. Hannah More* (3rd. ed, 4 vols, 1835); A. Roberts (ed), *Mendip Annals, or a narrative of the charitable labours of Hannah and Martha More, being the journal of Martha More* (2nd. ed, 1859); Privy Council Committee on Education, *Minutes and Annual Reports* (1839-99); Charity Commissioners, *Reports* (1819-1937); Charity Commissioners, *Analytical Digests*, 2: *schools and charities for education* (1842); H. Mann, *Census of Great Britain, 1851: Education in Great Britain* (1854); Charity Commissioners, *Digest of Endowed Charities, Gloucestershire* (1868), *Bristol and Somerset* (1873); *Reports of the Schools Inquiry Royal Commission* (C.3966), 1, 4, 5, 7, 14, 15, 20, 21 (1868-9); Board of Education, *Annual Reports* (1899-1944).

Chapter 11

Leisure and Recreation

General

R.V. Lennard, *Englishmen at rest and play: some phases of English leisure, 1558-1714* (Oxford, 1931); R.W. Malcolmson, *Popular Recreations in English Society, 1700-1850* (Cambridge, 1973); R. Longrigg, *History of Horse-Racing* (1972); W. Vamplew, *The Turf* (1976); R. Longrigg, *The History of Foxhunting* (1975); R. Longrigg, *The English Squire and his sport* (1977); A.R. Wright, *British Calendar Customs: England* (3 vols, 1936-40); C. Hale, *English Sports and Pastimes* (1949); R. Lavery (ed), *Recreational Geography* (Newton Abbot, 1975); R.C. Finucane, *Miracles and Pilgrims: Popular Beliefs in Medieval England* (1978); P. Cowley, *The Church Houses* (1970); B. Harrison, 'Religion and Recreation in 19th Century England', *PP*, **38**, 98-125; B. Harrison, *Drink and the Victorians* (1971); M. Girouard, *Victorian Pubs* (1975); A.B. Granville, *Spas of England and Principal Sea-Bathing places* (2 vols, 1841, repr. Bath, 1971); F. Alderson, *Inland resorts and Spas of Britain* (Newton Abbot, 1973); T. Kelly, *History of Public Libraries in Great Britain, 1845-1975* (2nd ed, 1977); T. Kelly, *Books for the People* (1977); J.A.R. Pimlott, *The Englishman's Holiday* (1947); A. Delgado, *The Annual Outing* (1977); J. Walvin, *Besides the Seaside* (1978); R. Mander, J. Mitchenson, *British Music Hall* (1975); R. Mander, J. Mitchenson, *Victorian and Edwardian Entertainment* (1978); G.F. Chadwick, *The Park and the Town* (1966); J. Walvin, *People's Game: a history of football* (1975); J.A.R. Pimlott, *The Englishman's Christmas* (Hassocks, 1978); A. Briggs, *Mass Entertainment: the origins of a modern industry* (Adelaide (Australia), 1960).

Local Sources and Studies

R.W. Dunning, *Christianity in Somerset* (Taunton, 1976); M.Q. Smith, *The Medieval Churches of Bristol* (Bristol, 1970); L.T. Smith (ed), *The Maire of Bristow is Kalendar* (*Camden Society*, N.S, **5**); C.B. Pearson (ed), 'Churchwardens Accounts of St. Michael's, Bath, 1349-1575', *SA*, **23**, part 3; **24**, part 3; **25** part 3; **26**, part 3; E. Hobhouse (ed), *Churchwardens' Accounts of. . . Yatton*, *SRS*, **4**; B.R. Masters, E. Ralph (ed),*The Church Book of St. Ewen's, Bristol, 1454-1584*, *BGRS*, **6**; J. Latimer, *Annals of Bristol* (Bristol, repr. 3 vols, 1970); J.H. Bettey, *Rural Life in Wessex, 1500-1900* (Bradford-on-Avon, 1977); G. Bradford (ed.), *Proceedings in the Court of Star Chamber relating to Somerset during the reigns of Henry VII and Henry VIII, SRS,* **27**; F.D. Wardle (ed), *Accounts of the Chamberlains of the City of Bath, 1568-1602, SRS,* **38**; F.D. Price (ed), 'The Commission for

Ecclesiastical Causes for the Dioceses of Bristol and Gloucester, 1574',
BG, **59**, 61–184; E.H. Bates Harbin (ed), *Quarter Sessions Records,
1607–39, 1646–60, 1666–76, SRS*, **23, 24, 28, 34**; T.G. Barnes, J.S.
Cockburn (ed), *Somerset Assize Orders, 1629–59, SRS*, **65, 71**; T.G.
Barnes, 'County Politics and a Puritan cause célébre: Somerset
Churchales, 1633', *TRHS*, 5th. ser, **9**, 103–22; I.E. Gray, A.T. Gaydon,
*Gloucestershire Quarter Sessions Archives, 1660–1889, and other official
records* (Gloucester, 1958); J. Aubrey, *The Natural History of Wiltshire*
(Newton Abbot, repr, 1969); E. Hobhouse (ed), *The Diary of a West
Country Physician (Dr. Claver Morris), 1684–1726* (1934); J. Woodford,
The diary of a country parson (Oxford, 5 vols, 1924–31); V. Waite, *The
Bristol Hotwell* (Bristol, 1960); B. Little, 'The Gloucestershire spas: an
eighteenth century parallel', *BGC*, 170–99; A. Hare, *The Georgian theatre
in Wessex* (1958); D. Gadd, *Georgian Summer: Bath in the eighteenth century*
(Bradford-on-Avon, 1977); B.S. Penley, *The Bath Stage* (Bath, 1892); A.
Hare (ed), *Theatre Royal, Bath: the Orchard Street Calendar, 1750–1805*
(Bath, 1977); K. Barker, *The Theatre Royal, Bristol, 1776–1966* (1974);
M.D. Fuller, *West Country Friendly Societies* (Reading, 1964); H. Coombs,
A.N. Bax (ed), *Journal of a Somerset rector. . .parochial affairs of the parish of
Camerton, 1822–32* (1930); S.C. Caple, *The history of Gloucestershire County
Cricket Club, 1870–1948* (Worcester, 1949); H. Meller, *Leisure and the
changing city, 1870–1914* (1976); K. Barker, *Entertainment in the Nineties*
(Bristol, 1973); K. Barker, *Bristol at play* (Bradford-on-Avon, 1976); B.M.
Wilmott-Dobbie (ed), *An English rural community: Batheaston with St.
Catherine* (Bath, 1969); B.M. Wilmott-Dobbie (ed), *Village life,
1883–1940: Batheaston remembers* (Batheaston, 1976); R. Jefferies, *The
Gamekeeper at Home and The Amateur Poacher* (1878–9, repr. Oxford,
1978).

Chapter 12
Public Opinion and Popular Beliefs

General

V. Alford, *Introduction to English Folklore* (1952); E. Hull, *Folklore of the British Isles* (1928); M. Baker, *Folklore and Customs of Rural England* (Newton Abbot, 1974); J.M. Vansina, *Oral Tradition* (1965); P. Thompson, *The voice of the past—oral history* (1978); K. Thomas, *Religion and the decline of Magic* (1971); F.C. Finucane, *Miracles and Pilgrims: Popular Beliefs in Medieval England* (1978); J.B. Russell, *Witchcraft in the Middle Ages* (Cornell (U.S.A.), 1975); J. Andersen, *The Witch on the Wall: Medieval Erotic Sculpture in the British Isles* (1977); A. MacFarlane, *Witchcraft in Tudor and Stuart England* (1970); R.T. Davies, *Four centuries of witch beliefs with special reference to the Great Rebellion* (1947); A.L. Lloyd, *Folk song in England* (1967); R.J.E. Tiddy, *The mummers' play* (Oxford, 1923, repr. Folcroft (U.S.A.), 1969); J.S. Bratton, *The Victorian Popular Ballad* (1975); J. Goody (ed), *Literacy in Traditional Societies* (Cambridge, 1968); R.A. Fothergill, *Private Chronicles: a study of English Diaries* (Oxford, 1975); A.J. Lee, *The Origins of the Popular Press* (1977); G.A. Cranfield, *The development of the provincial newspaper, 1700–1760* (Oxford, 1962); R.K. Webb, *The British working class reader, 1790–1848* (1955, repr. New York (U.S.A.), 1971); D. Read, *Press and people, 1790–1850* (1961); P. Hollis, *The Pauper Press* (Oxford, 1970); R.D. Attick, *The English common reader: a social history of the mass reading public, 1800–1900* (Chicago (U.S.A.), 1957); I. Jackson, *The Provincial Press and the community* (Manchester, 1971); J. Burnett (ed), *Useful Toil: autobiographies of working people from the 1820s to the 1920s* (1974); D. Vincent (ed), *Testaments of Radicalism: Memoirs of Working-class Politicians, 1790–1885* (1977); P. Horn, *The Victorian Country Child* (Kineton, 1975); M.L. Davies (ed), *Life as we have known it* (1931, repr. 1978); T. Harrison, *Living through the Blitz* (1976); S. Stewart, *Country Kate* (Kineton, 1971); S. Stewart, *Country Courtship* (Kineton, 1976); F. Thompson, *Lark Rise to Candleford* (Oxford, 1945); F. Thompson, *Still Glides the Stream* (Oxford, repr. 1976); G. Sturt, *Change in the Village* (1912, repr. 1955); G. Sturt, *The Wheelwright's Shop* (Cambridge, 1923); G.E. Evans, *Ask the Fellows who cut the hay* (1956); G.E. Evans, *Where Beards Wag All* (1970); G.E. Evans, *The days that we have seen* (1975); P. Jennings, *The living village* (1968); R. Blythe, *Akenfield* (1969); R. Page, *The Decline of an English Village* (1974); R. Samuel (ed), *Village Life and Labour* (1975); G. Robinson, *Hedingham Harvest* (1977).

Sources and Methods

W. Bonser, *Bibliography of Folklore* (2 vols, 1961, 1969); C. Phythian-Adams, *Local history and folklore: a new framework* (1975); W.F. Grimes (ed), *Aspects of Archaeology in Britain and Beyond* (1951), chapter 5; V. Eaton, 'The Festival Calendar', *LH*, **1**, 182–4; L. Dopson, 'Old People as sources of history', *LH*, **3**, 150–2; W.R. Iley, 'The Village memory', *LH*, **9**, 300–3; M. Pollard, 'Oral Tradition and local history', *LH*, **9**, 343–7; V.J.M. Bryant, 'Talking to Octogenarians', *LH*, **10**, 183–5; H. Newby, 'The dangers of reminiscence', *LH*, **10**, 334–9; D.M. Owen, 'The use of ecclesiastical records for secular subjects', *LH*, **5**, 44–50; W. Matthews, *British Diaries, 1442–1942* (Los Angeles (U.S.A.), 1950); J.S. Batts, *British Manuscript Diaries of the Nineteenth Century* (Arundel, 1976); J.D. Marshall, 'The analysis of diaries', *LH*, **9**, 294–9; W. Matthews, *British Autobiographies* (Los Angeles (U.S.A.), 1955); J.G. Muddiman, *Tercentenary handlist of English and Welsh newspapers* (1920); R.S. Crane, F.B. Kaye, *A Census of British newspapers, 1620–1800* (Chapel Hill (U.S.A.), 1927); R.T. Milford, D.M. Sutherland, *Catalogue of English Newspapers and Periodicals in the Bodleian Library, 1622–1800* (Oxford, 1936); G.A. Cranfield, R.M. Wiles, *A Hand-List of English Provincial Newspapers, and Periodicals, 1700–1760* (1961); K.K. Weed, B.P. Bond, *Studies of British newspapers and periodicals from their beginning to 1880: a bibliography* (Chapel Hill (U.S.A.), 1946); *Mitchell's Newspaper Press Directory* (1846 to date); *Willing's Press Guide and Advertisers' Directory* (1890 to date); R. Harrison, G. Woolven, R. Duncan (ed), *The Warwick Guide to British Labour Periodicals, 1790–1970* (Hassocks, 1977); G.R. Mellor, 'History from newspapers', *LH*, **2**, 97–101; K.A. MacMahon, 'Local history and the newspaper', *LH*, **5**, 212–7; P. Lucas, 'Sources for urban history 9: local newspapers', *LH*, **11**, 321–6.

Local Sources and Studies

K. Palmer, *Oral Folk Tales of Wessex* (Newton Abbot, 1973); R. Atthill, *Old Mendip* (Newton Abbot, 1964); E.S. Hartland, *County Folklore of Gloucestershire, Folklore Society Publications*, **37**; J.B. Partridge, 'Cotswold place lore and customs', *Folklore*, **23**, 332–42, 443–57; J.F. Nicholls, 'Bristol local customs', *Folklore Record*, **31**, 133–4; D.A.N. Todd, 'Mummers' Plays... from Bisley, Dursley, Gloucester, Minchinhampton, Wickwar, Gloucestershire', *Folklore*, **46**, 361–74; K.M. Briggs, *The Folklore of the Cotswolds* (1975); I. Waters, *Folklore and Dialect of the Lower Wye Valley* (Chepstow, 1973); R. Whittock, *Folklore of Wiltshire* (1976); W.H. Ashby, 'Somerset witch tales', *Folklore Journal*, **5**, 161–2; M.A. Hardy, 'The evil eye in Somerset', *Folklore*, **24**, 382–3; E. Vivian, F. Mathews, 'The Folklore of Somerset', *Folklore*, **31**, 239–49; J.P.E. Falconer, 'A medieval talisman from Swainswick, Bath', *Folklore*, **53**, 165–6; I. Gatty, 'Christmas Play at Keynsham, Somerset', *Folklore*, **56**, 246–8; R.L. Tongue, 'Traces of fairy hounds in Somerset', *Folklore*, **67**, 233–4; R.L. Tongue, K.M. Briggs, *Somerset Folklore, Folklore Society Publications*, **114**; K. Palmer, *Folklore of Somerset* (1976); C. Sharp, C.L. Marson, *English folksongs from Somerset* (Taunton, 5 vols, 1904–19); M.F.

Stieg (ed), *The diary of John Harrington, M.P., 1646–53, SRS,* **74**; E. Hobhouse (ed), *The diary of a West Country physician. 1684–1726* (1934); E.A. Fry (ed), 'The autobiography of the Rev. Elias Rebotier, Rector of Axbridge', *SA,* **40**, 91–112; H. Coombs, A.N. Bax (ed), *Journal of a Somerset rector. . . parochial affairs of the parish of Camerton, 1822–1832* (1930); B. Tillett, *Memories and Reflections* (1931); A.H. Parsons, 'My life in Bromley Colliery, 1917–22', *BIAS,* **3**, 26–7; B.M. Wilmott-Dobbie (ed), *Village Life, 1883–1940: Batheaston remembers* (Batheaston, 1976); W.H. Potter, *A Victorian boy looks back at Bristol* (Bristol, 1960); M.E. Boole, *At the foot of the Cotswolds* [Wickwar] (1923); R.W. Harvey, *A Bristol Childhood* (Bristol, 1976); L. Lee, *Cider with Rosie* (1959); L. Lee, *I can't stay long* (1975); Gloucestershire Community Council, Local History Subcommittee, *I Remember* (Gloucester, 3 vols, 1965–77); R.W. Harvey, *A Bristol Childhood* (Bristol, 1976); I. Bild, C. Thomas (ed), *Bristol as we remember it* (Bristol, 1977); P. Dallimore, G. Rawlings (ed), *Up Knowle West* (Bristol, 1977); I. Bild (ed), *Looking Back on Bristol* (Bristol, 1978); Bristol Public Libraries, *Early Bristol Newspapers: a detailed catalogue. . . up to and including the year 1800* (Bristol, 1956).

Bibliography: II
Primary Sources

This section on manuscript and other primary sources covers only the major record offices, libraries and museums within or concerned with Avon: it does not include national repositories such as the Public Record Office (see *Guide to the Contents of the Public Record Office* (3 vols, 1963–8), the British Library (see T.C. Skeat, *The Catalogues of the Manuscript Collections in the British Museum* (2nd ed, 1962) for printed catalogues of the British Museum collection of MSS.), and the House of Lords Record Office (see M.F. Bond, *Guide to the Records of Parliament* (1971).) Avon historians should also be aware that some out-county record offices have substantial deposited collections relating to parts of the county area: it is hoped to cover these in future numbers of *Quest*. Details of out-county record offices are given in *Record Repositories in Great Britain* (5th ed, 1973). Some important collections of MSS. still remain in private hands, and personal approach must be made to the owners: some are listed in the *Reports* of the Historical Manuscripts Commission and the National Register of Archives, and the local record offices usually have copies of those reports relating to MSS. in their area. Access to such records is entirely at the discretion of the owners, and local historians have a duty to their successors not to antagonize the owners of MSS nor to disarrange the MSS more than absolutely necessary.

In all the libraries, record offices and other institutions whose holdings are listed in this section, more detailed catalogues of and indices to their holdings exist, which local historians should consult before beginning their researches, including small collections not mentioned below. Users of these repositories are also advised to write to the archivists, librarians or curators before their first visit, enclosing a stamped, addressed envelope for reply: this will save time for everyone concerned, and may avoid disappointment if records are only available given due notice, especially during evenings or on Saturday mornings. Users should also equip themselves with a knowledge of the form, content and handwriting of documents before their first visit: archivists are always willing to advise in cases of difficulty but cannot be expected to undertake detailed research in order to answer enquiries either by post or in person. Finally, users should note that most record offices insist on the use of pencils for taking notes.

AVON CENTRAL REFERENCE LIBRARY

Address: College Green, Bristol BS1 5TL

Telephone: Bristol (0272) 26121

Reference Librarian: G. Langley, B.A., F.L.A.

Facilities: Microfilm readers and photocopiers are available. A minimum 24 hours notice is required before manuscripts can be made available.

Opening hours: Monday–Friday, 9.30–8.00
Saturday, 9.30–5.00

Access: Adjacent car-parking facilities are at short-stay meters: the nearest long-stay car-park is in Canon's Marsh. Buses run from Temple Meads B.R. station to College Green.

Major Collections of MSS

C.T. Jefferies: Collection of MSS, etc., relating to the history of Bristol, including Bristol wills and pedigrees of local families (Vol. 11), and papers relating to the African slave trade (vol. 13) and to Somerset (vol. 15) (7945–62).

H.T. Ellacombe: Collection of MSS etc. relating to local history, mainly of the Bitton and Kingswood area, 1512–1896. (4414–30).

The Southwell Papers: Collection of many letters, papers and documents relating to the municipal and other affairs of the City of Bristol, 1665–1777, and to the affairs of the Hon. Edward Southwell. (11152–61).

Miscellaneous Historical MSS

Account of merchandise imported into Bristol 1774–1788 (21259).
William Adams, Chronicle of Bristol, 1623–1648 (25486).
Bristol Library Society, registers (of loans), 1773–1857. (7453–529).
Collections of miscellaneous documents relating to Lewin's Mead
    Unitarian Chapel, 1827–1909 (19535).
Journal of an intended voyage in the ship Black Prince from Bristol to
    the Gold Coast... commencing April 24, 1762 (4764).
James New, An account of the houses and inhabitants of the Parish of St.
    Philip and Jacob in... Bristol, 1781 (21769).
Christ Church, Poor-rate book, 1795 (22620).
St. Nicholas (with St. Leonard's) Church: Account of G.W. Braikenridge,
    Churchwarden, Easter 1811–Easter 1812 (18105); Records of
    assessments on the Parish of St. Nicholas, 1811–1812 (18098–104).
Isaac Cotterell, Classified list of all the merchants and tradesmen in
    Bristol in October 1768 (21353).
L.H. Dahl, Stapleton past and present (1920–1931) (20499–50).
Richard Smith, Bristol Theatre: a collection of playbills, MSS etc.,
    1672–1843 (7976–80).
Jacobs Wells Theatre account book, 1741–8 (11204).
Michael Edkins, Ledger book, 1761–1786 (20196).
Bristol College: Agreement, balance, letter books etc., *c.* 1830
    (11644–51).

Joseph Haskins: Rental accounts of the fee farm and other rents arising out of the Spring Garden Estate in the Parish of Temple, Bristol... 1738–1750 (4414).

Annals of Bristol and extracts from William Worcester's manuscript (copy of MS lately in possession of Alderman Page) N.d. (9075).

Annals of Bristol from AD 1232–1784, with a calendar of the Mayors, Sheriffs etc. of Bristol from AD 1216–1701 (16767).

[Other similar calendars and annals of Bristol are also held].

Minutes of meetings of the Society for the Reformation of Manners, held at the Mint, March 1699–April 1705 (10162).

MSS. etc. relating to the Bristol Institution, arranged by John Latimer, first half of 19th century (26065).

Merchant Taylors Society: Charter and ordinances of the Bristol Merchant Taylors 1597–1640 (4788); Officers 1671–1818 (4765–6); Roll of apprentices 1674–1754 (6529).

Regulations of the Bristol Company of Whitawers, Pointmakers etc., *temp.* Charles II (4768).

Wire-drawers and Pinmakers Company, Minute books, 1493–1797 (5029–30).

Kingswood Enclosure Commissioners, Minute book, 1779–1784 (13381).

Tolzey and Pie Poudre Courts, Actions 1700–1758 (6580–90).

Under-Sheriff of Bristol, Receipts, payments, letters etc., 1759–70 (5331–2).

'Milford' (Ship): Papers, 1761 (21257).

Robert Rankin, Tables of the probabilities, expectations and values of lives in the City of Bristol and parishes of Clifton, St. George, Kingswood, 1824 (6160).

'Sybil' and 'Success' (Ships): Accounts and papers, *c.* 1779–86 (21258).

Caleb Dickinson, Copy-book of his letters, 30 August 1757–27 September 1758 (19718).

Mercers and Linendrapers Company's book, containing copies of oaths, lists of masters and members, accounts etc., 1647–1728 (4939).

'Tryall' (Privateer): Ledger, 1757–60 (21256).

'Southwell' and 'Dreadnought' (Privateers). Papers, 1746, 1758 (4991).

Committee book containing the minutes and orders of the partners concerned in the copper trade... in the name of Joseph Percival and the Copper Company, 1762–9 (4771).

Copies, Transcripts Etc

E.G.C.F. Atchley, Calendar of the deeds at All Saints Church, Bristol. (23037).

Andrew Hooke [probable compiler], Biographical notes etc. on the bishops, deans and prebendaries of Bristol, *c.* 1740 (5009).

Walter Calvert, editor, Bristoliana: being a collection of anecdotes, legends, memoirs and witticisms of the celebrities who resided in Bristol, *c.* 1888 (21951).

MSS relating to the Abbots of St. Augustine's, Robert Fitzharding and his descendants and Bristol Cathedral, transcribed by Samuel Seyer and others (4835).

Miscellaneous extracts relating to the trade of Bristol in the reign of Queen Elizabeth, copies from the manuscript collections of Lord Burleigh (22832).

Henry Bush, Account of the municipal government and local institutions of Bristol, *c.* 1825 (4762) and State records relating to Bristol (4760).

Documents relating to the ecclesiastical history of Bristol, being official transcripts from the archives of the Vatican, 1823 (5019).

Catalogue of Bristol deeds 1293–1792 (4941).

St. George Adult School: General register 1903–4 (23133) and Minute books 1912–19, correspondence 1913–1918 (23132).

G.W. Braikenridge, Collections for Bristol: MS notes, extracts, illustrations towards forming a complete history of Bristol, 1326–1874. 30 vols in 36 (9966–10001).

BATH CITY RECORD OFFICE

Address: Guildhall, High Street, Bath, BA1 5AW.

City Archivist: R. Bryant, Esq.

Telephone: Bath (0225) 28411, ext. 201.

Office Hours: Monday–Friday: 8.30 a.m.–1.00 p.m., 2.00 p.m.–5.00 (4.30 p.m. Friday).

Access: The nearest car-park is small, in Walcot Street, but the Guildhall is within a few minutes walking distance of the larger car-park in Charlotte St., the bus station in Manvers St., and Bath Spa B.R. station. Follow signs for Bath Abbey, which is immediately south-west of the Guildhall.

City Records

Charters, 1189–1973; Commissions etc., 1275–1662; Deeds, 1218–1900; Council Minutes, 1631–1978; Hall Notice Books, 1776–1895; Chamberlains' accounts, 1568–1684 (printed to 1602 in *SRS*, **38**); Treasurers' accounts, ledgers and vouchers, 1685–1978; Town Clerks' Accounts, 1748–1840; Oaths and Admissions of Councillors, 1755–1834; Freemen's Rolls, 1712 to date; Freemen's Accounts, 1776–1880; Militia Orders, Papers and Lists (St. James), 1795–1830; Loyal and Volunteer Association records, 1792–7; Poll Books, 1832–57; Electoral Registers, 1832–1978; Voting papers, 1841–71; Parliamentary Election papers, 1796–1967; Bath Corporation Bills, electoral rolls, 1925, 1937; Apprentice Registers, 1697–1707, and Indentures, 1735–1885; Court of Record, 1706–1834; Court of Requests, 1785–8; Court Leet, 1801–69; Quarter Sessions: Sessions Books, 1683–1785; Quarter Sessions: Court Rolls, 1776–1971; Quarter Sessions: Court Papers, 1786–1835; Petty Sessions, 1851–69; Court of Summary Jurisdiction, 1875–1933; Assize of Bread, Beer and Wine. 1777–1811; Alehouse Recognizances, 1776–1814; Coroners' Inquests, 1776–1835;

Pauper Examinations, 1758–1825; Rate Books and Valuation Lists from 1766 (City parishes), 1775 (Walcot), 1777 (St. Michaels), 1779 (St. James), 1784 (Abbey), 1796 (Lyncombe and Widcombe), 1818 (Bathwick), 1821 (Twerton).

Minutes and other records of Council Committees: Bath Act, 1789–1832; Baths and Pump Room, 1774–1969; Borough Property, 1837–1971; Scudamore Charities, 1652–1835; Children's, 1947–1966; Civil Defence, 1935–60; Electric Lighting, 1888–1948; Electric Trams, 1899–1908; Finance, 1851–1974; Fire Brigade, 1891–1968; Gaol, 1857–78; Health, 1930–74; Housing of Working Classes, 1894–1968; Libraries, 1914–74, Markets, 1837–1960; Mental Health, 1872–6, 1941–62; Parks and Cemeteries, 1891–1973; Planning, 1926–64; Rating, 1926–67; Sanitary Committee, 1904–30; Surveying, 1851–1962; Waterworks, 1769–1968 (incl. Water Rentals, 1777–1926); Watch Committee, 1836–1966. (Many of the above series include subcommittee records.)

Bathwick Police records, 1835–51; Walcot Police records, 1766–1822.

Maps and Plans, 18th–20th centuries.

Bath Urban Sanitary Authority, 1872–1904.

Bath School Board: minutes, 1882–1974; papers, 1870–1974, log-books and visitors' report books for the following schools: Bathforum (1863–1926), Kingsmead (1942–3), Lyncombe (1954–63), Oak Street (1895–1946), St. Michaels (1865–1911), Weston (1863–1933), Weymouth House (1862–1949).

Bath Poor Law Union

Minutes, 1836–1930; Minutes of sub-committees, 1862–1923; Case Books, 1894–1927; Letter Books, 1863–1903; Guardians' Declarations and Attendance Book, 1894–1929; Bye-Laws, 1841–8; Accounts, 1849–68; Ledgers (General), 1836–1909; (Parochial), 1848–1910; Registers of Removals, 1845–63 (outside Union), 1878–85 (to Workhouse), 1903–18 (to other Institutions); Relief Order Books, 1886–1928; Returns, 1877–9, 1891–1905 (weekly), 1905–9 (fortnightly), 1907–14 (weekly); Report and Register Books, 1851–1915; Health Record Books, 1911–8; Vaccination Officers' Reports, 1871–1914; Miscellaneous papers, 1894–1900; Pauper Children boarded out: registers, 1869–1918; reports on homes, 1882–1923.

Deposited Records

(a) *Anglican parishes:*
Northstoke: registers, 1655–1975 (CMB)
Twerton: registers, 1682–1923(C), 1684–1942(M), 1538–1659, 1668–1895(B), 1825–1970 (Banns); confirmation lists, 1877–1938; select vestry minutes, 1819–1911; Parish Council minutes, 1894–1911; Overseers' minutes, 1896–1903; Sanitary Committee minutes, 1886–90; School Board minutes, 1884–1902; Terriers, 1840; Tithe accounts, 1829–80, 1890; Churchwardens' accounts, 1741–67, 1819–1905; Settlement and removal orders, certificates

and examinations, 1709–97; Apprenticeship Indentures, 1740–87 Weston: registers, 1538–1951 (CMB); Churchwardens' accounts, 1739–1836

(b) *Methodist Churches:*
Bath Circuit: accounts, 1792–1805; minutes, 1838–1962; baptismal register, 1839–62; school registers and records, 1817 to date; Baptismal registers, minutes, accounts, school records, correspondence etc. for the following churches: Batheaston (1878–1968), Box (1868–1971), Claremont (1935–54), Corston (1903–62), Freshford (1906–38), Hinton Charterhouse (1903–66), Inglesbatch (1879–1967), Kingsdown (1871–1966), Larkhall (1891–1971), Midford (1903–63), Milk Street (1876–1951), New King Street (1792–1950), Saltford (1865–1926), Twerton (1854–1949), Walcot (1815–1954), Westgate (1865–1971), Weston (1888–92).

(c) *Presbyterian Church:*
Trinity: minutes, registers, communicant rolls, 1920–73.

(d) *Private deposits:*
Bathwick Estate Company: deeds, 1780–1910; Royal Bath and West and Southern Counties Society: Minutes, 1777–1960; Correspondence, 1777–1960; Accounts, 1777–1805; Subcommittees' Minutes, 1777–1954 (The valuable library of the Society has now been transferred to the University of Bath Library.) Miscellaneous small collections.

BATH REFERENCE LIBRARY

Address:	18 Queen Square, Bath BS1 2HN
Telephone:	Bath (0225) 28144
Librarian:	Mrs. M. Joyce, Dip. Lib.
Access:	Queen Square is within walking distance of Bath Spa B.R. station and the Bus station in Manvers St. A large long-stay car-park is just round the corner in Charlotte St.
Opening hours:	Monday–Friday, 9.30–7.30; Saturday, 9.30–5.00.

Business Records

W. & F. Dawson, printers: specimens, *c.* 1853–*c.*1869.
J. Eveleigh: business accounts and records, 1788–1803.
Wallbridge Mills, Frome: dye pattern books of West Country woollen cloth, 1750–ca. 1850.
Stevens & Bailward: pattern books of West Country woollens, 1768–75; bill book, 1762–96.
Post Office: Walsingham MSS, 1784–92.

Catalogues
William Beckford, Lansdown Tower, 1845.
Charles Godwin, library, *c.* 1870.
Marshall's Library, subscribers, 1793–9.

Diaries
Daniel family of Bath, East Frome and Pennard, 1770–1923.
Anne H.J. Jones, 1837–40.
Major-General Richard O'Donovan, 1819–23.
John Stone, town clerk of Bath, 1838–99.
Emily Wood, 1877–8 (Bath to Australia and back).

Journals
John Curry, overseer of Walcot, 1811–31.
John Parish, 1807.
G.E.M. Singers-Bigger, 1925–6, and MSS relating to Sarah Grand.

Tours
Anon, Tour into several English counties, 1725.
T. Moy, Tour to Isle of Wight and the West of England, 1810.

Biographies
R. Jones (clerk of works to Ralph Allen), Autobiography, n.d.
C.W. Shickle, Revd. Joseph Glanvill, 1920.

Records of Bath societies
Church Institute, 1914–7; Church School Managers' Union, 1876–91;
Eclectic Society, 1828–34; Field Club, *c.* 1865–*c.*1900; Literary Club,
1862, 1902–39; Male Voice and Orpheus Glee Clubs, 1889–1929;
Philharmonic Society, 1885–90; Royal Literary and Philosophical
Society, 1875–1933; Royal Literary and Scientific Institution, 1825–7,
1932–59; Old Bath Preservation Society, 1909–39; Socratic Society,
1920–33; Southern Dispensary, 1849–1911; Theatre Royal, 1770–7,
1828.

Antiquarian Collections (Bath)
Many, of varying value, including MSS of or relating to Ralph Allen, T.S.
Cockerell, R.E.M. Peach, C.P. Russell, Rev. C.W. Shickle, Mrs. Sarah
Siddons, S. Sydenham and W. Tyte.

Antiquarian Collections and Historical MSS (North Somerset)
Survey of impropriate tithes of Chewton Mendip and Emborough, 1798;
collections of Revd. F.J. Poynton, particularly relating to Kelston;
correspondence and memoranda of Revd. John Skinner, rector of
Camerton.

BATH: VICTORIA ART GALLERY

Address: Bridge St, Bath BA2 4AT

Telephone: Bath (0225) 28144

Curator:	Miss J. Knight
Opening hours and Access:	As for Bath City Record Office
Holdings:	Large collection of local topographical prints and drawings, 18th–20th centuries, and a smaller collection of Bath coins, 10th–11th centuries, and trade tokens, 17th–19th centuries. Notice in advance is required for the use of both these collections.

BATH AND WELLS DIOCESAN BOARD OF FINANCE

Address:	Diocesan House, The Old Deanery, Wells, Somerset, BA5 2UG.
Telephone:	Wells (0749) 73308 or 73747
Office Hours:	Monday–Friday, 9.00–5.30.
Car-parking:	A small cark park is available in the Deanery Courtyard.
Chief Officer:	H. Parkes, Esq., Assistant Secretary.

Records

Diocesan Board of Finance, Minutes, 1912 to date;
Diocesan Dilapidations Board, Minutes, 1924 to date;
Diocesan Conference Reports, 1870–87; Minutes, 1898–1970;
Diocesan Synod, Minutes, 1970 to date;
Diocesan Board of Education, Minutes, 1838–1913;
Diocesan Church Building Society, Minutes, 1836–44, 1889–1913;
   Secretary's Day Book, 1837–42;
Diocesan Curates Fund Society, Minutes, 1854–76;
Diocesan Branch of the Clergy Pensions Institute, Minutes, 1894–1944;
Wells Archdeaconry Clerical Charity, Minutes, Correspondence and
   other records, 1738 to date (unsorted).

BRISTOL CITY MUSEUM AND ART GALLERY

Address:	Queens Road, Bristol BS8 1RL
Director:	N. Thomas, M.A., F.S.A., F.M.A.
Opening hours:	Monday–Saturday, 10–5 (except Bristol Industrial Museum: Saturday–Wednesday, 10–12, 1–5).

The collections are organised into several departments listed below. The reserve collections are normally accessible by appointment with the Curator of the appropriate department: Agricultural and Social History (ASH); Applied Art (AA); Archaeology and History (A & H); Fine Art (FA); Technology (Tech).
Schools intending to use the loan collections or material on Museum and Art Gallery premises should contact the Head of the Schools Department.

Buildings and displays

(a) City Museum and Art Gallery, a fine early 20th century building, houses the main reserve collections (AA, A & H, FA), and displays of local paintings and drawings, local ceramics and silver, local prehistoric and Roman archaeology and local maps. (Tel. No: 299771)

(b) Blaise Castle House, Henbury, an early 19th century house in a landscaped park, contains the reserve collections and displays of the Department of Agricultural and Social History (ASH). The park includes a 19th century watermill. (Tel. No: 625378)

(c) Red Lodge, Park Row, a 16th–18th century furnished house (AA) (Tel. No: 299771)

(d) Georgian House, Great George St., a late 18th century furnished house (AA) (Tel. No: 299771)

(e) St. Nicholas' Church and City Museum, St. Nicholas St., a 14th–18th century church housing displays of local church plate, topographical drawings and photographs and artifacts illustrating the development of Bristol *c.* 850–1550. Facsimiles of local brasses are available for rubbing (A & H). (Tel. No: 292412)

(f) Kings Weston Roman Villa, Long Cross, Lawrence Weston, and the Sea Mills Roman Site, Roman Way, Sea Mills, (both 3rd–4th centuries) excavated foundations and mosaics at the former (A & H)

(g) Thomas Chatterton's House (1748), the birthplace of the poet (ASH) (Tel. No: 23975)

(h) Bristol Industrial Museum, Prince's Wharf, a 1950s warehouse, houses displays of local transport and some machinery (Tech) (Tel. No: 299771)

Other archaeological sites are owned by the City, e.g. Blaise Castle and Clifton Down hillforts, Brandon Hill civil war defences, and the Castle Vaults.

Reserve Collections

(a) Artifacts

  (i) Provenanced local domestic (e.g. furnishings, toys), agricultural, costume, corporate (e.g. civic, insurance, Friendly Societies) and trades material (ASH)
  (ii) Provenanced local archaeological material (Palaeolithic to Post-Medieval) (A & H)
  (iii) Provenanced local industrial machinery and products, local transport (Tech)
  (iv) Locally made and used ceramics, glass, silver and furniture (AA)
  (v) Local numismatics including tokens, military and commemorative medals (A & H)
  (vi) Provenanced architectural details (A & H)
  (vii) An excellent collection of local topographical paintings and drawings (FA)
  (viii) Local militaria (ASH)
  (ix) Local Personalia (ASH)

N.B. Much of the rest of the collections may have strong local connections e.g. some of the ethnographic material.

(b) Printed Matter

  (i) Maps of Bristol and the surrounding area (A & H)
  (ii) Topographical prints (FA)
  (iii) Bristol trade cards, union certificates, etc. (ASH)

(c) Photographs

  (i) Bristol buildings, mostly in the city centre—both prints and black and white slides (A & H)
  (ii) Bristol shipping and other industries (Tech)
  (iii) Local postcards (ASH)
  (iv) Graveyard records of the Action Group for Bristol Archaeology (A & H)

(d) Manuscripts

  (i) Bristol sites and monuments index (A & H)
  (ii) Notes and other documents related to local excavations, and field and buildings surveys including Bristol Archaeological Research Group records and the AGBA (A & H)
  (iii) Documents relating to the collections of the Museum and Art Gallery and its predecessors

BRISTOL DIOCESAN HEADQUARTERS

Address: Church House, 23, Great George St., Bristol BS1 5QR.

Telephone: Bristol (0272) 292231

Archivist:	Miss P. Fulwood
Opening hours:	Monday–Friday, 9.00–5.00.
Access:	Great George St. is off Park St. Metered car-parking is available in the street. For long-stay car-parking and access from outside Bristol see under Bristol Record Office.

Holdings

Diocesan Board of Finance and subcommittees, minutes, 1920 to date; Church Trust Deeds.

BRISTOL RECORD OFFICE

Address:	The Council House, College Green, Bristol BS1 5TR
Telephone:	Bristol (0272) 26031, ext. 442
Search-room hours:	Monday–Thursday, 8.45–4.45; Friday, 8.45–4.15; Saturday, 9.00–12.00 (by appointment, notice to be given by noon on Friday)

Means of reference

A general *Guide to the Bristol Archives Office*, compiled by Elizabeth Ralph, was published by Bristol Corporation in 1971. Part I describes the official archives of the Corporation of the City and County of Bristol, ranging from charters and custumals, administration, financial and judicial records to transferred records of former statutory authorities such as the local board of health and school boards (The archives of the Incorporation of the Poor and its successor Board of Guardians were destroyed during World War II). Part II lists estate and family records, business and trade records, solicitors' collections, records of institutions and societies and antiquarian and composite collections.

Summaries of principal accessions since 1971 can be found in successive *Transactions of the Bristol and Gloucestershire Archaeological Society* published after that date. Other published guides are noted with the appropriate records listed below. Only significant new deposits are mentioned as work is currently in progress on a composite supplement which it is hoped will be available in typescript in 1978.

Access

The Record Office is situated in the Council House at the end nearest the Cathedral. Metered car-parks behind the Council House cater only for short-stay visitors: the nearest long-stay car park is at the New Bristol Centre in Frogmore Street. Buses from Temple Meads (B.R.) station run to College Green.

Facilities

The record office is equipped with a microfilm reader and the visitor may be directed to consult certain major series of Corporation records on microfilm. A limited number of microfilms from the Public Record Office are also available. (These do not include the 1841, 1851, 1861 and 1871 census returns for Bristol which are available at the Central Library adjacent to the Council House.) In addition, the office is equipped with a microfilm camera and a xerox photocopier, so that copies of documents can be supplied. Group visits can be accommodated, by prior arrangement. All postal enquiries should be addressed to the City Archivist.

The office's reference library includes the publications of the Bristol Record Society, the Bristol Branch of the Historical Association, the Bristol and Gloucestershire Archaeological Society and *Notes on Bristol History*, published by the University of Bristol Extra-Mural Department, which may be consulted, but priority is given to record users over those wishing solely to consult published sources which are available in the Avon Central Library.

Official Records

City and County of Bristol

Constabulary: registers of constables, occurrence books, minutes, reports, etc. 1836–1974.

Engineer's Department: minutes, accounts, register of shareholders, correspondence and plans of Ridgeway Park Cemetery Co. 1868–1968; plans of parks and recreation areas 1910–68.

Fire Brigade: log, record and occurrence books, and photographs 1900–74.

Health Department: reports 1875–1973.

Museum and Art Gallery: minutes, registers, letter books, accounts, papers and correspondence relating to Bristol Library Society, Bristol Institution for the Advancement of Science, Literature and the Arts, and Bristol Museum and Library 1643–1960.

Planning Department: plans of sewers, drains and houses submitted to the local authority for approval to construct 1851–1948.

Port of Bristol Authority: minutes, reports, letter books, registers of arrivals, departures, imports and exports 1791–1971.

Social Services Department: registers of births, baptisms, deaths and adopted children, and creed registers for Eastville Institution 1868–1952.

Public Records

Hospitals: case books, casualty books and maternity registers for Bristol Royal Infirmary 1836–1948.

Inland Revenue Valuation Office: field survey books and revaluation maps 1901–49.

Probate: *see* Anglican Diocese, below.

Registry of Shipping and Seamen: agreements and crew lists of ships registered at the port of Bristol 1863–1913.

Anglican Diocese

Details of diocesan, capitular and probate records deposited in the Bristol Record Office are given in *Diocese of Bristol: A Catalogue of the Records of the Bishop and Archdeacons and of the Dean and Chapter*, compiled by Isabel M. Kirby and published by Bristol Corporation in 1970. The diocesan registrar regularly transfers to the record office additional records in series.

Parish

The Bristol Record Office has been appointed the diocesan record office for parish records of the Archdeaconry of Bristol, while the Wiltshire Record Office is the diocesan record office for parish records of the Archdeaconry of Swindon in the county of Wiltshire. Records of the former archdeaconry are listed in *Guide to the Parish Records of the the City of Bristol and County of Gloucester*, by Irvine Gray and Elizabeth Ralph (Bristol and Gloucestershire Archaeological Society Records Section Publications, volume 5, 1963). Many more parish records than are indicated have since been deposited and an up-to-date list of parish registers deposited in the Bristol Record Office, with covering dates, can be purchased.

Catholic Diocese

Diocese of Clifton: confirmation registers 1857–1903.

Nonconformist

A survey of free church records in Bristol and Gloucestershire will be published in due course. Of the Bristol records, only those which have been deposited are listed, the following denominations being represented: Baptist, Congregational, Methodist, Prebyterian and Society of Friends.

Unofficial Records

Family and Estate

Butcher MSS.: deeds, papers and correspondence of the Butcher family, including papers of Alderman Edmund Butcher, M.D., relating to the Bristol Riots, 1676–1954.

Cann MSS.: correspondence, papers and photographs of Alderman Percy W. Cann, former Lord Mayor of Bristol, 1895–1972.

Gibbons MSS.: correspondence and other papers of John King, surgeon, Maria Edgeworth, novelist, Thomas Haynes Bayly, dramatist and lyricist, and Gibbons family 1790–1941.

Hunt MSS.: deeds and papers of William Hunt of Northcote House, Westbury on Trym, 1650–1950.

Business and Trade

Bankers: minutes, correspondence, etc. of Miles Bank 1832–1913.

Brewers: Courage (Western) Ltd.: minutes, accounts, registers, etc. of

Bristol Brewery, Georges & Co. Ltd., Bristol United Breweries Ltd., and other constituent breweries 1803–1962.

Chocolate Manufacturers: catalogues of machinery and related correspondence sent to H.J. Packer & Co. Ltd. 1907–63.

Insurance: Norwich Union Insurance Society: insurance plans of Bristol, Bath and Gloucester by Charles E. Goad, civil engineers, from 1887 with revisions to *c.* 1970.

Merchants: ledgers, papers, plans and photographs of Poole Bros. & Galbraith, sand, gravel and coal merchants, 1845–1966.

Ropemakers: ledgers, deeds, correspondence, etc. of Joseph Bryant Ltd., including Stephen Bros. & Martin Ltd., 1764–1974.

Surveyors: maps, surveys, sale particulars, land steward's reports, accounts and deeds of J.P. Sturge & Sons 1672–1889.

Transport Industry: minutes, accounts, registers, etc. of Western Wagon Co. Ltd. 19th-20th centuries.

Solicitors' Collections

Meade-King & Co.: minutes, accounts, register of boys and inmates, etc. of Stokes Croft Educational Foundation & Almshouses 1722–1933.

Institutions and Societies

Bristol Friends of Humanity Society of Coopers: minutes, accounts, roll call books and miscellaneous papers 1832–1971.

Bristol Municipal Charity Trustees: minutes, leases, ledgers, journals, cash books, rentals, surveys and plans relating to Trinity Hospital, Foster's Almshouse, Queen Elizabeth's Hospital, Dr. Thomas White's Charities including Temple Hospital, Alderman John Whitson's Charities including Red Maids' School, Alderman John Merlott's charity and Alderman Henry Bengough's charity 1512–1906.

Bristol Teachers' Association: minutes, yearbooks, etc. 1871–1959.

Clifton Club: minutes, accounts and registers 1818–1967.

Colston Hall Sunday Evening Services for the People: minutes, accounts and programmes 1892–1942.

Friends' First Day Schools: minutes, reports, accounts, etc. 1810–1963.

Lady Haberfield's Almshouse Trust: minutes, accounts, deeds, etc. 1880–1950.

National Union of Sheet Metal Workers, Coppersmiths, Heating and Domestic Engineers: minutes and papers 1872–1972.

Rapier Players: minutes, accounts, licences, correspondence, programmes and production photographs 1924–72.

BRISTOL UNIVERSITY LIBRARY, SPECIAL COLLECTIONS

Address: University Library, Tyndall Avenue, Bristol BS8 1TJ

Telephone: Bristol (0272) 24161

Senior Assistant Librarian:	G. Maby, Esq.
Opening hours:	Monday–Friday, 9.00–5.00
Access:	Buses run from Temple Meads B.R. station and the Bus Station to the Bristol Royal Infirmarary (walk up St. Michael's Hill), Park Row (walk up Woodland Rd) and Queen's Rd (walk up University Rd). On-street car-parking is restricted in the University precinct: the nearest long-stay car-park is in Park Row.

Major Local History Collections

Brunel MSS: letter-books, sketch-books, calculations, accounts and diaries of I.K. and H.M. Brunel, 1830–66. Clifton Suspension Bridge Trustees: minute-books, letter-books, cash books, share registers, annual reports, working plans, drawings and views, 1798–1953. Pinney MSS: accounts, family and estate papers, correspondence, 1650–1948 (mostly Dorset and West Indies, but some Bristol items). Paget MSS: accounts, correspondence, etc., 1611–1911 (mostly Somerset, but including Kilmersdon now in Avon). Bristol Moravian Church: archives, 1760–1893. Somerset Miners' Association: minutes, accounts and correspondence on mining accidents, compensation, industrial diseases, politics and welfare, 1868–1964. Napier-Miles of Kingsweston MSS: correspondence (mostly musical) and some family papers, 1884–1935, Symonds of Clifton Hill MSS: correspondence and family papers, 1844–1946. University (-College) Archives: archives, 1876–1978 (many items still held by Registrar and Secretary's departments). In addition there are numerous small collections and individual items.

GLOUCESTERSHIRE RECORD OFFICE

Address:	Worcester Street, Gloucester GL1 3FW
Chief Officer:	Brian S. Smith, M.A., F.S.A., County Archivist
Search Rooms:	Worcester Street Monday–Friday, 9.00–5.00, also Thursday, 5.00–8.00. Saturdays by appointment only (from Spring, 1979).
	Shire Hall, Westgate Street, Gloucester (for official archives only, see pp. 158–60) Monday–Friday, 9.30–1.00, 2.00–4.30.
Telephone:	Main Search Room: ⎱ Gloucester (0452) Shire Hall Search Room: ⎰ 21444

Location: The Record Office is situated in Worcester Street
about 10 minutes walk from the railway and bus
stations. Worcester Street branches off from
Northgate Street and the Record Office entrance is
just past the railway bridge. Limited car parking
space is available at the Record Office.

Services and facilities

Anyone interested in local history may consult the records and no fees
are charged by the Record Office for historical research. It is helpful to
write or telephone before making a visit.

The Record Office will move in 1979 to Worcester Street, where all
records are available except official archives from mid or late 19th
century. The latter comprise County Council, District Council and
Quarter and Petty Sessions records, as well as the records of 19th century
boards, including Guardians, Highway and School Boards. At Worcester
Street and Search Room contains an extensive local history library and an
archivist is always on duty.

The list of records given below is only a short list of those relating to the
area of Avon which was formerly in Gloucestershire.

All postal enquiries should be addressed to the County Archivist. The
record office has photocopying and microfilm equipment and access to
photostat and plan-printing cameras, so that copies can be made for
students. There are also microfilm readers and a microfiche reader for
public use.

Official

County Quarter Sessions

Gloucestershire Quarter Sessions Archives, 1660–1889 by I.E. Gray and
A.T. Gaydon (Glos. County Cpuncil, 1958) is still available from G.R.O.

The records include court order books, highway and footpath
diversion orders, records of houses of correction (including Lawford's
Gate), land tax assessments, registers of electors, deposited plans of
public under-takings (roads, railways, harbours), and inclosure awards.
The guide gives brief details of each class of record and more detailed
lists are available in the Record Office.

County Council

Some official records of the Gloucestershire County Council,
1889–1974, are deposited in G.R.O. They include the minutes and
accounts of the council and its committees, and departmental records
such as schools records. The latter include the records of Bitton and
Kingswood and Oldland School Boards, minutes of school managers for
Bitton, Dyrham and Hinton, Oldland, Siston and Yate, and log books
and admission registers of various individual schools.

District Authorities

Records of pre-1974 district authorities include those of Kingswood U.D.C. and some of Mangotsfield U.D.C., Thornbury R.D.C., and Warmley R.D.C. The records of Kingswood U.D.C. comprise minutes of the Local Board of Health, 1890–94, and of the U.D.C., 1894–1944, general ledgers, 1920–1959, and rate books from 1914.

Boroughs

Charters, deeds, borough, charity and poor law records survive for Chipping Sodbury and Thornbury *c.* 1230–1938.

Petty Sessions

Petty Sessions records survive for the following courts: Lawford's Gate, 1818–1962, Thornbury, 1880–1966, and Chipping Sodbury, 1905–1963.

Poor Law Unions

Minutes and ledgers of the Boards of Guardians survive for the following Unions: Chipping Sodbury, 1836–1947, Thornbury, 1836–1936, and Warmley, 1897–1931.

Coroners

The records of the South Gloucestershire coroner deposited in G.R.O. are not yet open to the public. An account book for inquests held by William Joyner of Berkeley, coroner for the county of Glos., 1790–1823, gives details of inquests in the south of the county (D260).

Diocese

A catalogue of the records of the bishop and archdeacons: records of the diocese of Gloucester, vol. 1., was compiled by I.M. Kirby (Gloucester Corporation, 1968). The records include the bishop's 'act books' dealing with administration of the diocese, papers of the consistory court, clergy presentments, faculties for church building, glebe terriers, marriage licence allegations, tithe maps and bishop's transcripts of parish registers. More detailed lists of some of the records are available in the Record Office.

Some parishes in the Bristol area were affected by diocesan boundary changes in the 19th century; for details see Kirby.

Parish

The *Guide to the parish records of Bristol and Gloucester*, by I. Gray and E. Ralph (*BGRS*, 1, published in 1963) lists all parish records, many of which were or have since been deposited in B.R.O. or G.R.O.

Nonconformist

A 'survey of Free Church records' (not yet published) includes lists of records of churches and chapels now in Avon, many of which are still kept by the churches.

Courts of Sewers (D272, D392)

Minutes, 1543–1848, accounts, surveys, maps, court papers, legal and other papers of the Commissioners of Sewers for the Upper and Lower Levels of Gloucestershire [land drainage of Severn Vale], 17th—19th centuries; and of the Commissioners of Sewers for the Ladden Brook Valley, 1862–1903, and of the South Gloucestershire Drainage Board, 1886–1940.

Severn River Authority (D2785)

Severn River Authority reports, files, press-cuttings and glass negatives of sites *c.* 1910–56, some out-county but chiefly relating to land drainage, coastal defence and fishing rights below Tewkesbury. Includes Severn Barrage Committee reports 1933, 1945; contracts *c.* 1930–65; annual reports 1951–60.

Bristol Avon River Authority (D2882)

Ladden Brook Commission of Sewers and Yate Internal Drainage Board, minutes 1863–1973, accounts 1863–1959, rate books 1943–63, correspondence, maps and papers, *c.* 1863–1912.

Family and Estate

Beaufort of Badminton (D2700, D3022)

Deeds of Badminton estates, 1743–95, Bristol, 1610; copy journal of Henry 3rd Duke of Beaufort, 1728; personal account book of Charlotte Sophia, Duchess of Beaufort, 1809–1827.
N.B. The family and estate papers have just been transferred to the G.R.O. but are not available until catalogued.

Blathwayt of Dyrham (D1799, D2659)

Manorial records of Dyrham and Hinton, 1571–1868; deeds of Dyrham and Hinton, including manor of Dyrham and Dyrham Park [1375], 1511, 1570–1846; deeds of Hawkesbury, Thornbury, Sodbury, Tormarton, 1642–1860, Bristol and Barton Regis, 1543–1703, 1847, Bath, 1732–1851, Lansdown and Weston, 1573–1742, Langridge, 1566–1767, 1844–1910; maps of Dryham and Hinton, *c.* 1715–*c.* 1850, of Bristol, *c.* 1830–47, of Langridge and Weston, 1846.
Estate surveys and valuations, 1704–1892; rentals, 1735–1855; leases of Dyrham and Hinton, 1577–1871; leases of Bristol, Bath, Langridge and Weston, 1579–1891; estate accounts, vouchers and correspondence, 1592–1935, including building of Dyrham Park, 1692–1706; architec-

tural drawings of Dyrham Park, *c.* 1700–1800; household inventories, 1601–1940; household and domestic vouchers, 1659–1907.

Papers and correspondence of Wm. Blathwayt, Secretary at War, 1668–1717 (diplomatic correspondence, *c.* 1656–1717, in British Museum); diaries and journals, 1703–1936.

Chester-Master of Almondsbury (D674)

Barton Regis hundred court rolls, 1606–1830; manorial records of Almondsbury, 1340, 1452–1690, of Hempton (Almondsbury) and Northwick (Henbury) 1466, 1677–1828, of Barton Regis, 1553–1751, and of Brimsham (Yate) 1384–1464, 1540–1682; deeds and leases of Almondsbury, Bristol: St. Philip and St. Jacob, Bristol: St. George, Henbury, Olveston, Winterbourne, Yate, 1254–1884.

Accounts of St. Augustine's Abbey, Bristol, 1491–1507; rent roll of estates of Philip Grene and John Kemys in Bristol, 1498/9; survey of Almondsbury and Olveston, 1811; maps of Almondsbury 1842–71.

Legal papers relating to Kingswood Forest, 1598–1661, and to Almondsbury tithes, *c.* 1756–1807; leases and papers relating to coalmines at Bristol: St. George and Kingswood, 1764–1875.

Codrington of Dodington (D1610)

Deeds of Dodington, 1587–1861, Marshfield, 1574–1827, Sodbury, 1602–1919, and Wapley and Codrington, 1618–1921; estate rentals, 1800–1847, 1873–1920; estate accounts, 1757–1849, 1879–1946; plans of estate in Dodington, Marshfield, Old Sodbury, Wapley and Codrington, 1744–1820; family settlements and correspondence, 1721–1927; household accounts, 1823–1850.

Estate, legal and financial correspondence, 1793–1938; personal and family correspondence, 1793–1914.

Political papers relating to election of members of Codrington family as M.P.s for Tewkesbury, 1761–1864; correspondence of Sir Gerald Codrington, as chairman of Thornbury Division Conservative Association, 1886–1924; accounts and registers of Royal Gloucestershire Hussars Yeomanry Cavalry, Dodington and Marshfield Troop, 1830–96.

Codrington of Dodington (D3059)

Settlement and trust papers relating to William John Codrington and family (a junior branch of the main Codrington of Dodington family), 1802–1898, referring in part to property in Gloucestershire but chiefly to securities.

Ducie of Tortworth (D340)

Manor court rolls of Tortworth, 1370–73, 1389–1482, 1508/9, 1667, 1680, and of Wickwar 1533, 1638–1642, 1646–1667; deeds and leases of Charfield, Cromhall, Tortworth and Wickwar, *c.* 1596–1875.

Estate records, 1587–1844, 1885–8, including accounts, 1848–1863;

maps of the manors of Cromhall Abbotts, 1760, Tortworth, 1760, and Wickwar, 1759; other estate plans, 1823–1839.

Ducie, Moreton and Reynolds family correspondence, 1626–1820, including correspondence of Reynolds family relating to Naval matters, 1704–1804.

Hale of Alderley (D1086)

Manor of Tresham and Saddlewood in Hawkesbury, draft court rolls, 1652–4, survey, 1786; deeds of Hawkesbury (including Hillesley, Kilcot and Tresham), Henbury, Oldbury-on-Severn, Rangeworthy, Wickwar and Yate, 13th–19th cent.

Estate rentals and accounts, 1733–1858; leases, 1544–1873; maps of Hawkesbury, 1767–1883; family settlements, Hale and related families, 1674–1865; other family papers, including correspondence, 1599–1887, and diaries, 1740–1855.

Business (legal, banking and merchant) papers of Hale and related families, 1697–1800; official papers of Sir Matthew Hale, 1640–76.

Howard of Thornbury (D108)

Honour of Gloucester court books and papers (Thornbury area), 1639–1851; hundred of Thornbury court books, 1612–1852; manor of Thornbury, court rolls, 1352–1458, 1580/1, 1612, court books, 1671–1908 and other records, 1671–1934; manor of Oldland (in Bitton) court papers, 1759–1903; manor of Mars (in Falfield) court roll, 1461–79.

Leases and estate papers, 1646–1907; maps of manor of Oldland (Bitton) 1766 and 1845, of manor of Thornbury, 1830.

Jenner-Fust of Hill (D908)

Manor of Hill court rolls, 1355–1761; deeds *c.* 1230–1905; map, 1659; Hill Court estate papers, 1868–1931.

Newton of Bitton (D1844)

Correspondence, estate and legal papers of the Newton family of Barrs Court, Bitton, 1626–1761, including papers relating to coal-mining at Bitton and Kingswood, legal documents relating to Kingswood Chase, and a large number of letters to Sir John Newton, 1660–1694, about estate business in Bitton and Lincolnshire.

Since the Newton family also has estates in Lincolnshire, some papers are deposited in Lincs. R.O., and these refer to the Bitton estate as well.

Osborne and MacLaine (D3330)

Correspondence and estate papers of Osborne and MacLaine families, 17th–19th cent., including deeds of Almondsbury, Bristol, Henbury, Oldbury, Olveston and Thornbury; family papers of Osborne, MacLaine and related families (Tayer, Lampney, Tyler and others).

Thurston of Thornbury (D866)

Deeds of Thornbury, 1587–1851; estate accounts, 1706–1894; family correspondence and other papers, 18th–19th cent.; Thornbury school records, 1634–1879.

Solicitors

Goldingham and Jotcham, Wotton-under-Edge (D654, D2830)

Deeds and family papers, including those of Arnold of Chipping Sodbury, Manning of Cromhall and others; deeds relate to Charfield, Cromhall, Falfield, Fishponds, Hawkesbury, Oldbury-on-Severn, Rockhampton, Thornbury and Yate, 16th–20th cent.

Wells, Hodsman, Crossman & Co., Thornbury (D1606, D1628)

Deeds and papers of Lloyd family of Thornbury, 1713–1880, and related families, including Harford of Bristol.

Office papers, including family and testamentary papers of clients, and deeds, 1522–1916. Clients include MacLaine of Thornbury, Fisher of Olveston and Collins of Thornbury.

Office letter books, accounts including J.M. Baxter of Alveston, solicitor, and rentals, 1822–67; inclosure accounts and papers, Almondsbury, 1795–1816, and Frampton Cotterell, 1824–31; Thornbury Grammer School accounts, 1870–1908; parliamentary election papers, 1874–1886; maps of Alveston, 1840, and Thornbury, 19th cent.

NAILSEA BRANCH LIBRARY

Address:	Somerset Square, Nailsea, Bristol, BS19 2EX.
Telephone:	Nailsea (02755) 4583
Librarian:	Miss A.J. Atkinson
Opening Hours:	Tuesday, Friday, 10–1.30, 2.30–8.00. Wednesday, Thursday 10–1.30, 2.30–5.00. Saturday 9.30–1.30, 2.30–5.00

Holdings

(a) *Nailsea Parish Council records:*

Churchwardens': accounts and rate-books, 1714–1905, and bills and vouchers, 1793–1830. Vestry Minutes, 1762–1861. Surveyors of Highways accounts, 1843–55. Overseers of the Poor: Rate-books and assessments, 1837–1927; Account-books, 1679–1819, 1896–1927; Bills and vouchers, 1799–1812, 1911–18. Settlement examinations, 1758–1832. Removal Orders, 1761–1841. Bastardy examinations and orders, 1763–1835. Pauper examinations, 1798, 1816. Apprentice Indentures, 1783–1834. Lists of paupers, 1955, 1891–1914. Militia Orders, 1799–1816. Parish Council Minutes etc., 1895–1961. Parish Council Accounts, bills and vouchers etc., 1895–1964. Parish Council Correspondence,

1889–1962. Nailsea Area Town map, 1957, and plans, 1949–64. Allotment registers etc., 1895–1966. Playing Fields Committee Minutes etc., 1945–62. Registers of electors and jurors, 1910–4, 1955–6. Nailsea School Accounts, 1912–35.

(b) *Miscellaneous MSS.:*

Durbin family papers, 1879–82. Boulton family and business papers, 1936–60. Nailsea Enclosure Award, 1818.

(c) Ordnance Survey 6″ and 25″ local sheets, 1902–49.

(d) Transcripts and photostats of Nailsea parish registers, Tithe Map and Award, 1851 Census, and Churchwardens' Accounts, 1714–95.

(e) Copies of theses and other works relating to the Nailsea area.

SOMERSET RECORD OFFICE

Address:	Somerset Record Office, Obridge Road, Taunton, TA2 7PU, Somerset.
Telephone:	Taunton (0823) 87600
Chief Officer:	County Archivist (address impersonally)
Hours of opening:	Monday–Thursday: 9.00 a.m.–12.45 p.m., 1.45 p.m.–4.50 pm. (Friday to 4.20 p.m.) Saturday: 9.15 a.m.–12.15 p.m. (by appointment).
Office hours:	Monday–Thursday: 8.30 a.m.–12.45 p.m., 1.45 p.m.–5.00 p.m., (Friday to 4.30 p.m.) Saturday 9.00 a.m.–12.30 p.m.
Location (from Avon) (by car):	A38 (or M5 to Junction 24) or A361, which joins A38 at Walford Cross, towards Taunton. Follow A361 right after ½ mile (signposted Barnstaple) and in 2 miles enter Taunton. Obridge Road is second left after 30' sign and is currently (1978) marked 'Obridge Link'. The record office is the first building on right-hand side and has a lay-by (5 cars) in the centre front. The area is a residential one and there are no restrictions, other than those suggested by natural courtesies, on parking in the road immediately opposite.

(by rail):   The record office is less than ½ mile (7–8 minutes walk) from the station by way of Priorswood Road. Obridge Road is both first and second (but take second) turning on the right after the Gardeners' Arms and is signposted 'Obridge Link' as above. The station is on the bus route between town centre and office (see next entry)

(by bus):   There is a regular town service from the centre of Taunton (the Parade), distance 1¼ miles; bus numbers 274, 275, 276 (Dorchester Road). Stop is Lyngford Road, which is opposite Obridge Road. For station bus stop turn left out of entrance and left again at main road and cross road to far side of railway bridge.

Means of reference

The record office has not published a general *Guide* to its holdings, but an up-to-date summary of Main Manuscript Accessions for the previous twelve months has appeared in the *Proceedings* of the Somerset Archaeological Society since 1960. Offprints of these lists will be found in the main libraries in the Bath, Wansdyke and Woodspring District Councils. Any sectional publications of relevance (whether still in print or not) are noted in the appropriate entries in the section relating to Record Holdings below.

More detailed information on individual collections of documents can be found in the various typescript calendars, catalogues and lists available in the search room and access to these can be pinpointed by way of the office's indexes. Two members of staff (one being a professional archivist) are permanently on duty in the search room to supervise the use of records, to assist users and to guide them to less obvious sources.

In the lists of holdings below only substantial deposits have been noted, but it may be safely assumed that all parishes in the county will be represented in the office's indexes to a greater or lesser extent. The amount of material, however, may vary from parish to parish by force of external circumstances.

Users of the office

Individual visitors who have not attended previously are advised to write in advance to introduce themselves to the County Archivist and to explain the subject of their interest. This serves not only to establish their *bona fides*, but also to enable appropriate records to be produced in readiness or to save a wasted journey if material is non-existent or insufficient.

The record office has a second search room which can accommodate group visits (from schools, local societies, etc.), but prior arrangements must be made in all such cases.

Postal enquiries about records available are answered, but extended research cannot be undertaken, although every effort will be made to answer reasonable specific questions.

Ancillary facilities
The record office has two microfilm readers and an ultra violet lamp, which can be made available to users by direction of the search room staff. It also possesses a photocopying machine, from which copies can usually be supplied on the spot.

The contents of the office's reference library were summarised in volume 104 of the *Proceedings* of the Somerset Archaeological Society and this general description still holds good. Its main feature is its extensive holding of printed calendars of public record publications.

Record Holdings
Official

County Council
The record office holds minutes of and reports to Council, minutes of some Committees and many departmental records. Its holdings of records from the Education Department include log books, admission registers and (less frequently) managers' minutes for schools (now closed) in the county, dating from 1863, and returns relating to staff, buildings, curricula, etc., for all schools in the county area taken over under the 1902 Education Act.

The County Nursing Officer deposited minutes and annual reports of the County Nursing Association, 1902–1957, and minutes for Banwell, Locking and Christon, Congresbury, Hewish and Puxton, Long Ashton, Midsomer Norton, Peasedown St. John, Weston-super-Mare and Winscombe District Nursing Associations, from 1908.

District Councils
Clevedon rate books, 1853–1951.

Poor Law Unions
Records for 17 of the former 18 Unions created within the county in 1836 are represented in the office's holdings, the exception being the records of the Bath Union [for which see Bath City Record Office]. A general scheme of classification has been applied to the whole series and this is described in the introduction to the published *Handlist of Records of the Boards of Guardians* (1949). This *Handlist* is now out of print, but should be available for reference in major libraries.

Avon parishes are to be found in parts or the whole of the Axbridge, Bedminster and Long Ashton, Clutton and Keynsham Unions. The main class of record—minutes of the Board—survive from the creation of the respective Unions to 1930 in the case of the three last named Unions, but those for Axbridge date only from 1859.

After the abolition of the Unions in 1930 and the transfer of functions to the County Council, the Area Guardians Committee created by amalgamation of former Unions continued to produce comparable records to 1948, when the operation of the old poor law finally ceased. Records of Keynsham and Clutton Institution will be found under the Frome Area Guardians Committee, while Weston-super-Mare gave its name to another Area Committee which covered the Somerset seaboard from Burnham northwards.

Turnpike Trusts

The record office holds a set of 1″ O.S. maps on which all turnpike roads in Somerset have been plotted. An accompanying (typescript) survey gives details, by Trusts, of legislation, lengths of road controlled as defined in the various Acts and notes of relevant deposited plans. The survey also contains a catalogue of the records held for eleven trusts in the country, including the Bath Trust, for which there are minutes or draft minutes, 1757–1878, maps, 1787, 1827, and general papers, reports, etc., 1809–1880.

Highway Boards

These were established under the 1862 Highways Act, whereby individual parishes lost the administration of their own highways, and ceased to exist after the Local Government Act, 1894. Minutes and ledgers are held for the Clutton, Keynsham and Long Ashton Boards, generally from 1863.

Somerset River Authority

Records of pre-1930 drainage and navigation bodies inherited by the Authority, including the Northern (Wrington) Division, 1761–1934, the Yatton, Banwell, North Weston and Worle and Kewstoke juries of sewers, 1774–1937, and the Avon, Brue and Parrett Fishery, 1866–1950.

Public records held by appointment under Public Records Act, 1958

Quarter Sessions. The first county record office was established by the Justices of the Peace in a building adjoining the Cathedral at Wells between 1616 and 1618, and not surprisingly the main groups of records now surviving date from the same period, although there are limited survivals from as early as 1537.

An *Interim Handlist of Somerset Quarter Sessions Documents* was published in 1947. This is now out of print, but should be available for reference in major libraries. A separate *Handlist of Somerset Enclosure Acts and Awards* was published in 1948 and is still obtainable from the Somerset Archaeological Society, The Castle, Taunton. The administrative orders from the surviving court order books for the reign of James I (covering 1607–25), Charles I (1625–39), for the Commonwealth (1646–56, supplemented by the sessions rolls, 1656–60) and for part of the reign of Charles II (1666–76) have been published by the Somerset Record Society in volumes 23, 24, 28 and 34 and the enrolled deeds of bargain and sale (1537-Commonwealth) similarly in volume 51.

Indexes by persons, places and subjects to the sessions rolls, 1607–1616, 1660–1726, and an (indexed) handlist of deposited plans of public undertakings (roads, canals, railways, etc.), 1791 onwards are available in the record office search room and highway diversions have been indexed onto the office's general topographical index.

Other categories of record accessible on a topographical basis are: jurors' lists (which also give occupations and occasionally in the 19th cent., ages), 1697, 1748–66, 1810–65, land tax assessments, 1766–67, 1782–1832, registers of electors, 1832–1973, alehouse recognizances (broken series), to 1828, and bridge papers, generally 19th cent.

Petty Sessions. The few divisions in the county which have transferred records include the Long Ashton Division for which court registers, 1859–1920, and registers of licences, 1874–1922, survive.

Coroners. Records of H.M. Coroner for the Northern Division, from 1926 (restricted access).

Probate. Estate Duty Office copy wills proved in courts in the diocese of Bath and Wells, 1812–1857 (arranged chronologically and subdivided in alphabetical blocks; indexed by personal names, but not places). The original probate records were largely lost in the bombing of Exeter in 1942; *see* J.S.W. Gibson, *Wills and where to find them* (1974) for survivals.

Collieries. The National Coal Board has transferred pre-nationalization records for former colliery undertakings. Under the thirty year rule these are now almost all available for study, with the exception of records involving compensation.

The records consist on the one hand of a large number of volumes (minutes, wages books, sales, etc., accounts) chiefly for the Bromley and Pensford Collieries, from c. 1900, but including more limited records for collieries in the Norton Radstock area from 1860, and on the other, deeds and leases including some relating to coal, for Camerton and Dunkerton, 1670–1929, and Timsbury, 1657–1899, and correspondence, agreements, plans, etc., relating to the Jarrett and Beauchamp families' mining interests in Camerton, Dunkerton and Wellow, 1840–1938.

The record office has also received additional mining records separately deposited by the Beauchamp family, including minutes of the Colliery Owners' Association and some records relating to wages, 1936–1946, correspondence, 1913–1946, and deeds and leases, 1712–1920 [many in poor condition].

Public Records Presented

Schools. Architects' plans of schools or extensions to schools submitted with applications for building grants to the central government, 1841–1902, including 40–50 schools in the Avon area of Somerset.

Diocese

The Lord Bishop has deposited the majority of the pre-1900 diocesan records, including surviving archdeaconry and Peculiar records, in the record office. Certain limited classes—notably the faculty deeds—required for current office purposes remain in the Diocesan Registry in Wells. Apart from Abbot's Leigh in the diocese of Bristol, the county of Somerset and the diocese of Bath and Wells were co-terminous in the medieval and modern periods.

Parishes now in Avon lay in the deaneries of Bath and Bedminster which made up the archdeaconry of Bath and in parts of the deaneries of Axbridge and Frome in the archdeaconry of Wells.

The parishes of Yatton (with Kenn) and Easton in Gordano were Prebendal Peculiars and Banwell, Churchill and Puxton together formed a Peculiar of the Dean and Chapter of Bristol.

Such Bishop's registers as survive between 1309 and 1558 have been calendared and published by the Somerset Record Society in volumes 1, 9, 10, 13, 29–32, 49, 50, 52–55. Some, but not all, of the surviving marriage bonds between 1645 and 1755 were published by A.J. Jewers in his *Marriage Allegation Bonds of the Bishops of Bath and Wells* (1909). No printed *Guide* to the diocesan records exists, but a brief, although not entirely reliable, survey was commissioned by the Pilgrim Trust in 1946.

MS. Handlists are available in the record office for the main categories of record where a simple, single description is insufficient: e.g., court and visitation act books, 1458–1905, deposition books, 1530–1733, licence books, 1537–1837, Peculiar records, 1619–1864, and clergy lists, 1526–1831. Other groups of single purpose records have remained in chronological series and do not require individual treatment: e.g. marriage licence bonds, 1574–1899, presentation deeds, 1573–1899, meeting house certificates, 1736–1851, ordination papers, 1745–1837, and benefice returns, 1814–1837; the bishop's transcripts were originally in this form, but were subsequently re-cast into a parochial arrangement.

Certain series are conveniently accessible on a topographical basis, either because they have been indexed onto record office indexes, e.g. meeting house certificates, ordination papers, exchanges of glebe and the limited series of faculty papers and nominations of schoolmasters, surgeons and midwives; or because of their internal arrangement, e.g. glebe terriers, 1571–1693, benefice returns and visitation act books. The latter are arranged alphabetically by parishes within the separate deaneries and have the added merit of recording in English details of the matters presented. They relate almost entirely to the bishops' primary or triennial visitations and survive most fully between 1600 and 1640.

The general contents of the deposition books are briefly described in the *Proceedings* of the Somerset Archaeological Society, vol. 108, pp. 170–71 and a limited number of interesting cases (by parishes), including some for the parishes in the archdeaconry of Bath, are there noted.

The entire diocesan series of tithe apportionment maps and awards prepared as a result of the 1836 Tithe Act and largely confirmed between 1838 and 1844 is held.

Parish

The record office is the designated diocesan record office for the diocese of Bath and Wells, and the Bishop's Directions for the 'Care of Parish Records' are printed in the current *Diocesan Hand Book*. An *Inventory of Parochial Documents* in the diocese was published by the County Records Committee in 1938 at a date when few records (and no registers) had been deposited. Since the designation of the office over 240 parishes in the diocese have deposited registers and other parochial documents, both civil and ecclesiastical, and there remain a further 20 parishes which had previously deposited records, excluding registers, and which have not subsequently extended their deposits.

The following parishes, now in Avon, are included in the first category: Backwell, Banwell, Camerton, Churchill, Clevedon, Congresbury, Dunkerton, Englishcombe, Flax Bourton, Foxcote, Hinton Blewett, Hinton Charterhouse, Langridge, Long Ashton, Midsomer Norton, Nailsea, Puxton, Radstock, Swainswick, Tickenham, Uphill, Wellow, Worle, Wrington, and Writhlington, together with the divided parishes of Compton Martin, West Harptree and Ubley; and in the second category: Chew Magna and Walcot.

Registers only from the 19th century have been deposited by the Bath parishes of Lyncombe St. Mark and Widcombe St. Thomas a Becket and Weston-super-Mare Christ Church.

Catalogues to a standard form are available in the search room and up-to-date lists of registers deposited can be purchased at cost price (plus postage).

Nonconformist

Minutes, sufferings books, etc., of the Somerset Quarterly Meeting of the Society of Friends, from 1656, including minutes of the (united) Bristol and Somerset Q.M., 1784–1936.

Unofficial

Family and Estate

Dickinson of Kingweston (DD/DN)

Business letter books and accounts of Graffin Prankard, a Bristol merchant, 1712–1755, and correspondence and accounts of his son-in-law, Caleb Dickinson, 1736–1783.

Gibbs of Barrow Gurney (DD/GB)

Deeds, etc., of Gibbs family estatees in Barrow Gurney and Flax Bourton, 1740–1924, and for the Gore family estates in Barrow Gurney, 1547–1780, and composite volumes of Gore family correspondence, accounts and legal papers, etc., 1521–1814.

Gordon of Naish House (DD/PN)

Deeds of the Naish House Estate in Gordano parishes, 1599–1880;

maps of the manors of North Weston, 1741, 1840, and Easton in Gordano, 1824, 1828; surveys, etc., of the manor of Portbury, 1723–1784.

Gore Langton of Newton Park (DD/GL)

Deeds and leases (including some coal) for Brislington, Corston, High Littleton, Marksbury, Newton St. Loe, Stanton Prior, Twerton and Wellow and for Cold Ashton and Doynton, *c.* 1290–1912.
Court rolls, books or papers for Brislington, 1586–1598, High Littleton, etc. 1568–1587, Newton St. Loe, 1667–1720, and Wellow, 1701–1730.

Hippisley of Ston Easton (DD/HI)

Deeds and leases, 13c.–1906; maps and surveys, 1766, 1794; court and compotus rolls, 1460–1613 (scattered dates), overseers' accounts, 1635–1685, all for Cameley.

Kemeys Tynte of Halswell (DD/S/WH)

Deeds, leases, etc., for Chelvey, Chew Magna, Nailsea, Regilbury in Nempnett Thrubwell, Pensford and Wraxall, 16c.–1900. Court rolls or court books for the manors of Chew and Regilbury, 1553–1653. Rentals and surveys (limited) for all above places, between 1670 and 1798.

Mogg of Farrington Gurney (DD/MGG)

Deeds of High Littleton and coal leases, agreements, etc., relating to mines there and in Timsbury, Midsomer Norton and Farrington Gurney, 1689–1842.

Popham of Hunstrete (DD/PO: DD/POt)

Deeds, leases, etc., for Marksbury, Compton Dando, Chelwood, Farmborough, Timsbury, Pensford, Publow and Chew Magna, 1541–1877. Manorial records (limited) for most of the same, 1627–1841.
Hunstrete estate accounts and vouchers, 1649–1846; field books and cropping records, 1824–1844; agent's letter books, 1843–1852; surveys, registers of leases, *c.* 1740–1871, and maps for most places, various dates between 1758 and 1866.

Poulett of Hinton St. George (DD/PT; DD/SS)

Deeds, leases, etc., for Yatton, Kenn, Kingston Seymour and Walton in Gordano, 1352–1816; rentals, 1792–1802; surveys, *c.* 1660, 1798; map, *c.* 1780.

Rees-Mogg of Temple Cloud (DD/RM)

Deeds, etc., of estates, including coal interests, in Clutton, Hinton Blewett, Timsbury, Paulton and Midsomer Norton, 1621–1880; survey of Clutton, 1754.

Samborne of Timsbury (DD/SA)
Deeds of estates, including coal interests, of the related families of Samborne and Savage in Timsbury and Midsomer Norton, 1546–1911.

Sexey's Hospital, Bruton (DD/SE)
Deeds, leases, etc., of the hospital's estates in Lyncombe and Widcombe, 1539–1805; estreats, 1554–1570; estate papers and correspondence of Hugh Sexey relating to this estate and to other property, including Stalls Parsonage, in or near Bath, *c.* 1600–1615.

Skrine of Warleigh (DD/SK)
Deeds of Bathford, 1597–1838; court rolls, 1592–1606; survey, 1606, with customs, 1584. Papers relating to building works at Warleigh, 1811–1815; map, 1792. Letters written by Richard Graves from Claverton, from 1754.

Strachie of Sutton Court (DD/SH)
Papers of John Strachey, F.R.S. (1671–1743), relating to the production of his county map (1736) and his projected county history, with his collected papers on general, local and natural history and genealogy.
Deeds, leases, etc., for Chew Magna and Stowey, 1639–1902; maps, 1793, 1832; agreements, correspondence and accounts relating to Woolley gunpowder mills, 1733–1809.
Estate and household papers and accounts, 1731–1900; personal papers, correspondence, etc., of various members, 18–19 cents., including literary papers of Sir Edward (1812–1901); Radstock coal accounts, etc., 1853–1897.

Waldegrave of Chewton (DD/WG)
Deeds, leases, books of grants, etc., for Radstock, 1647–1827; manorial records for Radstock, Midsomer Norton and Kingston Seymour, 1579–1605, for Radstock alone, 1734–1824, and for Kingston Seymour alone, 1767–1812; surveys for Radstock, various dates between 1696 and 1806, and maps, 1759, 1806; Radstock coal mining records, *c.* 1850–1900, and correspondence about initial mining there, 1779–1788.

Walker Heneage of Coker Court (DD/WHb)
Deeds, leases, etc., for Bath, Bathampton, Batheaston, Bathford and Twerton, *c.* 1160–1670 (calendared to 1470 in Somerset Record Society vol. 73, *Medieval Deeds of Bath and District*); court rolls for Batheaston, 1418–1431.

Wyndham of Orchard Wyndham (DD/WY)
Deeds, leases, etc., for East and West Rolston in Banwell, 1525–1795; survey, 1649.

Solicitors

Foster of Wells (DD/FS)
Leases for Compton Martin, 1715–1834; deeds of coal mines (Dowling family) at Bishop Sutton in Chew Magna, etc., 1716–1829, and colliery accounts, 1850–1853; papers relating to the sale of Smyth Pigott estates in Yatton, Kenn, Congresbury and Kingston Seymour, 1857, 1914; farm and general accounts of Thomas Knyfton of Uphill, 1757–1796, and architectural plans of Uphill House, 1853.

Osborne, Ward & Co., of Bristol (DD/OB)
Deeds of Twerton (mills), 1813–1891; deeds and papers of the Kington family of Wraxall, 1670–1880; deeds of copper mill at Stanton Drew, 1608–1825, and litigation papers involving the Copper Co., 1851–1853.

Other deposited records

The Church Commissioners (DD/CC)
(Bishopric estates). Deeds, leases, manorial records for the manor of Banwell, 1662–1904; survey, 1634; map, 1828, rent rolls (also relating to Churchill and Worle), 1826–1852.
(Chapter estates). Deeds, leases, etc., for Congresbury and Winscombe and for Pucklechurch in Gloucestershire, 1618–1866, and charter for Pucklechurch, 950; manorial records for Winscombe, 1277–1865, and for Congresbury and Pucklechurch, 1381–1865; surveys, rentals, etc., various dates between 1650 and 1865; map of Winsocmbe, 1792.
(Prebendal estates). Parliamentary surveys for Easton in Gordano and Yatton, 1650; records of the manor of Yatton Rectory, 1756–1876.

Miscellaneous holdings

Reproductions of records elsewhere
Microfilm copies of the 1851 and 1871 censuses and the series of non-parochial registers (in the Public Record Office) for the whole of Somerset, including Bath.

Ordnance Survey maps
Full sets of the 1st edition (surveyed 1882–1888) and 2nd edition (revised 1900–1903) of the six inch maps for Somerset and near complete set (for the Avon area) of the 2nd edition twenty five inch.

WOODSPRING MUSEUM

Address: Burlington St., Weston-super-Mare, Bristol BA23 1PR

Telephone: Weston-super-Mare (0934) 21028.

Curator: Miss J. Evans

Opening Hours: Monday-Saturday, 10–1, 2–5.

Holdings

(a) *Maps:*
Bowen's map of Somerset, 1760; Day & Masters map of Somerset,
1″ to 1 mile (photographs available), 1782; Ordnance Survey, 1st
edition, 1″ to 1 mile, 1811; Ordnance Survey, 1st edition of 25″ to 1
mile (Sheets XI, XII, XVIII, XIX) including Brockley, Backwell, E.
Congresbury, Wrington, Dundry, Chew Magna, Shipham,
Churchill, Blagdon, W. Harptree, etc., 1885; Wm. Sander's
Geological Map of the Bristol coalfields (covering most of Avon at
scale of 4″ to 1 mile, this is plotted from the tithe maps and therefore
shows all field boundaries as they were in 1840), 1862; Geological
Map, Old Series, 1817; Tithe map of Kingston Seymour, 1847;
Milton enclosure award, 1793; Kewstoke enclosure award, 1857.
Also, Ordnance Survey 6″ maps for Woodspring District with O.S.
finds marked, together with card index.

(b) *Documents:*
A few, e.g. Bleadon cottage title deeds; Chemists' prescription
books, 1876–1947.

(c) *Lists:*
Listed buildings in District of Woodspring; Scheduled Ancient
Monuments in District of Woodspring.

(d) *Local History Files* (Mainly on Weston itself, but also on Clevedon
and Portishead):
1805 Congresbury Charter (xerox of copy in Bristol Record
Office); Bailey articles in 'Weston Mercury'; copies of writings of
George Bennett (Banwell antiquarian 1812–30); Files on
individuals, e.g. Hans Price, architect in Weston and Clevedon.

(e) *Topographical Material:*
Various illustrations and prints, predominantly of Weston
(catalogue available); Photographs of some of the Buckler &
Braikenridge drawings in Taunton (*c.* 1820–40); Old photographs
e.g. Long Ashton, Hutton, Worle, Weston; Slide collection of 800
illustrations of Old Weston.

(f) *Family Portraits:*
Smyth-Pigott family of Brockley (30 portraits from Col. Thomas
Pigott (1660) onwards, and some documents of the Smyth-Pigotts;
Paynes of Uphill Manor (2 miniatures); Weston characters (40
painted *c.* 1848); Sheppard family of Kewstoke 1860s; Lucas family,
Blackwell House—oil painting by Rippingille 1829.

(g) *Air Photographs:* Various

(h) *Building Plans: c.* 15,000 plans of houses built, or proposed, in Weston *c.* 1860–1937 (not yet indexed).

(i) *Newspapers:*
Weston Gazette—from 1904 onwards; *Weston Mercury*—from 1904 onwards.

(j) *Objects:*
Assorted materials from the District, from archaeological to items such as the Banwell 16th century fire hooks and late 18th century fire-engine, and the work of Charles Summers (1827–1878), a Victorian sculptor, and Weston-Clevedon-Portishead light railways. Products of local industries, e.g. Royal Potteries of Weston-super-Mare, 1836–1961, and catalogues. Wesuma Ware. Elton Pottery. Contents of Chemist's shop, 1900.

(k) *Tape Recordings* of elderly inhabitants.

INDEX

(J.S. MOORE)

This index does not include the names of contributors (which are given in the 'Note on Contributors'), the authors and titles of books included in Bibliography I (except for printed editions of historical texts), and the source-materials listed in Bibliography II.

Compound place-names are indexed under the first element in common usage, e.g. *Iron* Acton, not *Acton*, Iron. Composite entries are indexed under key-words, followed by a dash; the repetition of the key-word within the entry is indicated by a full colon.